STEADY EDDIE

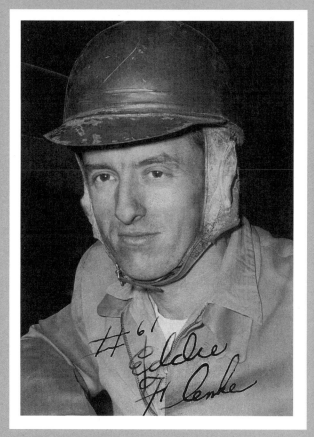

Marge Dombrowski Collection

STEADY EDDIE

Memories of Ed Flemke, Modified Racing's Fastest Professor

Edited by Bones Bourcier

COASTAL 181
PUBLISHER

Layout and Production *Jim Rigney*
Copyediting/proofing *Sandra Rigney, Cary Stratton*
Photo Archives *MaryRose Moskell*
Book Design *Sandra Rigney*
Cover Design *Joyce Cosentino Wells*

PHOTO CREDITS
Front Cover *John Grady*
Back Cover (from the top) *Mike Adaskaveg, Carolyn Flemke Collection,
    Mike Adaskaveg, Lawlor Family Collection*
Chapter Openings (unless author supplied)
Mike Adaskaveg (John Stygar, Ron and Paula Bouchard, Eddie Flemke Jr.,
    Carolyn Flemke, Bruce Cohen)
Dave Mavlouganes (Pete Hamilton, Gene Bergin)
Charlie White (Denny Zimmerman, Pete Zanardi)
Area Auto Racing News (Junie Donlavey)
Speedway Illustrated (Robin Pemberton)

ISBN 10: 0-9789261-1-0
ISBN 13: 978-0-9789261-1-3

For additional information or copies of this book please contact:

Coastal 181
29 Water Street
Newburyport, MA 01950
877-907-8181, 978-462-2436
www.coastal181.com

First printing April 2007

Printed in the United States of America

Contents

Editor's Note by Bones Bourcier

A unique book about a unique racer

In the footsteps of Steady Eddie: Editor Bones Bourcier at the Miss Washington Diner in New Britain, CT, February, 2007. *(Heather McIntosh photo)*

THE CONCEPT behind this project was simple, springing from three different beliefs. First, that a book on Ed Flemke was overdue. Second, that a standard, facts-and-figures bio was impossible, given the shoddy state of record keeping in Flemke's heyday. (Published guesses at his victory total range from 400 to 600, a *gap* of 200 wins. Racing has attracted many characters, but few competent file clerks.) Third, that Eddie's real legacy was the impact he had on others—family members, fellow drivers, team owners, mechanics, track operators, fans—from his jalopy roots to his tenure as father figure of the modified division.

So why not try something different? Why not round up folks from each of those constituencies, and let them tell Flemke's story? Pick a promoter, a few rivals, a car owner, a mechanic, a son, a daughter, and so on, and have each individual discuss a different aspect of the man. Then, bring in an editor to put things into roughly chronological form. (This is a good time to point out that I didn't write this book; I was just lucky enough to read it first.)

The end result was the 21 chapters you'll find on these pages, 21 viewpoints on 21 specific areas of Flemke's life, from 21 people who knew, respected, and loved the guy. We purposely left the tone conversational. Emotion, we figured, was more important than sentence structure, and there's plenty of emotion herein.

There are some thank-yous necessary, starting with those who contributed chapters. Then there were those who offered photos, anecdotes, and logistical help: John Grady, Dick Berggren, Larry Jendras Jr., Fran Lawlor, R.A. Silvia, Howie Hodge, Bill Balser, Val LeSieur, Phil Smith, Dave Mavlouganes, Brian and Eric Williams, Mike Kerchner at *National Speed Sport News*, Len Sammons at *Area Auto Racing News*, Don Thomas, Tom Ormsby, Margret Rosati, Mario Fiore, Nick Teto, Karl Fredrickson at *Speedway Illustrated*, Brian Danko, and Chris Goldsnider. If I've left anyone out, my apologies; please know that your help made a difference.

The gang from Coastal 181 came through, as always. Lew Boyd and Cary Stratton, Jim and Sandra Rigney, Joyce Wells, and MaryRose Moskell pour great energy into preserving the histories of our favorite racers and speedways.

Above all, my warm appreciation for the hospitality shown by Betty Vanesse and Marge Dombrowski; Carolyn Flemke, Kristy and Ken Boland, and Laurie Parsons; Christine Bowen and Eddie Flemke Jr.; and Paula and Ron Bouchard. They shine as brightly as any trophy Steady Eddie ever won.

It was on the start/finish line at Plainville Stadium, just after he'd won a 100-lapper, that I first shook hands with Ed Flemke. Our mutual friend Mike Adaskaveg made the introductions. Back then, Mike was writing and shooting photos for the *Meriden Record-Journal*. These days, he's an award-winning news photographer for the *Boston Herald*. He also got me my first writing gig, over 30 years ago. Having Mike provide the foreword for this book doesn't close the circle; it keeps it spinning.

I grew up in Southington, CT, where Flemke lived for years, so he was a hero of mine long before I met him at age 15. He was great to me personally, and always accommodating to me professionally. In a world as clannish as racing can be, acceptance was gold to a young, dumb

Shivering at Wall Stadium's 1979 Turkey Derby are, left to right, Eddie Flemke Jr., Bones Bourcier, and Ed Flemke. *(Pete Lawlor photo)*

columnist trying to make his way. I've always had the feeling that being seen as a kid who was "OK with Eddie" began the ripple effect of me being "OK with" Bobby Judkins, Ron Bouchard, Bugs Stevens, Richie Evans, Val LeSieur, Dick Berggren . . . the list goes on. Some of those guys gave me access. Others gave me jobs. All of them gave a future to a track brat who had fallen in love with writing about this sport and those in it.

So, you see, I owe a lot to Steady Eddie Flemke. This book doesn't square that debt, but maybe it's a small payment.

Foreword by Mike Adaskaveg

Life with Eddie: Victories, road trips, and lessons learned

THE STEADY CLICK-CLACK of tires crossing concrete slabs kept track of the Chrysler's speed as the New State Thruway's white ribbon blended into the black asphalt of the Massachusetts Turnpike. A huge, chrome-trimmed steering wheel dwarfed the driver, who, from my back seat view, appeared too small to be controlling such a beast. But control it, he did, Lucky Strike in one hand, a calm grasp of the wheel in the other.

Mike Adaskaveg

I couldn't help but think how easy highway driving must be for Eddie Flemke, who just an hour ago had wrestled the Judkins #2X through a motley field of coupes, Pintos, Vegas and Gremlins to win another modified feature at the Albany-Saratoga Speedway.

The words "State Line" glowed into the darkness from a green highway sign as the slowing click-clacks indicated it was time to make the customary post-race meal stop, this time at the greasy spoon we referred to simply as "the Stateline diner."

Flicking the butt away with his left hand, grabbing a wad of cash from the glove box with his right, Eddie smiled as if stopping for truck-stop food had been the goal of his whole day: Wake up. Work on cars. Gather up the kids. Drive to Malta, NY, from his home in Southington, CT. Help Bobby Judkins set up the car. Barely qualify in a heat race. Do a lot of thinking. Turn a few bolts. Take the lead with two laps to go. Collect the cash. Spend it at the Stateline diner.

Eddie's carload of five was soon complemented by another carload of five, along with Bobby hauling the #2X and whoever he had riding with him. The gang took over the joint and ordered just about everything on the menu. Much later, as the last sips of coffee were taken, Eddie waved the check to the new waitress. (There always seemed to be a new waitress at Stateline, every week.)

"Will you be paying, sir?" she asked.

Eddie shot back, "Don't you know my name?"

"Um, no," she replied cautiously.

"My name's Crime," Eddie said, his face deadpan, "and Crime don't pay."

Then he handed her the check and walked right out the door. The eruption of laughter from the tables was deafening.

Of course, Eddie had an incredible sense of timing. He waited just long enough in the parking lot, taking a few drags off another Lucky, before returning to pay the bill.

The knotted apple tree provided much-needed shade for a Sunday afternoon break from working on the bent-up jalopy stock car my mother's Italian family knew as the "Banana Wagon." Phil Salerno, a cousin of mine, was its driver. Instead of a number on the side, it had a banana, sort of a cheap way of advertising Phil's business, which was a produce stand.

I loved that car. For the kids I was growing up with, jalopy races were hip, cool, or whatever you said for "in" in the late 1950s.

But the elders had a different view.

They were in the vegetable business. My uncles, Carmen, Frank, and Mike, were farmers. Their cracked hands, muscled arms and sun-darkened skin were proof of how hard they worked every day. When it was time to pass a jug of homemade wine—made from Southington grapes —or take a rusty can opener to the rim of a can of Shaefer beer, the talk always turned to racing.

"Jalopies are for fun," they preached to me. "Midgets are real race cars."

They were in harmony in their message: Midgets were number one around here. If I wanted further testimony to that effect, I could go ask our neighbors, the Angelillo family, or their cousin Gene from Waterbury (who years later would own a pretty famous midget racer himself).

"George Flemke, *he's* the one you want to see drive," the elders declared.

They all looked up to George Flemke, Eddie's older brother. In their minds, he was the greatest local driver, winning midget races with his Ford V8-60. To my uncles and neighbors, that was as good as it got. Eddie, meanwhile, was still learning the ropes, racing in jalopy divisions like Plainville Stadium's sportsman class.

"Eddie is good, too," they'd say. "He'll move up to midgets some day. He's a good jalopy driver."

I knew my place and never spoke up. But my young brain knew different. I wondered: *Why sell the jalopies short? The stands are packed at Plainville and Riverside Park to watch cars just like the Banana Wagon.*

Eddie and the stock cars were both on their way up.

A couple years later, my quiet little neighborhood world was transformed. The Venetian blind factory on the corner went out of business, and, unbelievably, a bunch of guys building cars to race at Plainville moved in. They called themselves "The Lifters."

The sound of engines revving into the nighttime was a magnet for every kid in the neighborhood, including Clyde McLeod (who in time would work on Eddie Flemke's modifieds) and Stan Greger (who went on to be a great driver himself, winning dozens of Plainville features and three Riverside Park track championships). We'd line our bikes up at the windows of the old cement-block building, peering in. We could hear the guys inside talking, always about Eddie Flemke. By the way they talked, Flemke was everywhere. They told stories of him racing and winning at tracks we'd never heard of, in states we had yet to learn about.

Clyde was the big kid on the block. Everyone looked up to him, except the neighborhood parents. Clyde liked to burn old tires in his yard and light fireworks in the middle of the street, and he'd had a fascination with cars since he was tall enough to release the hood latch on the family Plymouth.

It wasn't long before Clyde brought out some pieces of sheet rock and chalked an oval right in the middle of a four-way intersection outside The Lifters' clubhouse. He dubbed it "Visconti Speedway," after the name of his street. As we lettered up our bikes with model paint, a fight began.

Every kid wanted to be Eddie Flemke.

Steady Eddie accepts a 1964 Plainville Stadium checkered from "Moneybags Moe" Gherzi. Moe, a great driver in his own right, had retired to become Plainville's race director. *(Tom Ormsby Collection)*

It was the biggest day of our summer vacation in 1965 when a bunch of us kids—me, Clyde, Stan, Johnny Angelillo, and a couple of others—lined up at the ticket booth at Plainville Stadium on a Wednesday afternoon. The gates were still locked, but we were stoked by the wafting aroma of fried hot dogs and French fries, and the anticipation of seeing Eddie Flemke and his "cent-sign" coupe in that night's big open competition show.

Exotic-looking cars with small bodies and big wheels, different from the usual bulky Plainville cars, were being towed along the dirt road to the backstretch pit gate. They were called "modifieds," some guy told our gang. Once the gates open and practice began, we saw the strangest car of all: a yellow-green coupe with the white letter "J" in a circle on the door. A guy named Don MacTavish was at the wheel. He was from up around Boston, and boy, could he drive.

As we begged for more hot dogs, our elders, who knew of our local loyalties, offered a cruel deal: If we cheered for MacTavish, the outsider, they would keep being the hot dogs coming.

No way. We'd rather starve.

MacTavish had a slick car, and he was fast, but our hero was Steady Eddie.

Come the feature, we kids suggested our own deal: If MacTavish beat Flemke, we told my uncle, we'd work on the farm for a week. But if Flemke beat MacTavish, we could load up on hot dogs before the concession stand closed.

Later that night, as the racers loaded up their cars, we pressed our stuffed bellies up to the pit fence yelling the drivers' names.

Eddie Flemke, the winner, waved and walked off into the darkness.

It wasn't until Stafford Speedway was paved that I met Eddie Flemke. Though we sort of moved in the same circles, I'd known him only by word of mouth or from reading the newspaper I delivered on my bicycle, the *Hartford Times*.

When I started writing a column for the then-popular *Illustrated Speedway News* at the ripe old age of 15, I figured it was time I talked to Eddie. Shy but confident, I introduced myself to him after a race at Stafford, and told him I wanted an interview. For me, this was a big deal.

"Here's my number," Eddie said. "Give me a call, come down to the house."

Eddie lived modestly in a small house on the north side of Southington. Nothing about the home would have revealed that its owner was a nationally known stock car driver. When I walked up to talk to Eddie, he was mowing the lawn in a T-shirt and work pants. Baby daughter Kristy was taking in the warm summer evening with her mom, Carolyn, on the steps of the porch.

This was Eddie Flemke? He was suburban dad, with a station wagon and a lawn that needed mowing, just like all the other fathers in the neighborhood. He even took time out to play with his daughter on the swing set.

I started by bringing up Phil Salerno and the Banana Wagon. Eddie told me how he met Phil: "I was passing the Banana Wagon, and the next thing I knew, I was through the wall. After the race, this big guy, Phil, walks up to me and says, 'You got me, now I got you. We're even.'"

Then Eddie laughed and explained that he had put Salerno into the wall in some earlier race.

"A few weeks later, I went to Riverside without a ride. Phil had a spare car and offered me a ride, so I said sure."

That night, Flemke won the feature, with what he called some "defensive" help from his temporary teammate.

"From that day on, we were the best of friends," Eddie recalled. "Salerno had a big crew. I'd fight them any day on the track, but not off."

Young writer and photographer Mike Adaskaveg, way back when. *(Mike Adaskaveg Collection)*

We got along right from the start. Eddie invited me to ride along to the races with him and his older kids, Eddie Jr. and Paula, who were about my age. The next night, we piled into the station wagon and headed for Malta, NY. Carolyn stayed behind, happy being the home-maker, the scrapbook keeper, the good mother to little Kristy.

I still remember that first trip. Steady Eddie always stayed a couple miles per hour above the speed limit. And his conversation seemed unusual to me; he fired questions back at anybody in the car who asked him questions. In the years to come, I would come to expect this sort of thing from Flemke. He was analytical, logical. He was a master of philosophy without ever having been formally educated in that science.

But as I said, my understanding of this came way down the road. On that day, on that trip to Malta, to us kids the ride was all about catching up to Bobby Judkins and his hauler, and stopping for a quick pre-race snack at a place called Dunster's.

I wasn't much more than 16 years old when Paula, Eddie Jr., and I took turns behind the wheel of my '68 Chevelle, driving to Utica-Rome Speedway on a rainy September morning. Eddie chose the back seat.

The wipers were slapping heavy drops from the windshield while Paula was at the wheel for the last stretch of the trip to Vernon, NY. Suddenly, the car in front of us went into a 360-degree spin on the drenched Thruway.

Eddie calmly delivered the orders from the back seat: "Don't touch the brake. Keep your foot on the gas. Steer *for* the spinning car."

Paula did exactly what her father said. In a matter of seconds—which seemed like a half-hour at the time—the other car crossed sideways in front of our bumper and looped harmlessly away. We continued on, but my heart was in my throat, as I'm sure was also the case with Eddie Jr. and Paula. Once we'd had a second to collect ourselves, Eddie quietly explained, "If you steer for a spinning car, it will be gone from that spot by time you get there."

I couldn't believe the connection I had just witnessed. It was a bond of trust between father and daughter.

Soon after I enrolled at Central Connecticut State College in New Britain, I began writing for the *Meriden Record-Journal*. As busy as I was, I still saw a lot of the Flemkes. In this same period, Eddie Jr. was just starting his own racing career. Each morning I'd park my car outside the house of Eddie Jr.'s mom, Christine, who lived close to the CCSC campus, and many nights I'd visit Eddie Jr. at the Quonset hut in the Milldale section of Southington, where he kept his coupe.

One night, just after he had raced at Riverside for the first time, I stopped to ask Eddie Jr. some questions. I wanted his assessment of the experience for a column I was writing. After that column ran, I again showed up at the shop, and saw his father standing there, backlit against the floodlights. I greeted Eddie the way all the local kids did: "Hi, Boss." But he walked right by, head down, never uttering a sound.

I asked Eddie Jr. what was wrong. "He didn't like what you wrote," Junior replied. "And he didn't like that I said what I said to you." For days, Eddie wouldn't speak to either me or his son. He was upset that between Eddie Jr.'s quotes and my writing, it appeared that he hadn't helped his son at Riverside, that he just sort of abandoned him there. But that wasn't the case at all; there were lessons taught and lessons learned, as you will see from Eddie Jr.'s chapter in this book.

We patched things up soon enough, and from that point on College Journalism 101 couldn't have taught me what Ed Flemke did. Our long drives to races became forums for debate on the subject.

"When you write a story about what goes on at Stafford," Eddie said, "think like the promoter. Pretend you are Jack Arute. Get into his head, see things the way Jack sees them. When you're writing about a driver, do the same thing. Try to see it from his perspective."

Eddie knew how to remove himself from a situation and look at it through other people's eyes. It concerned him that some in the racing media wrote great stories about drivers and tracks, but never took on the tough issues: safety, economics, and planning for the future of the sport. Eddie was always up for discussion on the topics, and controversy was good, he said, if it brought positive change.

"We're all in this together," I remember him saying.

Years flew by, and other episodes came and went, and then one day the shocking news arrived that Eddie Flemke had passed away. My last

Few in racing have ever had the discipline to step away and look objectively at a subject, the way Ed Flemke did. *(R.A. Silvia Collection)*

memories of him are pleasant ones: him working with Eddie Jr., building cars at their shop in East Hartford. One night he had called me from there—it was late, maybe 9:00 or 10:00 P.M.—and told me to stop by. When I got there, the pair were welding up a chassis, and Eddie proudly explained the ideas he and Eddie Jr. had, and how much more he and his son had to accomplish.

Then he was gone. I remember talking to Eddie Jr. after that horrible day.

"He had nothing," said the son. "No retirement, no savings. But that's the way he wanted it to be. He always said that you come into this world with nothing, and you should leave with nothing."

I knew that to be true. I'd heard Eddie say that many times over the years.

I visited Eddie Jr. just recently, and it was like "déjà vu all over again." When I walked into his Race Works shop after dark, I found Reggie Ruggiero bent over somebody's hot rod Chevelle, just like the one I had driven to Malta 35 years ago, and Eddie Jr. was snapping a few temporary fasteners onto a modern modified body.

Years had rolled by, but it was like we picked up right where we left off last time. I mentioned to Eddie Jr. that there hasn't passed a day when I haven't thought about his father, and the way he did things.

"He was so philosophical, and taught us so much," Eddie Jr. replied. "But we were 15-year-old kids, and we couldn't digest it all."

Everyone in this book—and many, many more people—had their lives changed in some fashion by Eddie Flemke. And it's also worth noting that lots of those mentioned in these pages might never have known one another if not for their shared experiences with Steady Eddie.

The fact that this book is being published more than 20 years after his death shows the important place Eddie Flemke occupied not only in the racing world, but also in the lives of everyone whose path crossed his.

No one has forgotten Ed Flemke, or the lessons he taught.

"We never knew we were getting lessons at the time, but today we do," his son said. "He's still here with us."

PART ONE

Out of Nowhere

The old neighborhood doesn't look like much today, and the truth is, it probably never did. The City of New Britain—which for a great chunk of the 19th and 20th centuries was not only the hardware center of Connecticut but also a major source of tools worldwide—has always been a blue-collar place, and in such places the emphasis is on function rather than form. The old factories —those of men like Frederick T. Stanley, who launched what evolved into The Stanley Works, and the Corbin brothers, Philip and Frank, whose holdings included the Corbin Screw Corporation—were built from brick, not because their owners found the reddish walls particularly beautiful, but because brick lasted. And the reason so many of the wood-frame houses which dot New Britain rose three stories was also a matter of utility: All those factory workers tended to come from immigrant families which stuck together as the years passed, so there was practicality in a home which could stack the parents on the ground floor, a son with his wife and kids directly above, and maybe some cousins up a couple of flights of stairs.

The area near the intersection of Allen and Oak Streets, where Jacob Flemke once had his auto repair shop, is the city in microcosm: the businesses mostly brick, the homes mostly three-story wood. Today it appears bleak, depressed. Even if you try to imagine the laughter put into the neighborhood by all those immigrant families—mostly Italian and Polish then, with some German—you keep coming back to the idea that these were always hard streets.

But here's the thing: Maybe the surroundings don't have to determine one's destiny. Maybe what counts most is the longing in the heart.

"I think desire is the outstanding thing in everybody's life," Jacob Flemke's youngest child, a son named Ed, once said. "And there's no limit on how far you can go, either, with that desire."

Already on wheels as a young man: Eddie Flemke in New Britain, CT, circa 1940. (*Carolyn Flemke Collection*)

So Eddie Flemke—born on August 27, 1930, and seemingly full of desire right from the start—turned those streets into a launching pad. And, Lord, how far he went.

It helped that his parents, both German immigrants, didn't comprehend limits, either. Wanda Flemke could not read an American newspaper, yet spoke English and four other languages fluently. Jacob, meanwhile, was conversant in six languages. Their children—in order, daughters Lydia and Betty, son George, daughters Marge and Dottie, and the pup, Eddie—did not lack for mental stimulation at home.

And, of course, there was dad's workplace. Today a generic maintenance building stands at 269 Oak Street, for so long the address of Jake's Garage. Jake's was where middle-class Joes brought their Hudsons and Fords for service, and passed the time doing the things men do in garages: chewing the fat, drinking an after-work beer, petting the dog—isn't there always a dog?—and discussing the issues of the day. Jack Vanesse, son of Betty Vanesse, the older of Eddie's two surviving sisters, frequented Jake's as a boy and remembers the men clearly: "They'd hand their empty beer bottles to the dog, and the dog would take them to the pile out back."

So there was plenty to keep young Eddie entertained. Still, his was hardly a childhood devoid of obstacles. You want hardship? Try this: Wanda Flemke died of a cerebral hemorrhage in 1937. "Mother went to bed one night, and she passed," says Marge Dombrowski, Eddie's other surviving sibling. At the height of the Great Depression, the idea of leaving six children in the care of their self-employed mechanic father was radical. Marge says, "The people from the state wanted to take us kids, and we had an aunt who said, 'I'll take the kids.' But my dad said, 'Nobody takes the kids. My children are going to stay together, with me.' And he worked hard to make that happen." The family moved from apartment to apartment, some of them in those three-floor walk-ups near the garage.

Then, in Eddie's teenaged years, something amazing showed up at Jake's Garage. It was a midget race car, just about the most exciting thing an American lad could imagine in the years just after World War II, when midget racing was the nation's most popular motorsport. The car belonged to Jacob Flemke's other son, George, well on his way to becoming one of the top drivers in the East. (A 1956 newspaper story called George "one of the all-time greats of midget auto racing," and lauded his "many victories this season, all the way from Daytona Beach to Lynchburg, VA.") No one seems quite sure how racing got its hooks into George, who died in 1997. The best guess is that the late Bert Brooks, a colossal open-wheel performer who called New Britain home for a time, was his primary influence.

Father Jacob, meanwhile, was an interesting case. He was a disciplinarian—"My dad taught us that you alone knew when you'd done something wrong," Marge says—and yet he had a bit of a wild streak. As a young man he had raced motorcycles, and according to family lore rode one across the United States, perhaps even setting some sort of long-forgotten speed record. He also had an active imagination: Betty remembers as a young girl listening to her dad proclaim that if the folks who built those darned contraptions called airplanes simply outfitted one with a large rotor on top, "the plane could go straight up and down instead of gliding in." Now, Betty was born in 1918, so Jacob Flemke was daydreaming about vertical-lift aircraft in, what, 1925, or 1928, or maybe 1932? Well, chew on this: The first truly viable helicopters, built by German and Russian aeronautical engineers, didn't fly until 1936.

Barnstorming on motorcycles, and daydreaming about flying machines? You start to get the idea that maybe the need for speed and tinkering which shaped Eddie Flemke came his way genetically. And once that midget of George's was added to the mix, was there any doubt that the youngest Flemke would be a racer? "I got to warm that car up one day," Eddie recalled in a 1974 interview, "and I knew I had the bug."

But instead of the elite midgets, Flemke turned to the more accessible stock cars—jalopies, folks called them—which were elbowing their way into tracks around New England. There are tales claiming he was foiled in attempts to race before he reached legal age, but the details are murky. It has long been accepted as fact that in 1948, at barely 18 years old, Ed Flemke won the first heat race he ever entered, at the now-defunct Cherry Park track in Avon, CT. And he soon found a weekly home at the Plainville Stadium, which had opened that same year and was thus every bit as raw as Flemke himself.

The jalopies were cheap to build and maintain. Good thing, because the purses in those early days were downright silly. Flemke often told the story of a night when he swept a track's entire card—winning his heat race, a semi and the feature—and collected $7 at the payoff window. By '51, things had improved, though not by much: A similar sweep put $39 in his pocket. But for a guy with desire, the stock car circuit was heaven. By sticking close to the United Stock Car Racing Club, run by the promotional team of Harvey Tattersall and his son Harvey Jr., a fellow could race Monday nights at Candlelight Stadium in Bridgeport; Tuesday nights at Riverside Park in Agawam, MA; Wednesday nights at the New London-Waterford Speedbowl, on the Connecticut shore; Thursday nights at Savin Rock in West Haven, CT; Friday nights at Plainville; Saturday nights at Riverside; and Sunday afternoons at Plainville again.

In 1952, at the height of the Korean War, Flemke was drafted into the United States Army. It was not a comfortable arrangement for either side. Uncle Sam preferred his men to stay close to their bases—in Flemke's case, Fort Devens in Massachusetts, Fort Dix in New Jersey, and Fort Jackson in South Carolina—but Eddie was drawn to the speedway lights. He went AWOL regularly, and on one such excursion broke his leg in a crash at Candlelight. His punishment included an extended stint in the military, and he served it at Fort Knox, KY. Naturally, he found racing nearby, including a track he remembered as "the Dust Bowl." The purses were outrageous, worse than the early payouts back home. "It cost us $2 to get in," he told writer Pete Zanardi. "I won my heat, the semi-final and the feature for $1.67."

What hectic years those were: Flemke was in the Army from 1952-54, somehow finding time to marry his New Britain sweetheart, Christine Errede, in '53. The couple had daughter Paula in '54, and son Eddie Jr. in '55. And the racing never stopped. In 1954—this time away on a legit weekend pass—Flemke collaborated with Buddy Krebs to win the Riverside 500, in which the top United stars annually paired for a unique "team race."

His military stint over, Flemke lived racing 24/7. Needing a ride for the 1955 season, he leaned on Richie Garuti, a pit-area pal since both were teenagers. Richie and his older brother, Ray, had for several years fielded a successful coupe, always carrying the #14 and sponsored by Ray's Garage, a beacon for racing fanatics in the Kensington, CT, area. The veteran Moe Gherzi, long a winner at tracks like Waterford, Riverside Park and Plainville, was driving the #14, but there was dissension in the Garuti camp. Broadcaster Jack Arute Jr.—whose father later formed a deep bond with Flemke, first as a partner/sponsor of the Garutis and then as owner of the Stafford Motor Speedway—was then a boy hanging around at Ray's, and watched it all happen.

"Ray and Richie didn't see eye-to-eye about drivers," Arute recalls. "Richie thought Moe's best days were behind him, and he wanted Flemke in the seat. Richie Garuti *loved* Eddie. Well, Ray, the stubborn big brother, insisted Moe was staying. So Richie, without anyone's knowledge, built a car in his own garage. One night he towed it over to Ray's. The new car had a #28 on the door, and Eddie Flemke's name on the roof.

"Ray looked it over, and finally he said, 'Why #28?' And Richie answered, 'Twice the car, and twice the goddamn driver.'"

That unhappy exchange had a happy ending: Across the next couple of seasons, Flemke and Gherzi drove their Garuti team cars to a pile of victories, including the 1956 Riverside 500, before Flemke took over as the outfit's sole driver. And Flemke was the Riverside champ in both 1956 and '58, once in the #28 and once in the #14.

Among the United stars of the day were tough guys like Jocko Maggiacomo, Benny Germano, George Lombardo, Jerry Humiston and Buddy Krebs. Also in the mix were three men whose names would come to be linked with Flemke's for . . . well, for all time. One was a young lad out of Glastonbury, CT, named Denny Zimmerman. The others were Rene Charland and Melvin "Red" Foote.

Charland, a French-Canadian living in Agawam, MA, had a permanent smile, a love for practical jokes, and an ever-present cigar. By the late '50s, he was already a towering figure. Photographer John Grady says, "Rene was one of the prime builders of short-track racing in the Northeast. He

was so approachable, so good with the fans, and so willing to help promote the sport."

Foote, from Southington, CT, was an absolute superstar at Waterford, where in 1953 he won an incredible 16 features and the track title. In '58, Foote grabbed seven more features en route to his second Speedbowl crown. Historian Dave Dykes calls Red "a legend amongst early New England racing personalities."

It was a stellar bunch, all right, but Flemke more than held his own. One yellowed clipping from the Empire Speedway in Menands, NY, another United haunt, shows just how strong he was. The year is uncertain, but the race report is dated September 15, and to that point in the season Flemke had won all but two of the features run at the track, this against the likes of Charland, Foote, Big Ed Patnode, and Dick Nephew.

It was a time in Eddie Flemke's life when, for better or worse, everything seemed to be in fast-motion. On the home front, he and Christine hit rough seas, separated, and were divorced in 1960; no doubt, his obsession with racing played a major role. He set up temporary residence just down the road in New Britain with his sister Marge, her husband, Joe Dombrowski, and their two daughters. And it was also in 1960 that Flemke began stepping away from the United circuit and toward NASCAR, which was making a serious push for control of modified racing up and down the Eastern Seaboard.

A car needs a great driver, so brothers Richie and Ray Garuti added Flemke to their stable in 1955. The combo was terrific on the old United Stock Car Racing Club circuit. This shot comes from Riverside Park. *(Shany Lorenzet photo, Dick Berggren Collection)*

Flemke's Studebaker "modified" sits on a trailer outside the New Britain home of Eddie's sister Marge, in February of 1960. It was hauled from there to Daytona, where it was destroyed in a 37-car crash. *(Marge Dombrowski Collection)*

One of his first big leaps into NASCAR ended in disaster, when Flemke took part in the 1960 modified/sportsman event at the year-old Daytona International Speedway. He was caught up in what the next week's *National Speed Sport News* called "the most spectacular accident in the history of automobile racing," a first-lap pileup which tore up 37 cars, flipping 17, and sent eight drivers to the hospital. Writer Benny Kahn described it this way: "Less than 90 seconds after the starter's green flag, one driver went out of control in the east turn and touched off a fantastic chain reaction. Dick Foley of Montreal, Canada, swerved and spun across the steep bank. Three cars speeding in his wake—Larry Frank, Ed Flemke and Al Hager—tried to avoid Foley and went looping and spinning. In a flash, an onrushing pack of cars were engulfed in the wild wreck. Cars went in every direction, crossways, sideways and high in the air, involving countless collisions . . . Ironically, Foley drove his car on the infield grass and came back on the track ahead of the crashing cars. Foley's car did not receive a scratch and he was able to restart the race and finish in 10th place."

Years later, Flemke replayed the melée: "Here comes a guy sideways in front of you, going 150 miles an hour. I figured if I hit him in the side, I'd kill him. So I turned right, myself and Larry Frank. I guess Larry and I were the guys who started the real mix-up."

The list of those involved read like a "Who's Who" of the period's stock car heroes. In addition to Frank, the 1962 Southern 500 winner, there were Grand National (now Nextel Cup) drivers Elmo Langley, Wendell Scott, Earl Balmer, and 1960 World 600 winner Joe Lee Johnson; NASCAR sportsman icons Ralph Earnhardt, Tiny Lund, and Reds Kagle;

New Jersey aces Bob Rossell, Jackie McLaughlin, and Wally Dallenbach; New Yorkers Bill Wimble, Will Cagle, Billy Rafter, and Dick Nephew; Tennessee stud Hooker Hood; and, of course, Eddie Flemke, the hot modified shoe out of Connecticut.

Come the summer of '60, Flemke was a fixture at NASCAR tracks like Norwood Arena, outside Boston, and at the fast five-eighths-miler at Thompson, CT, steering Benny Washburn's #15X and other rides.

On the track, he was winning. Off the track, he was establishing the contradictory persona—sly, yet helpful—for which he is still remembered.

First, the caring, mentoring Flemke. Among those Eddie took under his wing was a young driver named Billy Greco, who had won big at West Haven but yearned to make his bones at Riverside Park. Offered the seat in the famed Suffield Auto Parts #5 owned by Al Lango, Lou Colturi, and Munn Nigro, Greco wondered if he was ready. "I was a little afraid of it," he told writer Pete Zanardi. "It was a good car. Buddy Krebs was driving it, and they had fired him." According to Greco, Flemke "was the guy who made me get in it." Come the warm-up session on Greco's debut, "Flemke came over and said, 'I'll tell you how to get that car around. Go out there and drive the car as hard as you can into the corners. Spin it out.' That's what I did. I came in, and he said, 'Did you learn anything?' I said, 'I don't understand.' He asked, 'How far did you go into the corner before it spun?' I said, 'Pretty deep.' He said, 'Well, don't go beyond that,' and left it right there. That's how I won a lot of races with the #5. Those other guys would go into the corner, and I would listen to their motors. When they let off, I would go in further. I did it because I knew the car wouldn't

Benny Washburn's coupe was one of Steady Eddie's first regular NASCAR rides at the dawn of the '60s. *(Shany Lorenzet photo, Dick Berggren Collection)*

come around on me." Greco told Zanardi that Flemke was "probably the smartest race driver I've seen."

And then there was the scheming, mischievous Flemke, constantly using those smarts to his own advantage. One traveling companion, Bill Brown, can still see the gang in Norwood's pit area staring in curiosity as Flemke cranked away at a front-end adjustment bolt with a long-handled ratchet. What Brown knew, but the onlookers didn't, was that the socket on the end of that ratchet was so oversized that it spun freely, never grabbing the bolt. "Pretty soon," says Brown, "you noticed the other drivers and mechanics saying, 'Hey, maybe we need to turn that bolt, too.' They all started messing with their cars, and Eddie hadn't done a thing!"

The locations had changed—Norwood instead of Plainville, Thompson instead of Riverside Park—but Eddie Flemke's winning ways had not. His niece Susan, Marge's daughter, is grown now, but she still sees it all through a little girl's eyes.

"Our house was full of Uncle Eddie's trophies," Susan remembers. "It was up to me and my sister JoAnn to keep them all dusted, so we didn't like trophies. But, you know, it seemed like he was always coming home with another one."

"We didn't have everything, but we had what was necessary"

Growing up in the happy, hectic Flemke household

by BETTY VANESSE

Betty Vanesse is the second of six children born to Jake and Wanda Flemke, and the elder of Ed Flemke's two surviving sisters. Though she moved to Florida better than 50 years ago, she still rattles off names and locations from her hometown of New Britain, CT—not to mention assorted New England speedways—with alarming ease. Betty and her late husband, Van, served for years as the genial and very understanding February landlords for Steady Eddie and whatever New England-based racing folks happened to travel south with him for any given Daytona Speedweeks. Spry and sharp, Betty resides these days in Anderson, South Carolina, not far from her son Jack, who as a young man spent much of the summer of 1961, at the dawn of the Eastern Bandits era, on the road with his Uncle Eddie. Jack Vanesse later drove late models in South Florida.

Betty Vanesse

GROWING UP, there were six of us kids, four girls and two boys, and Eddie was the baby. There was Lydia, the oldest, and then me. Next came my brother Georgie, then my two younger sisters, Margie and Dottie, and finally Eddie. Today, there's only Margie and me.

Our father came over from Germany in, I believe, 1907. Mother came later, also from Germany, in 1913. Both of their families just happened to settle in New Britain, and eventually they met and were married and had children. There was a pretty wide spread in our ages; gosh, I was born in 1918, and Eddie didn't come along until 1930. And his older brother, George, was born in 1921, so even between the two brothers there was a gap of several years.

Scrapbook memories: Eddie "Honey" Flemke with father Jacob and older sister Dottie, sometime in the 1930s. *(Carolyn Flemke Collection)*

When my father first got to America, he went to work at Corbin Screw in New Britain. But while he was working there in the factory, he learned, on his own, to fix automobiles. So, as a self-taught mechanic, he ended up opening his own business, Jake's Garage. I still remember the address: 269 Oak Street in New Britain.

Mother never worked. Her job was to take care of the house, and, of course, with six children that was enough. And, I must say, my mother was a very good housekeeper and a wonderful cook. Back then, the neighbors used to say, "Give Mrs. Flemke a bone, and with that bone she'll make the most delicious soup!" Yes, there was always food on the table.

My father was apparently quite a daredevil. He loved motorcycles, and some people say he rode one across the country. I've heard stories about that, but unfortunately we have nothing down on paper about it. But I know he had a motorcycle with a sidecar, and one day he was giving one of my sisters a ride in that sidecar and my mother said, "No more." I guess she didn't like that very much.

We lived in several different places in New Britain. We never had a home of our own, always apartments. But, I'll tell you, we had a very happy life. We didn't have everything, but we had everything that was necessary. When Christmas came, we each got a toy, which was a big deal, and there would be candy and cookies. We managed pretty well. Like I said, we had what we needed. And, you know, we were very thankful for it.

We always had a dog in the family, although the dog was usually down at my father's garage. He'd always keep the dog out by the sidewalk, so if anybody came into the driveway the dog would bark and he'd know there was somebody stopping by.

Every Sunday morning, us kids went to church. Mother didn't always go—she used to say that with six kids, she needed a break—and I'm sorry to say that my father didn't always go, but they made us go. So every week, we had church and Sunday school, which I think was good for us. You know, Eddie was always very well-mannered, and I think those manners came from the way we were raised. Our parents were very big on the idea that you should watch your mouth and mind your manners.

Hanging out at Jake's garage, Eddie poses with two things every boy needs: a solid dad, and a reliable dog. *(left, Marge Dombrowski Collection; right, Betty Vanesse Collection)*

Our mother, sadly, died when Eddie was only seven years old. I suppose that each of us girls became even more of a big sister to him after that, simply because we had lost our mother and he was still so young. My father was certainly a big help, of course, but a lot of the household work fell to us girls, including looking after Eddie. Although, I have to say, because I got married just a year after our mother passed away, the other girls did more of that than I did, especially Lydia, because she was the oldest. But, yes, I did look after him. One day he came home and mentioned that the teacher had rapped him over the knuckles for something he'd done, and, boy, I went straight down to the school and I told that teacher a thing or two. I said, "You have to have some patience with this boy. After all, he has no mother at home." Eddie was the baby, and it was up to me and my sisters to watch over him. In fact, after I got married, my husband Van and I would take Eddie out on the weekends for that very reason.

Here's something people may not know: When he was growing up, our nickname for Eddie was "Honey." See, my brother Georgie had been called "Sonny" for a long time, so when Eddie came along we had to have a special name for him, too. So those were our brothers, Sonny and Honey. That was fine with Eddie until he began to grow a bit older. Pretty soon, he preferred that we just use his real name, and looking back I can understand why.

Eddie was a quiet young man, but he was such a lovable boy, almost *too* lovable. He was an upbeat kid. If he had any hobbies, I didn't notice them, because I was busy working all day; I had a factory job, making thermos bottles. I guess Eddie's main interest would have been hanging around at his father's garage.

That garage was a very busy place. My father had a lot of customers, and there were also a lot of fellows who would just kind of stop by to talk. Eddie and Georgie were usually there with their father, so I suppose it was natural that they learned mechanics along the way.

Eddie was always tagging along after his older brother, which I'm sure wasn't too much fun for Georgie because Eddie was so much younger. It took a little bit of time, I think, for Georgie to get used to that.

It was Georgie, of course, who first started racing, and that was in the midgets. To this day, I'm not really sure exactly how he got interested in that. There were a lot of racers in the New Britain area back then, including Bert Brooks, but I can't say who got Georgie so involved. I do remember that my father wasn't too pleased, although after he began to see that Georgie was so serious about it he began to accept the racing. In fact, after a while my father would even go along to the tracks, and during the week he would work on the race cars. He was very, very proud of both those boys. Now, he loved us girls, too, but just like any father, I suppose, his boys were tops in his mind.

I can remember going to a lot of races myself when Georgie was racing. Those midgets used to race all over the place: Cherry Park in Avon, Bridgeport, Danbury, West Springfield, Stafford Springs, just everywhere. I used to keep track of everything that happened by writing it all down. I must have done a good job, because the club that organized the midget races, the ARDC, would sometimes ask to look at my paperwork.

Georgie won an awful lot of races in those midgets. I'd be up there in the grandstands, screaming my head off.

Eddie followed Georgie around, too. I remember how much he admired Georgie's mechanical skill. He used to always tell people how good Georgie was at taking a car that was all torn up and putting it back together so beautifully. And, of course, following his older brother around was what got Eddie involved in racing.

Once Eddie was driving, I didn't go as much, because I was married. We did go to see him whenever we could, but he was just getting to the point where he was winning a lot of races when Van and I moved to Florida in 1950. I still saw him quite a bit, because Eddie often visited us in the winter, and whenever we got back to Connecticut we usually went to see him race. If I couldn't go for some reason, Van would always go. And our sister Margie followed Eddie's career very closely. Dottie wasn't as interested as the rest of us, but certainly we were all very proud of how successful Eddie became.

George Flemke was one of the premier midget drivers of the 1950s, winning up and down the East Coast. *(Shany Lorenzet photo, R.A. Silvia Collection)*

Jacob Flemke with one of his boy's mid-'50s coupes. Not a race fan at first, he warmed up as the years rolled on. *(Marge Dombrowski Collection)*

Watching Eddie race was always fun for me, unless it came down to real close competition. Then I would close my eyes off and on, and sort of peek at him. It's a hard thing to watch a loved one in a situation like that. But if he won, which he often did, I loved it.

I believe it was Eddie's personality, as much as anything else, that helped him in the very beginning of his career. He was very *willful*. He was strong-headed, just like all the Flemkes have been, German and strong-headed, so once he put his mind to racing, nothing was going to stop him. I feel like, since he was the baby and we had given him so much attention, he really wanted to show us that he could succeed. And that's funny, because until he started racing I never did see anything in Eddie that would have led me to believe he was so competitive inside.

Another thing about Eddie being stubborn and strong-headed: If you were Eddie's friend, he would do anything for you, but if you had a real disagreement about something, he could wipe you out of his mind completely. That was just his way. I remember a period when he and his brother had had words about something or other, and it took a *long* time before he finally spoke to Georgie or his wife, Fran. Many times I would say to him on the telephone, "Eddie, please call Georgie," but he refused to do it. He was always nice to me about it, but he'd say, "Betty, I'm not going to do that." Well, they finally straightened it out one day when we were all at Daytona. We were in the infield, and I knew that Georgie had a motorhome there, so I said, "Eddie, I'm going over to see Frannie.

The name on the door is "Little Eddy," a nickname announcers hung on Flemke in the jalopy days. And check out the sponsor: dear ol' Dad! *(Shany Lorenzet photo, Dick Berggren Collection)*

Would you like to come along?" He said, "No, you go ahead." So I went and visited my sister-in-law, and pretty soon came a knock on the door. It was Eddie. I excused myself, and I let Eddie and Frannie talk. Later that same day, he went and found Georgie, and they finally talked, too. I told him later, "Eddie, you made me so happy today." And it was such a good thing that they did talk, because the very next month Frannie passed away, and it was just over a year later that Eddie passed away.

But, you know, that was Eddie. For whatever reason, he just decided that particular day at Daytona that it was time for everybody to talk things out. He made up his mind, and that was that.

When my husband and I moved to Florida, we lived down near Miami for several years and then moved further north, to Port Orange and then Deland. Either way, Eddie would visit us whenever he came down for the races in February. And I understood how that was; racing came first, so I knew he came down more for the races than to see his sister. But that was fine with me, because at least I got to see him. I was always thankful that he was able to visit. He might have a whole gang with him, but I didn't care. Whoever he wanted to bring along, it was fine with me. I'd go out and rent extra beds so everyone could be comfortable, and I'd tell them, "Boys, don't worry about how the house looks. Just enjoy yourselves."

When we lived in the Miami area, they'd come down a week early. Eddie and his friends would do their own thing during the day, like going to watch jai-alai or maybe to the dog track. Then they'd come home in time for supper, and they'd either go back out or they'd sit and play cards. They'd do that for a week or so, relaxing, and then they'd head up to Daytona.

Later on, when we lived in Port Orange and Deland, Eddie would stay with me during the Daytona races. That was wonderful for me, because Eddie and Van got along so well. They would go off to the race track during the day, and then we'd have our evenings together. I'd cook dinner for Eddie, and for anybody he brought with him.

No matter how many years we did that, I still looked forward to it. Little brother was coming to visit, and that was so nice for me.

We couldn't have asked for a better brother than Eddie. He was such a wonderful guy. He was always so respectful of each and every one of us in the family, and we respected him so much. And, you know, no matter where I was living at a particular time—in Florida, or lately in South Carolina, or wherever—it seems like there's always somebody who's heard of him. His name comes up in conversation and people will say, "Eddie? Oh, of *course* I remember Eddie Flemke! I knew him very well. . ."

It makes me feel so wonderful that people remember him the way they do. In 2005 he was inducted into the New Britain Sports Hall of Fame, and I went home for the ceremony, along with my sister Margie, who lives near Fort Lauderdale. That was such a great visit, and it made me so happy, so proud, to see this happen in our hometown.

It's a special thing, to think that people still think so highly of him.

"As small as he was, he was a strong little shit"

Two New Britain kids, racing hard in the jalopy days

by GEORGE LOMBARDO

George Lombardo was a fierce competitor in the best days of the old United Stock Car Racing circuit, which during the 1950s and early '60s sanctioned racing at numerous short tracks throughout Southern New England and Eastern New York. Lombardo became a familiar face in victory lane at Plainville Stadium, the Waterford Speedbowl, Riverside Park and elsewhere. Having spent dozens of evenings battling with Ed Flemke, George now passes many of his afternoons with his late friend's son, Eddie Jr., lunching at the Race Works shop owned by the younger Flemke and Reggie Ruggiero. "I've known both of those guys since they started racing," Lombardo says. "Hell, I knew Eddie Jr. when he was just a little kid. Plus, this is a good way for me to keep connected with what's going on." Recently, the noontime meal at the Berlin, CT, chassis shop included a cake commemorating Lombardo's 82nd birthday.

George Lombardo

WHEN I FIRST REALLY GOT TO KNOW Eddie Flemke, I must have been about 22 or 23 years old. He was much younger, probably 17. The season was starting at Plainville Stadium, and he brought a car over there to race, but they wouldn't let him drive. Too young.

Now, I should add that I had already seen him around. I knew his father, and of course I knew his brother George, and I knew his sisters. Eddie was just a young kid, but you could tell he was smart. And eager, very eager. He loved anything to do with automobiles. In fact, I can remember him driving his father's Buick down the street, and when you saw that thing coming you'd swear nobody was in it. He was so young and so small, he'd be peeking through the steering wheel. I worried about that, so I said to George, "Hey, your little brother was driving the Buick." George said, "Oh, don't worry, he drives it all over the place." I couldn't believe it.

Eddie's father had a garage on Oak Street in New Britain, and I'd had my street car repaired there a couple times. This was back during World War II, and right after the war had ended. George said, "You ought to stop by more," so I did that. And this one night, I noticed that over in the corner he had this *thing* covered up under a canvas.

I said, "What's that?"

Well, George pulled that cover off, and underneath was a midget race car. It startled me. I had never seen one before. George, of course, was a very good midget driver, but none of my gang knew anything about racing at that point. But, boy, that was a nice machine, and I still remember that V8-60 engine under the hood. And then they actually started it up for me; it had what they called a "hot-shot" battery, so they just put the car up on jacks and turned the rear wheels by hand to get it going. I listened to that thing, and that was all it took. I got very interested in that car, and I couldn't wait to see it run.

Just after the war, midgets were really big around here. Oh, geez, they got some good crowds. In fact, Eddie loved them as much as I loved them. I started going to a lot of midget races, and I would see him there. Sometimes he'd go with his brother, and sometimes he'd get there on his own. That Eddie, boy, he got around. He didn't need many people to help him get places. He'd figure out a way. You could see already that he just *loved* racing.

Like I said, I went all over the place to watch George and everybody else, so before long I knew a lot of guys who ran midgets. But pretty soon, these stock cars came in; at first, everybody called them "jalopies." As I remember it, the first jalopy show around here was at Cherry Park in Avon, and it was hilarious: the wrecks, the rollovers, the rough-riding, all that stuff went over big with the fans. I was sitting in the stands myself, and I loved it. It was different. And it wasn't just the silly stuff; the racing was really good, too, very competitive.

Well, before long they were running those cars at other tracks, too, and I liked them. And pretty soon they announced that this new jalopy-style racing was going to come to Plainville Stadium, which had been a real good midget track. So I watched the jalopies run there a couple times, and it looked like a lot of fun. I decided that I wanted to do that, too.

Now, I always drove Buicks on the road, and there was a guy I used to know in New Britain named Leo Woitja, who ran Woitja's Garage and specialized in Buicks. Leo had an old '35 Buick, a big four-door sedan that he would take out on calls to push in any cars that had broken down on the road. I said, "Leo, would you sell me that car?" He said that first I had to tell him what I wanted it for. I told him I wanted to run it in the jalopy races. He said, "Fine. I'll *make* this race car, and you *drive* this race car." So right off the bat, I had a car owner. I never even had to buy the thing! He was my setup man and my mechanic, and what helped was that Leo knew everything there was to know about a Buick.

It was so easy for a young guy like me to get involved in racing back then. I didn't have much money—I was working as a well driller, just like I've been a well driller all my life—but, you know, I'll bet we didn't have a hundred bucks in that whole car.

I spent my whole first season in that car. That would have been 1949. The following year, Ray Garuti, who I knew from the midgets, said, "I'll build a jalopy if you'll drive for me." I guess I had done well enough to impress him, I don't know. I jumped into his #99, which was a 1935 Ford coupe he had bought from his neighbor. We won a bunch of races with that car at Plainville. We were sponsored by Arute Ford, which was operated by Frank Arute, Jack's brother. As everybody knows, Jack Arute eventually bought Stafford Speedway, and the Garuti brothers, Ray and Rich, were very successful in the stock cars for years to come.

But let me tell you a little bit about those jalopy days.

First, those cars weren't too fancy. The frame was stock, stock, stock. Our engine was nothing special, either, at least not right away; the sides were welded up where the block had cracked. Oh, we had an awful time in the beginning with the Ford flatheads heating up, and so did everybody else. But Ray and Rich Garuti knew a few things, so they put in a good cam and a lighter flywheel. Yeah, we were cheating right off the hop. Oh, those guys knew what distributor to use, how to bore out the jets in the carburetor, things like that. Hey, the rules said we had to use stock parts, and all our parts were stock when the Garuti brothers *got* 'em. They just didn't *stay* stock!

For safety stuff, we had nothing but a lap belt. The seat we used was the one that came with the car, I believe. It was covered in mohair, and Jesus, you'd get hot and that stuff would itch. For a uniform, we used a T-shirt and dungarees, and a helmet. That was one thing I had going for me: I had a good Cromwell helmet, from England, and back then that Cromwell was the very best. But, you know, I didn't care about safety, because I didn't think about danger. I never once imagined that I could get hurt in a race. That sounds crazy, I know, because back then there were lots of crashes, rollovers, fires. But never, ever in my life did I ever feel fear.

We raced with the United Stock Car group, Harvey Tattersall's club. It seemed like they controlled everything back then. They had Candlelight Stadium in Bridgeport, which was a tight track built around a ball field; I *watched* races there, but I never drove at Candlelight. And they had Savin Rock in West Haven, another very tight track built around a ball field, but it was right in a big amusement park, so it was a

George Lombardo was the prototypical 1950s stock car hero, a rugged man who won wherever he went. *(Shany Lorenzet photo, Dick Berggren Collection)*

fun, beautiful place to race. They had a board fence on the back side of that track, and if you went through that fence you ended up out on the trolley tracks. Sparky Belmont went through that fence one night, and here came that trolley car, blowing its whistle! Then there was Riverside Park, a tremendous, tremendous bullring, also in an amusement park. That track was a fifth-miler in those days, and so flat that I swore the third and fourth corners were actually banked the wrong way. Another United track was New London, which of course is now called the Waterford Speedbowl. It looked pretty much like it does now, except the very top lane, out next to the wall, was a very soft bed of crushed stone, which they thought would slow you down if you lost control. The trouble was, the track was banked and that top lane of crushed stone was flat, so if you slid up the bank you never slowed down until you hit the wall. Only then did you drop down into the soft stuff! But other than that, the track layout was just like it is now. To us, that Speedbowl was a nice, big track with lots of room compared to those ball fields.

My favorite place of all was Plainville Stadium. That was always a great track, a quarter-mile around with just a little bit of a bank. It had nice, wide corners, and I loved that, because that's where I had to do most of my passing. In my day, the fast cars always started in the back, so I always had to work my way up. Believe it or not, I once went to Plainville and started 40th in a *heat* race. That's right, a heat race! And I made the feature! Oh, you can't believe how many cars used to come to those jalopy races. The pits filled up, so they'd park 'em all over the grounds.

Don't forget, it was a different world back then. It wasn't easy to do the kind of traveling we did. There were no interstate highways—every-

An unidentified trophy girl hands the hardware to Flemke in the early '50s. *(Marge Dombrowski Collection)*

thing was back roads—so even going to New London or the Eastern States Fairgrounds in West Springfield was a haul. Today, as long as you know your interstates, you can go *anywhere* without a hassle. Not then. And, of course, we got the race car to the track using a tow bar.

Now, right along in this same time is when Eddie started showing up. It was only at Plainville in the beginning, and he did very well there, right from the start. He just had a lot of ability, and he was fast. Both of us were. Yes, Plainville was the place where we pulled up our pants and figured out what we were doing, and learned. Then it was on to Riverside, New London, *all* those places.

The difference was, some of us traveled around a little. Eddie started traveling, and it was like he never stopped.

Eddie and I had some great battles. Christ, pick any track, and we battled there. I had a lot of confidence in his ability, right from the start. Oh, we raced hard! And yet we'd help each other, too, off the track and even *on* the track. See, there were times when maybe I'd block a little bit for him, or he'd block a little bit for me, or one of us would let the other one back in line if he was trapped in the wrong lane. That's because we were friends. The promoters made us out to be rivals, but we never paid any attention to that. Eddie wanted to beat me, and I wanted to beat him, but we always got along. Yeah, there might be a time when we'd be going for the same spot and one of us would screw up, and the other would get mad. But never any hard feelings, never any bitter feelings. It

Gosh, think of all the feature wins divvied up by this pair! That's Jocko Maggiacomo looking on as Flemke does some carburetor surgery. *(Carolyn Flemke Collection)*

was a good friendship, always. Nothing on the track was so important that it was bigger than that friendship.

One thing I always noticed was that in those early days, Eddie had a very hard time driving for anybody but himself. That's because the other owners didn't do things the way he wanted them done. He was very advanced in the way he thought about things, which meant he was ahead of those other guys. Some owners had the latest, greatest equipment, but they didn't have the know-how. So he'd just build his own cars, and he'd make those damn things *go.*

The car was basic, and so was the driver. But both got the job done at the Waterford Speedbowl, where this shot was taken. *(Shany Lorenzet photo, Dick Berggren Collection)*

By this time, you still couldn't buy a damn thing made for racing, except for a special tire, the Ascot 716 made by Firestone. But if you tried really hard, you could *find* stuff, and Eddie was so good at that. Like, there were two brothers in Rhode Island, Sam and Cesar Litterio, who would grind cams right there in their little machine shop. You'd bring your cam, and oh, they'd put a grind on that thing. Those were the first racing cams I ever knew about around here, and Eddie found those guys pretty early on. That was all hush-hush; everything was a big secret in those days.

For the most part, we used what we could find in a junkyard, and the rest was all in the tricks you knew: what springs to put in which corner, how to put wedge in, what shock absorbers to play around with, stuff like that. And that was one of Eddie's strong suits: He knew all the tricks.

He was the first guy I ever saw cut extra grooves in the tires, looking for more bite. That worked. And because those old junkyard tires and recaps had thick, thick rubber, the right rear would get really hot; well, Eddie he had another trick where he would actually drill into the tread, especially around the shoulder, to cool that tire down. He understood, way before most of us did, that a tire was no good if it got too hot.

Skinny tires, a stock frame, a hopped-up flathead . . . and big-time sponsorship from an eatery not far from Riverside Park! *(Shany Lorenzet photo, Dick Berggren Collection)*

You know, for a few years—especially as the jalopy cars became modifieds—a lot of drivers and car owners were ahead of Eddie and me, equipment-wise. I mean, guys like Moe Gherzi, Jocko Maggiacomo, Moon Burgess, and Whitey Brainard were very advanced. They had very good cars, and they were great drivers. Next to them, we were like kids. But we caught up to them pretty quick. Caught 'em, and left 'em in the dust. That's the beauty of being young and dumb. We were chargers, and we were very determined.

In fact, I think the reason Eddie became so successful was his determination. This kid really, really *lived* for racing. In those early days, he had no time for anything else. If there was anybody who could find something new that would work, Eddie was the one. And, let's face it, he was a terrific driver, a real pusher. By that, I don't mean that he actually pushed people around on the track, although he would certainly do that if he felt it was necessary. What I mean is, he was a charger. He knew how to get that car around, and he would just come right up through the field. He was very, very good in traffic, and yet he also had the patience to win the long races. And as small as he was, he was a strong little shit. I was big, and very strong, which really helped in those days, because you needed to be strong with those cars. You had no

Left to right: United boss Harvey Tattersall Jr., car owner Ray Garuti, Flemke, flagman Al Parent, and co-owner Richie Garuti after another Riverside score. *(Carolyn Flemke Collection)*

power steering, and bad brakes, and cars that didn't handle, so you really had to muscle them. And Eddie could bull a car around, that's for sure.

That reminds me of something funny. You know, the good drivers were really in demand back then, because we would go to a place like Riverside Park and there might be 100 cars there. Well, naturally, some of the owners were worried that their cars weren't going to get into the feature, so they would ask the good drivers to qualify their cars, *plus* their own cars. I had nights where I ran every single heat race, a different car each time, and I know Eddie did, too. And then there might be two or three consi races, and we'd do the same thing there. There were no rules against that stuff yet. Then everybody would put their regular drivers in for the feature, and we'd beat 'em. It was crazy.

I got out of racing in 1966. I'd gotten married, and then along came the children, and I had to think about providing for my family. I needed money that I knew would be there, and to me that meant working. Then I went into business on my own—New Britain Wells—and I basically stayed away from racing altogether. I *had* to, because quitting was not easy. So I paid no attention to racing. Honestly, I didn't even keep up on how Eddie was doing. Oh, I knew he was still winning races, but the only time I knew more than that was if he and I happened to bump into each other at somebody's garage. We'd shoot the breeze, because we were always good friends. But outside of that, I just didn't know much about what was going on with him, or with racing, for a long time.

Now, years and years later, in the 1980s, I was driving down South Street in New Britain and I saw a midget sitting there. Turns out it belonged to Hank Stevens, who used to race stock cars with us at Waterford way back when. He had gotten into midget racing, and it just so happened that his car was parked there because he was driving a trailer truck for an outfit in town. I looked at that midget, and I liked it a lot. I said to Hank, "Geez, if you ever want to sell that thing, give me a holler." A few years later, he called: "You still want to buy that midget?" So I did, and for a few years I was a car owner. But no more.

My racing days are over, but I still go out to different tracks, just to watch: Waterford on Saturday nights, sometimes to Stafford, occasionally to Thompson.

Looking back, I had a good career. Sometimes I think I won in more oddball types of cars than any other driver I knew: a Chevy, a Ford, a Buick, a Dodge, everything. To me, it never made a difference what the hell I was driving, as long as it handled and stayed together. I'm proud of what I did. I won a *lot* of races.

But compared to Eddie, I never went too far from home. I dug wells, and he raced all over hell. Look how long he raced. Look at all the cars he drove, and how the cars changed in that time. Look at all the good times he had, and all the heartaches he went through.

But what I remember most about Eddie is that he came from the old school, just like I did. He could do it with nothing. *Nothing*. Just use your head, and make it work. He built his own cars, he came up with things that everybody copied—like the Flemke front end later on—and he kept on driving and kept on winning.

I'm telling you, he was really something.

"He was consumed by racing"

A rising young driver tackles matrimony and fatherhood

by CHRISTINE BOWEN

Christine Bowen (then Christine Errede) and Ed Flemke were married in 1953, by which time the new groom had become one of New England racing's genuine stars. She was by his side through what must have been a dizzying period: His stint in the military, parenthood, and as many as seven nights of racing each week surely kept them hopping. Though the couple split and eventually divorced in 1960, they shared a friendly oversight of two rambunctious children, daughter Paula and son Eddie Jr. Christine later married Paul Bowen, and the two are proud parents of another son, Ken Bowen. Christine still visits the area's speedways, cheering on Eddie Jr. in NASCAR Whelen Modified Tour events. Her fellow fans are likely unaware that the lady in their midst was something of a racing pioneer, having been one of the few female car owners in the rough-and-tumble, macho 1950s.

Christine Bowen

EDDIE AND I MET in a strange way. My father used to go to Eddie's father's garage on Oak Street in New Britain to have his car serviced, and I kind of knew him from there. And my parents used to take my brother and me to Cherry Park to watch George Flemke run with the midgets, so I knew a little bit about racing, too. But I was actually introduced to Eddie by a girlfriend of mine, who was going out with a friend of his. I was still very young, maybe 14 years old. Eddie was a few years older, and he was already racing when we met.

I was a New Britain girl, born and raised there. At the time we met, I was into baseball, roller-skating, tennis, and all kinds of sports. My big plan included going to college and becoming a teacher; math or science,

I wasn't sure, but teaching was my long-range plan. But, you know, plans change.

We were friends for a while before we got involved, because I was so young. But I'd see Eddie as I was walking to school; there were some shortcuts I could take, but if I went the long way it took me right past Eddie's father's garage. Naturally, once I'd met him, I would walk that way all the time, the way girls do.

Around this time, Eddie began teaching me how to drive. We used to go on the winding roads behind A.W. Stanley Park, in New Britain. I remember one time I was driving and Eddie pulled the steering wheel from my hands; it seems a tree was calling my name, and I was going right toward it. Needless to say, that ended my driving lesson for that day.

Eventually we began dating, which went on for a while, and in 1953 we decided we were going to sneak away to Massachusetts and get married, so we did. It was pretty spontaneous, and we were going to keep it a secret. *Ha-ha!* That didn't last. Then Paula was born in 1954, and Little Eddie in '55.

By then, Eddie had been racing for quite a while, and he was also in the Army. Of course, those two didn't always mix, but he didn't have a choice; he had been drafted in 1952, so he went into the service. But anytime he came home on leave, he would race, and sometimes he raced when he wasn't supposed to be away from the base. One night, racing in Bridgeport, he broke his leg and went to St. Vincent's Hospital, where the Military Police caught up with him. He had to make up some lost time over that incident; it was quite a few days, as I recall.

The funny thing was, after he made up that time, they actually made him an instructor at the mechanic's school at Fort Knox, Kentucky. By that time, our daughter Paula had been born, so she and I went down to Kentucky for a while. And I got pregnant with young Eddie while we were at Fort Knox, so I tell him that even though he was born in Hartford, he started out in Kentucky.

While we were out there, Eddie continued racing. We would go across the Ohio River into Indiana, and he would race at the dirt tracks there. This time, however, he had authorized passes to go racing.

Once we got home to Connecticut, we were right back into the swing of things, with Eddie racing all the time. I went to just about all the tracks, from Riverside and Plainville to Langhorne, Pennsylvania, and some tracks in New Jersey. I do remember some places better than others. For instance, Stafford was a dirt track then, and I remember sitting in the grandstands and getting hit by the flying dirt as the cars came out of the fourth turn. And I really enjoyed Plainville, which was a fun place in those days. But Riverside Park was always my favorite track; the atmosphere there was always so exciting. At Riverside, the cars

It's the mid-'50s, and Mr. and Mrs. Ed Flemke are posing in Victory Lane, a common occurrence. Christine sewed the white stripe on Eddie's dark work pants, giving them a genuine "driving uniform" look! *(Carolyn Flemke Collection)*

came onto the track through a gate in the third turn, across the infield from the grandstands, and every time I saw those cars pull out onto that track I'd get goose bumps.

Racing was what Eddie wanted to do, so I went along with it as best I could. Sometimes it was tough, because we had the kids, so I had to arrange the babysitters and things like that. But, you know, I felt like I should be there to support him. There were lots of times when we couldn't go together. He might have to leave for the track at two o'clock, and I'd drive up later, by myself or with the kids.

Racing was very different then. The wives were always in the grandstands, and *never* in the pits. Women simply weren't allowed. And the dress was different; you would never even *think* of wearing jeans. The women wore dresses and a lot of the men dressed up, too. We looked like we were going to the Kentucky Derby, not someplace like Plainville Stadium. In fact, somewhere I've got a picture from when Eddie won the Riverside 500 in 1954 with Buddy Krebs—it was a team race—and both Buddy's wife and I were wearing dresses and heels.

You had to learn to control your emotions at the track, because everybody seemed to know the drivers' wives, especially the wives of the drivers who won races. A lot of the fans knew where you sat, and they would *watch* you to see how you reacted. So I used to bring a three-ring, loose-leaf notebook with me, and I'd sit there and score the races, writing down the number of every car as it came across the line. That helped me contain how I felt—because I was too busy to be jumping up and down—and it also became a tool for Eddie. He would look through those pages later and he could see, lap by lap, who was moving up and how all that related to him.

Naturally, I knew racing was dangerous. I was at Plainville once, on Mother's Day, when one of the drivers was killed. But I could always compartmentalize; I could disconnect my worries while I was watching Eddie. It was worse when I stayed home with the kids, or when he was traveling far away and I didn't go along. Not being there is hard on any wife, girlfriend, or fiancé; if you're there, you can see what's going on, but if you're not there, you're just waiting for a phone call.

In the beginning, like everybody else, Eddie raced wearing just a T-shirt and work pants. Then I said, "Why don't you wear a nicer shirt, and maybe some black jeans?" He said he'd try that, so I sewed a white stripe down the side of those black pants. He shrugged it off at first, but I could see that he liked it. It was more professional.

You know, through those years when we were together, Eddie always worked a regular job. Racing alone couldn't support anybody back then. He was a very good mechanic—if somebody came to him with a problem, he knew what was wrong as soon as they turned on the engine—and that's how he earned his living. For a long time, he was the mechanic for the Heslin Dairy in New Britain, on Farmington Avenue. In fact,

This blue and gold coupe, a real looker for its day, was actually owned by Christine Flemke, making her a pioneer of sorts in the macho 1950s. *(Carolyn Flemke Collection)*

he kept the car right there. One night he asked me to start that thing up, and the garage door was closed, so pretty soon I was coughing from the fumes. I said, "Geez, if you want to get rid of me, just ask me to leave! This is killing me!"

Our lives were a bit different from the lives of the other couples we knew. They didn't go to the races, but, by the same token, we didn't go to social functions. I do think, though, that there was a little more *excitement* for us. They all got married, had kids, and stayed home. We got married, had kids, and traveled around a lot.

Still, there was a lot that we missed, a lot that we gave up. Just little things, like going out on a Saturday night, or going out for a nice dinner. In the off-season he did enjoy bowling, a competitive sport he was also good at; we would bowl as a family, going with his brother George, his sister Marge, their spouses, and my mom and dad. But Eddie didn't like being out on New Year's Eve, didn't like parties, didn't like to dance. I don't know that it was shyness; it's just that his preference was always racing.

I liked racing, too, I really did. While we were married, I was heavily involved with it. I kept his records, made scrapbooks, and ran around and got parts for him. I even owned his car at one point; that was the blue and gold #61. And I honestly enjoyed watching Eddie race. I always believed he was one of the best, if not *the* best. I know other people remember him the same way; once I was at Loudon, New Hampshire, watching Eddie Jr. race, and was wearing my Flemke sweatshirt. A fan across from me leaned over and said, "You know, I used to watch his father race, too. He was the greatest."

You know, they talk about racing being in your blood. I guess it really *was* in Eddie's. His father had raced motorcycles, and his brother George raced, and I'm sure they influenced him. Racing, I believe, was Eddie's first love. I didn't recognize that at first. That came later. In time, I could see that he was consumed by racing; it was his life. Racing came first, then the kids and the friends. I'm sure I was somewhere down the line.

Don't misunderstand me, Eddie was a good guy. But you know how people talk about the way racing can be someone's mistress? Well, it's true. The spouse tends to take a back seat when someone is that passionate about something. Eddie was always at the garage, or he was off with the race car.

We were divorced in 1960, but we remained friends, good friends. I mean, we had children together, and I never wanted to deprive the kids of being with their father, which they really enjoyed. And, you know, both of our kids ending up spending their lives around racing. I guess that was inevitable, because they went to so many races and spent a lot of time at his garage. Honestly, it wasn't what I wanted for them, but that's only because you always want what's best for your kids, and you want them to do better than you did. Again, I had seen how you could be totally consumed by racing, and I just didn't want that for them because I knew what it did to my life. You have to have a balance, and, fortunately, they both found that balance.

But, yes, Eddie and I were always friendly. You know, many years later Eddie Jr. was an usher at our friend Tony Altieri's wedding. I was there with my husband Paul, and Eddie was with his wife Carolyn, and we all sat at the same table. People seemed so amazed that we could sit there together, but we were fine with it. In fact, I babysat for Eddie and Carolyn's daughter Kristy, and they babysat for Kenny, my son with Paul. The fact that Eddie and I didn't get along as husband and wife didn't mean we stopped getting along as people. That, I think, made it so much easier for everybody, especially the kids.

When I look back on those old days, I'll think: It's too bad things turned out the way they did, but it was an interesting time. Yes, that's the right word: *interesting*.

"It was like he just had to get out and do this"

Full of energy, a young man fills his life with racing

by MARGE DOMBROWSKI

Marge Dombrowski is the fourth of six children born to Jake and Wanda Flemke, and the younger of Ed Flemke's two surviving sisters. Like all the Flemke girls, she watched both her brothers, first George and then Eddie, dive headlong into the booming New England auto racing scene in the carefree post-WWII years. Later, Marge and her late husband, Joe, and their two daughters, JoAnn and Susan, opened their Connecticut home to Eddie when he was navigating choppy post-marital seas. The children found the playful racer to be "more like a big brother than an uncle," in Susan's words. Marge resides today outside Fort Lauderdale, and both daughters live nearby. As is the case with her sister Betty, the Dombrowski home includes a liberal sprinkling of family mementos, heavy on photos from the glory days of the racer and brother the rest of us knew as Steady Eddie.

Marge Dombrowski

WHEN EDDIE AND CHRISTINE went their separate ways, he came to live with me and my husband Joe and our two girls, JoAnn and Susan. Joe and I were right there in New Britain, so Eddie just came to stay with us. We all loved him, and we loved looking after him. Part of that, I'm sure, was because Eddie had been the baby in my family, and I think maybe the baby of any family is always treated as being very special. But, you know, Eddie was just the kind of person you loved to take in. Even my husband loved him. Joe treated Eddie like a brother, or even better than a brother. Eddie just became part of our family.

I must say, he never, ever spoke badly about the marriage, or about Chris. He said that whatever had gone on was their business, and not

Family time! Young Paula and Eddie Jr. gather on the sofa with, from left to right, Joe Dombrowski, maternal grandfather Don Errede, father Eddie, and George Flemke. *(Marge Dombrowski Collection)*

the world's business, and that was that. And he was still a very good father to Paula and Eddie Jr., always.

In that period of his life, the late 1950s and into the early '60s, he was racing more and more, and traveling all the time. Instead of just going to the local tracks, he was racing at places like Norwood Arena, near Boston. He had so much energy; it was like he just *had* to get out and do this. Plus, it was his way of making a living, so the more he raced, the more money he'd earn. He didn't have a regular job when he lived with us, just the racing.

We'd go watch him when we could, but that wasn't always possible. Joe worked at Fafnir Bearing, right there in New Britain, and of course I had two young kids at home. So Eddie would go off to the track, but no matter where he was racing he'd almost always come home that night. He'd get home very late, so he might sleep until eleven o'clock in the morning. Then he'd be up, and before long he'd be gone again.

It was hard for me to not be at his races, because it was impossible to know what was going on. For example, in 1960 Eddie built a car for a big modified race they were having at Daytona. In those days, there was no TV coverage, and there was no such thing as cell phones or the Internet. Well, he ended up being involved in a 30-car crash, and it was two days before we knew about it! It was definitely easier when he raced closer to home.

By the time he came to live with us, Eddie was winning a lot of races, but it hadn't changed him at all. He took everything in stride, one

Mixing work with family duties, Flemke poses with his kids circa 1960, and cavorts with brother-in-law Joe Dombrowski in Florida during a Speedweeks visit. *(Betty Vanesse photos)*

day at a time. He was certainly making a name for himself, but it never went to his head. He never went around with a chip on his shoulder, never thought he was a big deal because he was Ed Flemke.

One thing I know was hard for him, because he told me this, was dealing with people who approached him for an autograph or to speak with him for an interview or something. That was all new to him. But after a while, he realized that it all went along with being a race driver, and he had a very good way of talking to people.

You know, racing was always so much a part of him. He and his older brother George built a car to race in the Soap Box Derby when Eddie was just a boy. I remember that thing had a wood frame, wheels from a carriage, and some rope to steer. Georgie was quite a bit older than Eddie, so I guess it was Eddie racing the car and George helping him. But I remember them running that car down Miller Street in New Britain, which had a double hill. And even when Eddie was just a kid on his bicycle, he was always riding around fast, skidding in the dirt and spinning a half-circle. Later on, he was never girl-crazy, the way some young guys are. It was racing, racing, racing. Build the car, drive the car, work on the car. That was his life.

I went to Eddie's races in the very beginning, way back at Cherry Park, but in 1949 Joe and I moved to North Carolina and later Florida for a while. But we moved back to Connecticut in 1956, so we did see a lot of Eddie's racing from '56 on.

Of all the tracks, I remember Cherry Park the best. Of course, I do have memories of Plainville, Riverside Park, Stafford, Waterford, Seekonk, and a few more, but for some reason I really recall Cherry Park. It was in Avon, CT, and back then that was way out in the country, and the ride from New Britain to Cherry Park was nice. It wasn't far, but it was still a nice ride. I remember watching George race there in the midgets, and Eddie in the stock cars.

Georgie raced midgets with a lot of very well known drivers, people like Bert Brooks and Johnny Kay, and it was nothing to have guys like them in our house. They were our friends. Eddie went in a different direction, toward the stock cars. The midgets were fading out, it seemed like, and the stock cars were the new thing coming along. In fact, personally, I think it was Eddie who really made that kind of racing popular in the New Britain area. Certainly, there were other drivers who came from there, and from the towns right around New Britain, but no one who became as well known as he did. People from the area really started following him, and I think that helped stock car racing become bigger.

Watching a brother race can be difficult. You sit there with a prayer on your lips, and with your fingers crossed all through the race. Only when something happened to knock Eddie out of the race could I ever sit and watch without being nervous. As long as he was out there, it was always crossed fingers and a prayer. And, you know, that never changed, even when I realized that he was very good. I understood that he knew what he was doing, but I still worried for him.

One thing I remember is that when we went to watch Eddie, we never booed any other driver. That's something we were taught by our father: "Don't boo another driver. Just make sure that when your driver is introduced, you holler louder than people holler for the other guys." So that's what we'd do. I also remember carrying these little horns when we went to Riverside Park, just so we could make even more noise.

After the divorce, Eddie would get the kids on weekends, and between his two and my two, the living room was non-stop action. They would be throwing balls around, and playing, and the house was rocking. We all had a great time. In fact, even when his own children weren't there, Eddie would sometimes be outside playing ball with my girls and the other kids from the neighborhood. And when the ice cream man came, he'd treat all those kids.

He was always up to something. Remember the Ballantine Beer logo, with the three rings? Well, one winter Eddie took his street car, spun that thing around, and made that Ballantine logo in the snow. The neighborhood kids couldn't believe it.

No, there was never a dull moment when Eddie was living with us.

In the end it wasn't that Eddie moved out on us, it was more like we moved out on Eddie. In 1961, Joe and I decided that we'd had enough of the snow and ice in Connecticut, so we went back to Florida. And it was right around this same time that Eddie met Carolyn, who became his second wife, so he still had somebody there, which was nice.

You know, Eddie never took his trophies out of the house, and I couldn't leave them behind, so I packed them all up and we brought them to Florida with us. Later on, once Eddie was settled in with Carolyn, we brought them back up there to him.

Once we moved away, we lost that regular contact you have when you live nearby. I knew he was still racing, but I'd sit and think: "I wonder where Eddie is this weekend?" We'd keep in touch when we could, but that's hard when you live so far apart and you're both busy doing your own thing. One thing that helped was that I had a friend who used to send me clippings from the New Britian paper, and we also got the *Speedway Scene* racing paper in the mail. We were always so happy to see Eddie's name in the headlines, which used to happen quite a bit.

When we did get home after that, we'd go to watch him race when we could. We saw him at other places, too. If he was racing at New Smyrna—or even if we knew he'd be there watching—we'd go see him. And one year my husband and I jumped into our van and drove up to see him at Martinsville. I remember spending several hours at a steak house near the track; young Jackie Arute was there, and we all sat there drinking coffee and telling stories.

Long after we'd been living apart, Eddie was still very much a part of our family. In fact, my two girls loved him so much that when they grew up and got married, they had their weddings in February because they knew their Uncle Eddie would be in Florida for the Daytona races.

Eddie was just a good guy. You know, we never, ever fought about things. Over the years, I had several arguments with my brother George —maybe because there were only three years between us—but I never argued with my kid brother.

Let me tell you what a considerate person he was. One night, Eddie was racing at Norwood Arena and he was involved in an accident with Bobby Allison. Eddie was hurt, and they put him in an ambulance. I hadn't gone to that race, but Joe was up there with him. Well, my father was in the grandstands, and by that time he was getting up there in age, probably in his late 60s. And Eddie would not let that ambulance take him to the hospital until he was sure his father understood that everything was going to be all right.

They checked him out in the emergency room and decided he was all right, so they let him go. Later that night, when they got home to New Britain, Eddie asked Joe to go into the house first, to prepare me. See, his face was black and blue, and his nose was swollen up, and he didn't want me to see him like that without being warned.

Here he was, all banged up, and he was considerate enough to think of his father and his sister.

After that crash he slept in a rocking chair in our living room for a couple of weeks, because with his nose so swollen he couldn't breathe lying down. And, you know, Eddie always had a little bump in his nose, so I believe he probably broke it in that crash.

Another night, years later, my husband couldn't come to the races with us for some reason, so my daughter JoAnn and I drove to Albany-Saratoga. Eddie said, "Where's Joe?" I said he was back in New Britain, that he couldn't get away that night. Well, Eddie said, "You're not driving back by yourself." So after the races, he drove us home.

He was always looking out for us. When he lived with us, he used to bring a bunch of friends over to play cards, probably a half-dozen guys in all. One night after they left, I pointed out to Eddie that the soles of their shoes had left little black marks on the floor. I wasn't mad about it or anything; I just mentioned it. Well, the next time they came over, Eddie made them all take off their shoes. He said, "My sister works too hard to keep this place neat for you guys to be messing up her floor." So they all went down to the cellar to take off their shoes, and then they came upstairs to play cards.

I'll always remember his sense of humor. He was full of jokes, all the time. I can still see him driving to the races, steering with his knee and playing cards at the same time! I was with him in the car more than once when he did that.

Eddie's favorite song was "My Way," and that was very fitting because he was so independent. As people in racing know, he was always interested in doing his own thing with his cars, and I know he bumped heads with NASCAR and some of the promoters because he was never afraid to tell people what he thought. He always did do it his way, like the song says.

If he could hear me talking about him now, he wouldn't believe it. He would never have expected in a million years that that he'd be in all these different halls of fame, or that people would still write about him. He was not that kind of guy. He would be proud of it all, yes, but I think he would be more proud of his children, and how far they've each come in life. Like I said earlier, success never went to his head.

To know that my brother is still remembered after all these years is so wonderful for me. Eddie was a very special person to those of us in the family, obviously. But it shows that he was a very special person to other people, as well.

PART TWO

Bandit Days

Tony Ferrante, one of NASCAR modified racing's most beloved car owners, remembers standing in the pits at New Jersey's Old Bridge Stadium in 1960 and wondering if he was in the company of a lunatic.

"I was looking at this one particular trailer, and I saw that it had Connecticut tags," Ferrante remembers. "Then I looked at this guy's car, a coupe with a little 327 cubic-inch engine. We were all running big blocks. Old Bridge had long straightaways, so you needed all the power you could get. I said to myself, 'This poor guy has got to be nuts. He came all the way from *Connecticut*'—remember, the highways weren't what they are today—'and he thinks he's going to race that thing against these guys? What a waste of time.' I thought he was crazy."

That poor guy was Ed Flemke, and all it took was one qualifying heat for Tony Ferrante to understand what racing people throughout New England already knew: Flemke was crazy, all right. Crazy like a fox.

"He started in the back," Ferrante says, smiling at the memory. "In the first turn, he passed four cars. Two of them got him back on the next straightaway. In the next corner, he went by three or four more. Again, a couple got back by him on the straightaway. But he was going forward."

The same scenario unfolded in the feature. Flemke didn't win that day—Ferrante doesn't remember exactly where Eddie placed, or for that matter, where his own car, piloted by Gentleman Jim Hendrickson, ended up—but that doesn't matter anyway. What matters is that Tony Ferrante has never forgotten the way that strange little car and its strange little driver inched their way forward, all day long, leaving some of the East Coast's most powerful modifieds in their dust.

"After the race, I walked over and introduced myself," Ferrante recalls. "I said to Eddie, 'Tell me something. How did you do that?' I remember he just shrugged his shoulders and said, 'Handling.'"

It was a sign of things to come. Ed Flemke had hit the road, and across the next few seasons a lot of folks were going to watch Steady Eddie go to the front, and wonder how on earth he did it.

Norwood Arena's move to NASCAR had opened up a world of possibilities. Running with Harvey Tattersall's United group had taken Flemke to a large number of tracks in the 1950s, but the Tattersall empire was essentially limited to Connecticut, Massachusetts, and Eastern New York. A coupe built to NASCAR specs meant that Flemke could not only run Norwood—which immediately became the Saturday night home to the Northeast's biggest names—but he could also haul to tracks from Canada to the Carolinas. For a young guy with racing on the brain and absolutely nothing tying him to home and hearth, this was heaven.

Flemke took to the highway, expanding his horizons mostly southward, racing both NASCAR-sanctioned tracks and independent ovals. He raced anyplace where his cars were legal and the money was right: the fifth-mile Islip Speedway and the Westhampton Speedway on Long Island, both gone now; the New Jersey track known first as Fort Dix and later as New Egypt Speedway; Wall Stadium, on the Jersey shore; and Old Bridge, which, as one of the few NASCAR tracks operating on Sunday, was capable of attracting big-names from everywhere: Miami's Bobby Allison, North Carolina's Carl Burris, Long Island's Hendrickson, home-state heroes Joe Kelly and Tommie Elliott, even New Englanders like Bill Slater and Joe McNulty.

When Flemke chose to stick closer to home—owing to weather, scheduling, maintenance delays, or maybe even financial issues if the previous weekend had gone sour—he still had options. His old United haunts were still operating, and the dirt track at Stafford Springs was going strong. But those occasions were rare. By the time the 1960 season had ended, Steady Eddie was a certified road dog.

And then came a weekend in early 1961 that really got things going. First Flemke won a 100-lapper in the Islip teacup on Saturday night; then he skipped down to Old Bridge for a Sunday afternoon 100, and won again.

As the story goes, someone in a position of authority at the Southside Speedway in Richmond, VA—the most educated guesses are that it was Nelson Royall, who owned Southside—happened to be at the Islip and Old Bridge events, hawking his own upcoming NASCAR shows. Wowed by Flemke's display, he offered the Connecticut racer a deal to come south the following week. Flemke accepted, and invited along a young Riverside Park graduate named Denny Zimmerman, whom Flemke had sort of taken under his wing.

The pair went to Southside and, for kicks and cash, ran another show

on the way home, this one at Fredericksburg, VA. Memories have grown foggy about how Flemke and Zimmerman fared on that first trip, but what happened next has never been forgotten.

Flemke had discovered in Virginia an exaggerated version of the same situation he'd faced at Old Bridge a year earlier. Just as he had managed to outrun most of those Jersey cars by relying on superior handling—using old chassis tricks he learned on the United circuit, and new ones he was inventing almost weekly—he found the Dixie fields to be easy pickings. Though many of the best Southern racers had fantastic engines, often built with parts and technical help from the nearby NASCAR Grand National (now Nextel Cup) teams, they were still relying on the same dirt-style chassis designs they had run for ten years. Flemke, schooled as he was on the tight fifth- and quarter-mile bullrings of New England, had never worried much about horsepower. Instead, he'd grown obsessed with getting his car to turn better than the next guy's. If he was building his own ride, he put all his effort into making it a flyweight; if he signed on with an owner, he immediately put that man's car on a diet, stripping and discarding anything that didn't seem necessary. By the time he headed to Richmond, he had it down to a science.

"Their cars weighed 3000 pounds," Flemke told writer Mike Adaskaveg years later. "Mine weighed 2100."

The ever-logical Flemke wouldn't have felt guilty about this. Surely, he

In the early '60s, this sight struck fear into the hearts of Southern racers. It's Steady Eddie in the wheelhouse of John Stygar's "dollar-sign." *(Mike Adaskaveg photo)*

viewed the whole thing as a lopsided fight, but not an unfair one. After all, everybody who ran a NASCAR modified in those days started with the same set of rules, the same junkyard parts, the same gutted coupes; what happened from there was up to the individual. It was the Southern racers, exercising their own free will, who had chosen power over handling. All Flemke had done was capitalize on how shortsighted they'd been.

Also appealing were the fat Southern purses, tailor-made for Flemke's Willie Sutton outlook on racing. Sutton, you'll recall, was the famous Depression-era gunman who, when asked why he insisted on robbing banks, reportedly replied, "Because that's where the money is." Flemke always sought out the dollars, too. From the start, he sacrificed track titles—and even NASCAR championship bids—by chasing the best pay-offs, and going "where the money was." In 1961, the big modified dough was in Virginia, and Flemke's bare-bones coupe was his Tommy Gun.

He won early and often, and so did Zimmerman, who by then knew and used many of Flemke's chassis tricks. Thrilled with things, Flemke suggested to his old United rival, Rene Charland, that he get in on the deal. Charland, who like Flemke loved the highway life, tagged along on the next jaunt to Richmond. Soon enough, another United pal, Red Foote, was part of the convoy, too. The boys had formed their own little circuit. Blasting out of Connecticut at midweek, they'd typically hit Fort Dix on Thursday, and then head for Southside in Richmond on Friday. Reversing course, they'd stop at the Old Dominion Speedway in Manassas, VA, on Saturday night, and then continue north for the Sunday afternoon program at Maryland's Marlboro Motor Raceway. As soon as the checkers dropped at Marlboro, they'd load their cars and tools in an insane rush, and point their tow vehicles toward New Jersey and Old Bridge's Sunday night show.

Naturally, the routine changed from time to time. If the schedule had occasional holes, they might be filled by dropping in at some dirt track along the way: Langley Field in Virginia, or Dog Track Speedway in Moyock, NC, or South Boston, VA (which, once it was paved in '62, became a more frequent Flemke haunt). And Zimmerman remembers a one-off Tennessee visit to what is now the Bristol Motor Speedway, though he can't recall how he and his friends fared. "It's a foggy memory," he says, laughing. "But I *can* tell you, the track certainly wasn't what it is today."

So frequently did Flemke, Zimmerman, Charland, and Foote ride off with the big money that race announcers dubbed them the "Yankee Bandits." Somewhere along the line, probably because someone noted that the foursome was also stealing lots of purses north of the Mason-Dixon line, the nickname changed. On the public address systems and in the racing press—and on into folklore—the gang became the "Eastern Bandits."

The shadow of the Eastern Bandits still looms so large—writer Pete Zanardi has accurately described it as a "pivotal chapter" in stock car rac-

ing—that it's easy to forget how quickly it all ended. The truth is, the Bandits carried out almost all their raids in a span of just three seasons, 1961-63. By the end of 1963, the Southern racers had caught up, equipment-wise, thanks in no small measure to the fact that Flemke, rather than hoarding his secrets, shared them with his Rebel friends.

They copied his skeletal roll cages, copied his chopped-up bodies, even copied—not just with Eddie's consent, but with his *help*—the pioneering split-spring "Flemke front end," a crude fix which proved to be a masterpiece of early-'60s chassis science. Zanardi says, "Denny Zimmerman told me not long ago, 'You know, I should be mad at Eddie. He gave it all away.'" And as the locals got faster, breaking up the Bandit foursome's lock on the top spots, it simply became less profitable for Flemke and his troupe to head south each week.

So Steady Eddie did what Willie Sutton would have done: He looked elsewhere for the handy money.

But what glorious times the Bandits had, Flemke in particular. In 1961, he was the dominant driver at Southside, also winning multiple features at Fredericksburg and Old Dominion. But he really came alive in '62, winning 17 features at the Manassas track, 11 of them *in a row*. (In the Labor Day 300 there, he lapped the field, beating Charland, Wes Morgan, and Bill Dennis, and the newspapers dubbed him "Mr. Unbeatable.") In 1963 Flemke continued to win in Dixie, but he also did especially well on the

This ride, owned by Eddie himself, saw action with the Bandits in 1963. His New Britain friend and traveling companion, Bobby Story, remembers, "Those Southern racers were so impressed with Eddie's cars. We were at Junie Donlavey's place one day, and the guys came out of the shop with tape measures to check out that Flemke front end. I was so proud of that, and so proud of Eddie." *(Shany Lorenzet photo, Dick Berggren Collection)* trip down there and back: He won seven Thursday night features and the track championship at Fort Dix (trouncing heroes like Will Cagle, Parker Bohn, Bob Rossell, and Herb Tillman), and counted a 100-lap score among his Sunday evening Old Bridge successes.

There were also two very special victories in the big Tobacco Bowl event at the Bowman Gray Stadium in Winston-Salem, NC, just a little over a year apart: one on December 30, 1961, and the other on January 1, 1963. The Stadium, as ever, was a tough little place in those days—its champions in the Bandit years, 1961-63, were Glen Wood, Perk Brown and Billy Hensley—and the Tobacco Bowl brought in some heavy-hitting outsiders. Well, Steady Eddie Flemke ran it twice, and won it twice. He beat George Dunn and Pee Wee Jones in 1961, and in '63, facing what the press called "numbing 35-degree weather," he topped Carl Burris and Rene Charland.

The "crazy" little driver who loved to get his cars handling was, quite simply, the toughest modified man of the era. Johnny Roberts of Maryland (1961) and Virginia's Eddie Crouse (1962-63) earned NASCAR modified championships. The Bandit king, Steady Eddie Flemke, earned bench-racing immortality.

The great tragedy is that accurate records of Flemke and his Eastern Bandits do not exist. Some of the tracks have closed, and other speedway bosses stupidly failed to maintain lists of race winners and even champions. Scrapbooks kept by Carolyn Flemke, his second wife—who met Eddie in '61—are revealing but incomplete. What could he have won across those three seasons? Fifty races? Sixty? More? Nobody knows, and no one ever will.

But here's one measure of what a force he was: When you mention to veteran car owner Junie Donlavey the 17 races Flemke won at Old Dominion Speedway in 1962, the courtly Virginian nods, grins, and says, "Yeah, but you really needed to see him at Southside. That's where Eddie was *tough*."

And Southside was the scene of one of the great Eastern Bandits moments.

As the story goes, Flemke and Charland were standing around one Friday night, waiting for the feature to start, when Rene, ever the joker, said to his friend, "You know, Eddie, I just can't understand that Grant."

Flemke replied, "Grant who?"

"Ulysses S. Grant," said Charland, referring to the great Civil War general. "It took him and all his men to defeat those Southerners. Now all it takes is you and me."

"Nobody back then was traveling like we were"

An insider's look at the early-'60s gypsy days of Eddie and the Bandits

by JOHN STYGAR

John Stygar had a long career as one of asphalt modified racing's best known car owners and mechanics. Always a quiet fellow, he let his equipment do the talking, and it sure spoke loudly. Stygar's most productive times came with Ed Flemke, first in the Eastern Bandits period when Flemke steered John's "dollar-sign" coupes, and later in a mid-'70s stint when Steady Eddie drove a powder blue #7 Stygar-built Pinto to multiple open-competition victories at Plainville Stadium, Waterford Speedbowl, and Seekonk Speedway. When Flemke was otherwise occupied, Stygar employed star drivers like Denny Zimmerman, Smokey Boutwell, Denis Giroux, and Bugs Stevens. And if no top-shelf chauffeurs were available? Well, then Stygar simply kept his car parked. "See, there really weren't that many good drivers," he reasons. "I always looked at it like, you've got three or four guys like Eddie, and everybody else is just learning." Stygar lives today, as he did then, in Manchester, CT.

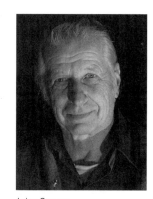

John Stygar

THAT WHOLE EASTERN BANDITS THING just sort of happened. At the start, it was all because Eddie said, "Hey, let's go here," and everybody followed along. There was no big game plan. We never thought about it being a big adventure, although I guess it was. We just loaded up and went. It was something that we tried, and it worked, so we kept on doing it.

But, boy, was it fun. The real Eastern Bandits period only lasted a few seasons, but I was with Eddie for that whole ride.

I first got tangled up with Eddie because I'd been partners in a stock car with another guy from Manchester named Donald Ponticelli. That was actually my first real involvement with racing. I was working at the time for a place in East Hartford that built and installed truck bodies; I worked on dump trucks, utility trucks, snowplows, stuff like that. Well, Ponticelli somehow got hooked up with Eddie, because Eddie lived in Manchester for a while back then, and he became our driver. We ran at Norwood and Thompson and a bunch of other NASCAR tracks, so this might have been around 1960.

Our car was the "dollar-sign" coupe. That gets a little mixed-up sometimes when people talk about those days; the "dollar-sign" car belonged to me and Donald, and we paid Eddie a percentage to drive it. Now, the "cent-sign" and "percent-sign" cars, which came later, belonged to Eddie. And, no, I honestly don't know why we all ran those crazy numbers. I can't remember.

The real reason we went south was that it was just easier to do more racing that way. Up here, the NASCAR tracks were Thompson, Norwood and Stafford, but Stafford was still dirt, so that was out because Eddie didn't like dirt. That left only two really good tracks. By going south, we had our own little circuit.

We'd basically make a big circle. We might start out on Long Island for a special show on Wednesday night, then head south to New Jersey on Thursday night, and down to Virginia on Friday night and Saturday night. Then we'd start coming north by running in Maryland on Sunday afternoon and New Jersey on Sunday night. And, geez, by then you're halfway home again.

That's pretty much how it went. We did a *lot* of racing in those days.

Obviously, that meant we were home just Monday, Tuesday and Wednesday at the most. For a lot of this time, we worked out of a garage in New Britain. It was owned by Bert Brooks, the great midget driver, but Eddie had a bay there and I had a bay. We kept the "dollar-sign" and the "cent-sign" there. That garage was like a meeting place; even if there wasn't much work to do, we all still hung around there.

I was lucky, because the people I worked for at the truck place were real good with me. I'd tell 'em on Wednesday, "Hey, I'm going to the races, I'll be back Monday," and they put up with me. I guess they figured that as long as I got my work done—and I worked a lot of overtime when I could, especially in the winter—it wasn't much of a problem. I guess I must have been doing something right.

For Eddie and I, it was pretty easy to travel. I wasn't married, and he was divorced. Eddie wasn't working in those years, just racing for a living, and, like I said, I could pretty much come and go from my job. So it was easy for us to just throw our bags in the car and go.

Anyway, all this running around was Eddie's idea, and then along came Denny Zimmerman and Rene Charland, and sometimes Red Foote.

Dennis was a quiet young guy, tall and thin. And he was very calm. He wasn't too flashy on the race track, and he never said very much.

Classic Stygar: Eddie collects the trophy from an unknown Fredericksburg official in 1961, while shy John (far right), probably thinking he's out of the frame, waits to load up his car and hit the road. (Bob Williams photo, Larry Jendras Jr. Collection)

Honestly, Dennis was just learning then. He was good, but he wasn't at Eddie's level. But he was really interested in getting better, and Eddie was always helping him along. And Denny Zimmerman, of course, turned out very good.

What I remember most about Rene is that he was always smoking that cigar and talking. He had all kinds of things going. He'd buy *this* and sell *that*, wheeling and dealing. And there was always a gimmick; he'd show up with all kinds of special oils and trick stuff. Oh, yeah, Rene was a barrel of fun. You know, Rene and Eddie were *very* different people. Eddie was a lot more serious, and Rene was a joker. But they got along well, and I'm sure part of that was because they were usually in two different classes. See, Rene was running for the NASCAR sportsman championship, and Eddie's car was a modified. The sportsman cars and the modifieds raced together, but they always started the sportsman cars up front. In fact, Rene helped Eddie quite a bit in some of those races. Let's just say that Rene sometimes did a little bit of blocking for Eddie, holding guys up until he got there. Rene didn't mind doing that, since he was kind of running his own race; even if he ran eighth or 15th, he could still be the sportsman winner, as long as he beat the other guys in that division. And Rene usually had the sportsman guys covered.

There was another big difference between Eddie Flemke and Rene Charland: Because winning those NASCAR championships was so important to him, Rene would go here, there, and everywhere for 10 extra points. With Eddie, it was all about the money. Wherever the best purses were, that's where we went, points or no points. But, the way it worked out, most of the time Rene was right there with us.

I know Red Foote is usually lumped in with the Eastern Bandits, but the truth is, Red didn't hit as many races as the rest of us did. He most-

Normally clean shaven, Eddie sports a bit of stubble in June of '63. Grooming time was a luxury on the hectic Eastern Bandits road trips. *(Bob Williams photo, Larry Jendras Jr. Collection)*

ly concentrated on the big shows, so I didn't see him as much as I saw Zimmerman and Charland. Red wasn't *as much* a part of our gang, and I didn't really know him very well. I kind of stayed close to Eddie's car, and I was always kind of quiet anyway, so I didn't have many dealings with Red unless he needed some help or something.

The Southern guys I remember most were Ray Hendrick and Sonny Hutchins. There were a lot of other good drivers down there—Runt Harris was one—but after all these years, it's hard to remember the names. Junie Donlavey always had a car there, usually with Sonny driving; in fact, Junie was running both the modifieds and the Grand Nationals quite a bit in that period.

Those Southern guys, they had some great motors: big Fords, Lincolns, a couple of Chryslers. Their cars were tanks—they used heavy axles for bumpers, heavy pipe nerf bars—but they did have some horsepower. We built our engines right out of a crate, nothing fancy, just stock parts and a good cam. But Eddie had a lot of chassis tricks, like his split-spring Flemke front end, where those guys had the old-style cross-spring. Plus, we had these little aluminum bumpers, and nerf bars made out of conduit, so our cars were nice and light.

We beat 'em with handling. If three cars passed Eddie on the straightaway, he'd pass *four* in the corners, down on the inside.

Actually, it was the same way with the New Jersey cars. We'd go to Old Bridge, which had *long* straightaways—longer even than a place like Thompson—and those other guys could really get going. But that track also had tight corners, so when it came time to turn, they slid up the track and, *shoo*, Eddie went right by 'em. That was that.

Handling and brakes, that's what we had. And it's not that we had special brakes—they were only stock Ford drum brakes—but Eddie knew a guy in Cromwell, Connecticut, who knew how to make up metallic brake linings. Nobody knew a thing yet about metallic linings, but we had 'em. And in some of those 100-lappers, those other guys would be out of brakes halfway through the race, but we were doing just fine.

No, we sure didn't have anything fancy. Don't forget, there wasn't any store-bought stuff. You know the only thing we could buy? Racing hubs and Frankland rear ends. Everything else either came out of the junkyard, or you made it yourself. Today, you can buy a car from one of the builders, and if you need anything else there's a parts catalog as big as the phone book. Heck, if you've got a big enough checkbook, you can go racing and not even own a welder! It was a little different back when we had the "dollar-sign."

How's this for fancy: For a long time, we towed up and down the East Coast with Eddie's street car, a Pontiac four-door! Big car, big motor. Boy, that thing went down the highway!

And you know, even though we put on a lot of miles every week, we had no real time frame, other than getting to the races. Even when it came to things like restaurants and motels, we had no real routine. Whenever we got hungry, we stopped and ate. Whenever we got tired, we stopped and got a room. Usually, Eddie paid for all that; he was really good that way. I think Eddie appreciated the work I did, so he paid for the meals and the rooms. Of course, we never got too fancy. As tired as we usually were, we'd just stop in a diner, and then we were happy with any motel that had a little square room and a bed. Sometimes, if we were on a tighter schedule for some reason, we might keep on pushing, with me driving and Eddie sleeping, or the other way around.

In the mornings, we'd do whatever maintenance needed to be done. Of course, that wasn't much, because those old coupes weren't too sophisticated. Once you had the basic car built and running, all you had to do was change the oil sometimes, air up the tires, and check the water. The biggest thing was the rear end; every track was a different size, so we'd have to change the gears. We'd do all that stuff at the motel, unless we were short on time. In that case, we'd hurry up and drive to the track so we could get signed in, pull the car into the pits, and start working on it. But, you know, as long as you didn't have a problem, you kept running what you'd *been* running. We might have had one spare tire and wheel between the three of us—Eddie, Rene, and Dennis—on some of those trips.

As much as we were gone, you couldn't expect to have a lot of regular help. I mean, not many people can be away from home that long every week. Sure, you might get a guy to come along every now and then, but most of the time it was just Eddie and me, plus Rene and his main guy, Freddy Rosner. Denny was usually by himself, without even a mechanic of his own. If Denny had a problem, Freddy and me would help him, that's all. Eventually, we picked up some helpers at different tracks. That's how it is when you're winning races: Everybody wants to be part of it.

October 1, 1961, and another Fredericksburg score. *(Bob Williams photo, Larry Jendras Jr. Collection)*

I've heard all these wild stories about how crazy the traveling was—like, how we supposedly worked on our cars as they were being towed down the road on a trailer—but, you know, most of those stories got blown out of proportion over the years. I mean, you're not going to get much work done going 50 miles an hour! So I hear those stories, and I just let 'em go. Let people believe 'em if they want to.

The biggest thing we had to worry about, really, was the cops. We got stopped several times for all kinds of things: lights that had burned out, speeding, whatever. Don't forget, we'd run through a lot of small towns where the cops don't have anything to do *but* stop you.

And it was a common thing to get stopped on the New Jersey Turnpike if you were towing a trailer. Down there, the widest your trailer could be was eight feet, six inches. We were *definitely* wider than that. Usually, we could deal with it pretty easily. See, years ago, you could get out of your car and talk to the cop while he checked you out. Well, when he went to measure the trailer, either Eddie or I would offer to hold one end of the tape. And while he was walking across the trailer to the other side, we'd cheat the tape; you know, move it in a little.

This one time, I got pulled over. Just like always, the cop said, "I think your trailer is over the limit on the width." We sort of shrugged and got out, and we were getting ready to do our little trick again with the ruler. But this time, there were *two* cops; the first one got his partner out of the patrol car, and the partner held the tape. Nothing we could do. Anyway, they asked me for my license so they could write the ticket. Well, earlier that week, at home, I was putting my license and registration away—I was using a different car or something, I don't remember—and I had mixed 'em up. I didn't have my license with me. So now we're over on the trailer width, and the driver doesn't have a license.

But we got lucky. The cop said to Eddie, "Do you have a license?" Eddie nodded yes. The cop said, "Good, you drive. Both of you, get in that car, and get out of here."

We did a lot of winning in those years. I mean, Eddie won a *ton* of races. We never kept track of how many, and I have no idea what the total might have been down there, but I'll tell you this: Everybody else had to beat us, and they knew it. We won everywhere: Old Bridge, Southside, Manassas, South Boston, Marlboro, you name it.

I do remember winning two big New Year's features at Bowman Gray Stadium. That was kind of interesting; Eddie and I were used to going south, so that was no big deal, but now we were loading up in the winter and driving through the snow to go racing!

Bowman Gray was a tiny track, flat, a bullring built around a football field. And I remember it was pretty cold down there, too, but at least there wasn't any snow. As I recall, there weren't many cars there—I mean, who's ready to go racing in the winter?—but most of the really good guys were there because they paid pretty decent.

Years after the Bandits era closed, John Stygar was still fiddling with modifieds. Here he adjusts the idle speed in 1975, while a shaggy Clyde McLeod looks on at left. *(Mike Adaskaveg photo)*

But you know, there were a couple of tough times, too. We were at Southside one night when Eddie rode up over somebody's tire and flew up into the bleachers. He actually went right up *over* the fence, and landed up in the stands. Nobody was sitting right there in that spot, thank God. That was the Gray Ghost car, which was painted just in primer. And the funny thing is, believe it or not, that car wasn't wrecked too bad at all. The chassis wasn't bent, and the body just had a few dents. We probably could have raced it, but I think maybe the oil pan, the gas tank, the radiator or something had gotten torn up, so we were out. If I'm not mistaken, we took that car over to Junie Donlavey's place, fixed it, and raced it the next night.

We always had a place to work on the car, because those people down there just *loved* Eddie. The fans accepted him, and the racers really seemed to like him. I'm sure that's because Eddie was the kind of guy who would help anybody. And, you know, part of the reason he did that was just to make things easier on himself. See, some of those guys were dangerous, and if he got 'em handling better it made them easier to race with. He was going to beat 'em anyway, and he knew that.

I remember those Southern guys checking out our cars every week, looking for our secrets. When you're winning, *everybody* checks you out. And we just let 'em look. What are you going to do? But between us letting them look at our stuff and Eddie helping everybody in the pits, we showed 'em how to catch up to us, and eventually they *did* catch up to us. They built newer cars, lighter cars, and with all their horsepower they got to the point where they were tough competition.

Now we had to some decisions to make. Once those guys finally had good cars, the only way we were going to keep winning was to build better, more expensive engines. Either that, or buy engines from those

Southern guys. Either way, we didn't have the money to do that, and we knew it.

That was the beginning of the end of us going down there every week. There just wasn't as much money to be made. The real Eastern Bandits period was over by 1964. Oh, we still went down there quite a bit, but not like we had earlier.

The other reason we stopped traveling south so much was that the Northern tracks were building up. There was a pretty good NASCAR circuit coming together in the Northeast; Norwood and Thompson started paying better, and so did Utica-Rome. Pretty soon, Albany-Saratoga came along, and there was good money there, too. And, like I said, Eddie was always a guy who looked at the dollars, so it just made more sense to stay closer to home. Fewer expenses.

But, you know, we still traveled a lot. We ran at Norwood Arena, near Boston, and we spent a lot of time at Utica-Rome and Albany-Saratoga over in New York. Sometimes Eddie ran my car, and he also ran his "cent-sign" a lot. Yeah, we cut back on the highway miles, but we still got around for a few years. In those days, we'd have Little Eddie with us sometimes, and Eddie's daughter Paula. They were just kids.

Once Stafford was paved in 1967, Eddie went and drove for Bobby Judkins, and he and I didn't do much together. I ran a few small shows here and there with different drivers, but I always seemed to have trouble. But Eddie and I stayed friends. In fact, he and I *always* got along very well. Sure, we had a few arguments, but not many considering all the time we spent traveling together. It always worked out. I always looked at it like, whether it was my car or his car, he was the driver and I was the mechanic, so whatever he wanted, I gave him.

Eddie was such a great driver. One of the things that made him so good was that he was so *calm*. I never really saw him get mad.

Whenever he went out in warm-ups, he'd line up behind the best guy there—Ray Hendrick down South, maybe Bugsy up here—and he'd follow him around, but he wouldn't *pass* him. This put the idea in that guy's mind that Eddie wasn't real fast. Then he'd drop away, pick up another fast car, and do it all over again. In the heat race, same thing. By the time the feature rolled around, he knew how his car was going, and he also knew how *your* car was going. From there, he just figured out a way to pass you. Even if you tried to mirror-drive him, he stayed cool. He'd wait, wait, wait, stay on your bumper, and eventually you'd slip a little. And when that happened, zip, he was *gone*.

It's nice how people still talk about that Eastern Bandits period. It was a long time ago, but it really was a big, big deal. I mean, *nobody* back then was traveling like we were. Most guys who raced at New London just raced New London; most guys who raced on the dirt at Stafford didn't go anywhere else. We went *everywhere*.

"He was as good a friend as I had"

In the tire tracks of the master, on the track and on the highway

by DENNY ZIMMERMAN

Dennis Zimmerman is best remembered by New England race fans for two things: his 1971 Rookie of the Year glory in the Indianapolis 500, and his role as Ed Flemke's original Eastern Bandits traveling partner. Born in 1940 and raised in Glastonbury, CT, Zimmerman discovered racing as a boy when he and his father visited Pennsylvania's Nazareth Speedway. With his dad's help, he became a Soap Box Derby phenom, reaching the prestigious finals in Akron, OH. Says Zimmerman, "I think I'm the only kid who ever ran in the Soap Box finals in Akron and went on to race at Indianapolis." He first met Flemke in the late '50s, and together they wrote coupe-era history before Denny switched to URC sprints and, ultimately, Indy cars. A corporate jet pilot in his post-racing years, Denny boasts, "I've never had a real job." He lives in Suffield, CT, with his wife, Ruth.

Denny Zimmerman

THE ONE STORY THAT SAYS it all about Eddie Flemke, as far as I'm concerned, comes from the Eastern Bandits days. We were at Manassas, Virginia, for a 100-lapper. Eddie was leading, and I was second, and we were just running away from the rest of the field. I was all over Eddie, and I just *knew* I could pass him; I mean, I really felt like I was quicker. But every time I'd jump outside to pass him, he'd pull away just a little bit, and then he'd point to his helmet. I'd see that, but I didn't think about it too much. In another lap or two, I'd be back on his tail, trying to pass, and just he'd squirt away again. I was getting pretty frustrated.

Well, the Manassas track, Old Dominion Speedway, had a bad bump coming off the second turn, just as you started down the back straightaway. That bump was a real jolt to the car, especially if you ran through there as hard as I was running. And finally, that's what got me: The quick-change gears in my car let go from all that pounding, and I fell out of the race.

What Eddie had been telling me by pointing to his helmet was, "Use your head. You've got it made. Relax." He was trying to let me know that he could have been going a lot faster than he was, but he didn't want to tear up *his* car. Eddie went on to win the race, and I'd have been second if I only listened to him. He said to me later, "Geez, I was trying to tell you to take it easy."

That was Eddie Flemke.

The story of how I got involved with him in the first place is a pretty good one, too. As a teenager I was living in Glastonbury, Connecticut, and working in a Sunoco gas station for Johnny Georgiades, who was a really fine local driver. He ran for the Sunnyside Racing Team—that was Johnny, Wally Post, and a guy who raced as "Freddy J."—and they all congregated right there at the gas station. I went down there and asked for a job just because I wanted to be part of that group. I ended up building my own car, a coupe, and taking it to Riverside Park in 1957. I raced that car there, and a few times at Plainville, for a couple of years. I tried to race it at Waterford, too, but I kept getting kicked out because I wasn't old enough.

In my second year of racing at Riverside Park, I was running along one night in the feature, minding my own business, and suddenly here came Eddie Flemke's car, shooting out of the infield in a cloud of dust at the end of the backstretch. He'd gotten tangled up with another car, I guess. Well, I never saw him until it was too late; I ran up over his wheel, got upside down, and was knocked unconscious. The medics were concerned because it took a long time for them to bring me around, so I spent that night in the hospital. In fact, I remember waking up to find Ed Patnode, one of the great Riverside drivers, lying in the bed next to me; he was there for a hernia operation. We spent a long time talking, until the doctors came along and released me.

Well, I guess Eddie felt guilty about that accident—which he shouldn't have, because it was just a racing thing—and he decided he was going to make it up to me. He started helping me at various tracks as I began branching out from Riverside Park. One of those tracks was Norwood Arena. I ran there quite a bit in 1960, the year they switched to NASCAR, and, you know, I did absolutely *nothing* at that place. I don't think I ever even won a consi there. In fact, a little while back they held a reunion for the old Norwood gang, and I was surprised when they invited me. I didn't think I deserved to be there. But I do remember Eddie helping me an awful lot at Norwood, and that's how our relationship began. He really took me under his wing.

That's a little bit strange to me, looking back, because even though

That's Eddie's "cent-sign" coupe on the ramp truck, and almost certainly one of Zimmerman's modifieds on the trailer behind it, bound for who knows where. *(Betty Vanesse Collection)*

he was seven or eight years older than me, Eddie was still a young man then. He was in his late 20s when I first raced against him, and maybe 30 by the time he really started helping me. You don't think of a guy being a mentor at that age, but I guess that teaching quality was just *in* him. And he was my teacher all the way through that Eastern Bandits period.

In the beginning, the Bandits consisted of just two drivers: Eddie and me. This was in 1961. The two of us were at Islip for a 100-lapper, and Eddie won it. Then we went down to a show at Old Bridge, and Eddie won there, too. Well, the promoter from Southside Speedway in Richmond was there, and I guess he liked what he saw. He invited us down for a big show he had scheduled; actually, he invited *Eddie* down, and Eddie asked me to come along. That sounded like fun to me, so we hauled down there.

You know, I honestly can't remember how we finished that first night at Southside. I guess everything was happening so fast for me that the first few nights all blend together a little bit. But I'm sure we did pretty well. Southside was just a little bullring, which was perfect for Eddie and me. Those Southern guys had big, heavy, strong cars with lots of power. They'd shoot down the straightaways like dragsters, but they'd just *park* in the turns. Oh, they didn't handle at all. When we saw that, we knew it was easy-pickings time, and we were right.

I do remember that when we left Southside on that first trip, we stopped on the way home at a Saturday-night track in Fredericksburg, Virginia. It was a nice little bullring, a flat quarter-mile or maybe even just a fifth, so again it was right up our alley. We didn't race at Fredericksburg Speedway very often—I guess maybe it didn't pay as well as Manassas—but when we did run there, we did well. In fact,

Fredericksburg was where I won my first NASCAR race a few weeks later. Eddie was there, but he fell out for some reason and I won the race.

Anyway, when we realized how well we could do at these Southern tracks, we decided we ought to start going down there on a regular basis. Then Rene Charland showed up, and Red Foote showed up, and basically it's us four—Eddie, me, Rene, and Red—who are remembered as the Eastern Bandits.

I'm sure Eddie told them, "Hey, boys, you need to be part of this. We've got a good thing going." That was just his way. We could have kept this secret to ourselves, and the two of us could have won even more races, because there were plenty of nights when Red or Rene ended up beating us. But that wasn't Eddie's way. He was so above-board, all the time, that it wouldn't have occurred to him *not* to tell those guys about it: "Yeah, come on down! We'll all run up front, and we'll have a great time!"

And, you know, we did have a great time. We had Rene there with us, and in addition to being a good, hard-charging driver he was a fun-loving guy who always had a story. For instance, if you asked him, he'd say he never spun anybody out, the problem was that the other guys all backed into him! Red was different; he was a quiet, unassuming guy, but a very good driver who got the most out of his equipment. I got along well with both those guys, and with John Stygar and Freddy Rosner, too. You know, I owe a lot to John and Freddy, because they helped me anytime I needed it. Those guys were two excellent mechanics.

As for Eddie, he and I were very close. Yes, he helped set up my car and helped instill confidence in me, but there was more to our relationship than that. He was as good a friend as I had. We were together so much back then. I mean, days at a time.

At the height of the Bandits, everything started at New Egypt on Thursday. From there, we'd usually drive through the night to Richmond, and we'd often stay in this little cabin-type motel down there. We'd get up and go visit Junie Donlavey, who always let us use his shop if we needed to work on our cars. Then we'd race Southside on Friday night, Manassas or South Boston on Saturday night—depending on who had the bigger race—and Marlboro, Maryland, on Sunday afternoon. We'd wrap it up with Old Bridge on Sunday night. Then we'd head back to Connecticut, work on the cars a bit, and start all over again the following Wednesday or Thursday.

Of those tracks, Southside and Old Bridge were my favorites. They were two very different places—Southside was a bullring, and Old Bridge was a half-mile with long straightaways—but I just seemed to go so well at those two tracks. If Eddie had a favorite, he never mentioned it to me. He just ran well wherever he went.

Naturally, the promoters loved us. We'd even get appearance money; not right away for me, because I wasn't as big a name as Eddie

was, but after a while it came. It's just a wild guess on my part, because I can't recall for sure, but I got maybe $50 a night. Eddie was probably getting more. When you think about it, that was pretty good money back then.

There are several of those Southern drivers who stand out in my mind: Ray Hendrick, Ted Hairfield, Runt Harris, Sonny Hutchins, Perk Brown, and a few more. Hendrick was probably the most gifted of the bunch; he was just so talented, like Eddie was. Yes, Ray was the dominant guy, but they all had their nights when they were hard to beat.

But, you know, for the most part we blew their doors off, again and again.

Of course, we had our share of hard times, too. In 1961, Eddie talked me into going to the big New Year's race at Bowman Gray Stadium in Winston-Salem, a race he ended up winning. I had just sold my car to a guy from Norwalk, Connecticut, but I only sold it on the condition that he let me run it one last time, in this race at Bowman Gray. Well, I crashed that car really badly, and severely injured my foot. Later on, incidentally, that injured foot ended up keeping me out of the military draft. But I felt so bad for the guy I'd sold the car to that I ended up building him another one, and then I drove that car for most of the '62 season.

I never minded the schedule or the traveling, because I looked at it like I was getting an education. Even then, my main goal was to race at Indianapolis, and I knew all this racing was a great way to work toward that. The guys who made it to the Indy 500 in those days were all short-

Zimmerman at Old Bridge, last stop on the weekly Bandit trail, after which the boys could relax a bit. "I remember all of us eating fairly regularly in a diner right near Old Bridge, late on Sunday nights," Denny says. "Wally Dallenbach was still in his modified days, and Wally Jr. [born in May of 1963] was still a tiny baby in his mother's arms." (Denny Zimmerman Collection)

track drivers, so the way I looked at it was, if *they* can do it, why can't I? I knew I just needed to work for it, and running all those races became my preparation.

Yes, we put in a lot of hard miles. One time, I actually fell asleep at the wheel on the New Jersey Turnpike, towing a car, and fortunately I woke up when I drifted into the median. But it wasn't too bad. When everything worked out, we'd all follow one another on those Southern trips, but I also remember traveling by myself quite a bit because each of us was ready to leave at a different time. For a while, I used to tow my car while Eddie and John Stygar towed his, but later on, probably in the second or third year of the Bandits, Eddie got a ramp truck. He'd load his car on that truck, and tow my car along behind him. And this is kind of funny to remember, but if we happened to be racing down around Norfolk—maybe going to Langley Field, or Moyock, North Carolina, two dirt tracks we ran a few times—we actually traveled by ferry boat! The Chesapeake Bay Bridge hadn't been built yet, so we just towed our cars onto the ferry and off we went. I'd get seasick every time.

The thing that helped Eddie so much, in addition to his driving ability, was that he was always ready to improvise. Nothing bothered him. Anything that came up, he'd just deal with it.

I'll give you a couple examples.

One night at Manassas, he was driving his own "cent-sign" car, so I jumped into John's "dollar-sign." Well, I got tangled up with another car and I turned over, but it was just a slow, easy roll that didn't seem to

After Denny's maiden run at Indy, his old friends threw him a party. That's Zimmerman on the right, greeting new arrivals Eddie Flemke and Pete Hamilton. It's a rare shot of Steady Eddie in a suit and tie! (*Carolyn Flemke Collection*)

hurt anything. A couple of other cars got wrecked worse, I guess, because they threw the red flag. My car had landed back on its wheels, so I drove it around to the frontstretch and got ready for the restart. Eddie was standing there beside his car, and he noticed some water pissing out of my radiator. Somehow, something must have poked a small hole in it, and now I had a leak. Well, Eddie just reached into his pocket, pulled out a pack of cigarettes, and crumpled the tobacco out of those cigarettes right into the radiator. A few seconds later, the leak stopped.

His greatest improvisation, of course, was the Flemke front end, that split-spring setup. We were getting ready to leave Bert Brooks's garage for another weekend of racing, and Eddie was waiting for a spring he had ordered from Superior Spring, up in Hartford. Well, when it finally got there, the spring was too short. Eddie thought for just a second, and he said, "We can fix that." He cut that spring in half, and now he had two small springs. He had to modify the front cross-member a little bit to make everything fit, and he added two stacking bolts so each side would be adjustable. He had that thing designed and built in no time at all, and it worked so well that everybody in modified racing copied it.

I had no idea, of course, that the term "Eastern Bandits" would become such a big deal. Even today it's something people want to talk about. And I do miss those days. For my racing career, that was Basic Indoc—meaning "basic indoctrination"—into so many things: how to drive a race car, how to *feel* a race car, and, thanks to Eddie, how to think about setting up a race car. The Eastern Bandits period taught me that in racing, the setbacks would come, but if I learned from those setbacks, success would follow. And it did. I started driving sprint cars in 1966, and from there on just kept on climbing until I made the Indy 500 in 1971.

I don't believe Eddie ever saw me drive an Indy car, not in person. In fact, I don't think he ever even watched me run a sprint car. Once I moved on, he was still too busy racing to come out and see me. But I know he was proud of me, and that makes *me* proud. After I won the Rookie of the Year award at Indianapolis, they held a party for me in Glastonbury. Eddie showed up, and that was the first time I'd seen him since the 500. I'm not sure he said anything to me when he first walked in, but I could see the pride in his face. I told him, "Well, I guess your student did pretty good."

Looking back, I'd have to say he was one of the very best drivers, all-time. No question about that. Eddie was as good as anybody ever at getting through traffic, and I have never known another race driver *anywhere* who was so good at staying out of trouble. I think I could count on one hand the times I saw him involved in an accident, and we're talking about a *lot* of races. Oh, there were things he had no control over; one night at Southside Speedway, his throttle stuck and he went straight into the first turn wall and destroyed his car. But in terms of getting into an accident that could have been avoided, Eddie just didn't do that. If there was a way around that wreck, Eddie found it somehow.

I'm sure that if he had ventured outside of the modifieds and gone into Indy cars or Grand Nationals or whatever, he'd have been very successful. But I think what stopped him from doing that is that he had a family, and that meant a lot to him. It was important to him to take care of Little Eddie and Paula; he saw that as a very big responsibility. He was earning a living doing what he liked, and he didn't want to take a chance by trying something different.

I enjoy the fact that our names are still linked together. I was fortunate enough to accomplish quite a bit in my career, but it seems like every story that involves me sooner or later gets back to the days I spent with him. And, believe me, I'm proud to be associated with Eddie Flemke. I'm proud of the friendship we had, and proud to have raced and worked with him.

As a race driver, he taught me everything I knew. He just didn't teach me everything *he* knew.

"They really did a job on us"

The Eastern Bandits era, from a Southern perspective

by JUNIE DONLAVEY

Junie Donlavey has fielded winning stock cars at every level of the sport, from modifieds (winning up and down the East Coast) to late model sportsman (copping multiple 300-milers at Daytona in what is now the Busch Series) to NASCAR's Cup division (in which his trademark #90 Ford, with Jody Ridley aboard, scored a David vs. Goliath victory at Dover in 1981). Universally respected, Donlavey has watched an amazing list of drivers slide into his cars: Dixie icons like Sonny Hutchins and Bill Dennis, NASCAR legends like David Pearson and LeeRoy Yarbrough, genuine characters like Dick Trickle and Ken Schrader, and one-off cameo shoes like Indy 500 champion Johnny Rutherford and DIRT modified ace Kenny Brightbill. Yet Junie, a few years past 80 now, looks back on his friendly early-'60s battles with Eddie Flemke and the Eastern Bandits as "some of the best times I've ever had."

Junie Donlavey

BEFORE HE EVER CAME DOWN HERE with his Eastern Bandits, I knew all about Eddie Flemke. I had seen him run up North a few times when we took our modified up there, and I knew all about the races he had won. Yes, I sure knew about Flemke.

In that time just before they came down here, we had a nice bunch of tracks running the modifieds. We ran at Norfolk, at Manassas, down at South Boston, and of course at the Southside Speedway right here in Richmond. We had Ray Hendrick, Sonny Hutchins, Runt Harris, Ted Hairfield, and some top-notch chauffeurs running in this area. Great drivers. We had a pretty good little circuit going. Everybody ran coupes and sedans; my cars were mostly coupes.

Sonny Hutchins, the legendary Virginia gasser, beside the Donlavey #90 coupe. Look closely, and you'll see Junie himself in the white hat, just to the left of Sonny's checkered flag. *(Bob Williams photo, Larry Jendras Jr. Collection)*

I can't say for sure exactly who was driving my car when Eddie first came down here. I mean, I'm 82 years old now. When you get to be this age, you'd better have your thinking cap on when you get up in the morning. Sometimes you can hardly find your way to the office! Really, I had so many drivers, and the years all kinda run together, so to put each driver with a certain year is hard to do. But it was probably Sonny Hutchins, because he was my modified driver for a long time.

Sonny was a terrific race driver. In fact, later on, when I ran late models and Grand National cars—which are the Nextel Cup cars today—Sonny ran that stuff for me, too. He was also a fun guy who just *loved* to race. Money didn't mean a thing to him; I mean, he'd have driven that car for free. He just enjoyed it that much. You know, we *all* enjoyed it back then, so we were a perfect match. The best part about Sonny, from a car owner's standpoint, was that he never complained. He went out and ran his laps, and if the car ran good, that was fine. If it didn't run good, he'd just tell us what he thought we needed to do. He never let racing get to him to where he was aggravated with it. Yes, sir, he was just as good as they came.

Southside Speedway was a small, flat track that took a good-handling car and a lot of driving skill to get around. Manassas was a little bit bigger, with a pretty good bank; yes, Manassas was fast. South Boston was pretty much like it is today, fast and with a little less banking than Manassas. South Boston was dirt when we first ran it, but then they paved it in 1962.

Anyway, back to Eddie. I guess it was the promoter from the Richmond track, Southside Speedway, that first brought him down here. That man's name was Nelson Royall. In fact, they also used to call that track Royall Speedway before they called it Southside. You know, the good promoters back then would bring drivers in; the gentleman who ran the Richmond Fairgrounds track for years, Paul Sawyer, used to pull his own short-track car all over the country, so he would see some of these top guys, too, and bring 'em in to run at the Fairgrounds and at his other track in Norfolk. But whoever it was that brought in Flemke and those boys, probably Nelson Royall, sure brought in a good group.

When they came down to this area—Eddie, Red Foote, Denny Zimmerman, and Rene Charland—they really did a job on us. Oh, they were so fast on the short tracks around here! All four of them were tremendous drivers, and they all worked very hard on their cars, too. But the other thing I remember is, they all had different make-ups, different personalities.

Rene was a fun guy, and easy to get along with. The first time you met him, it was like meeting up with a friend you had known for years. I don't think that man ever had a conversation with anybody he didn't think he already knew! He was just a nice guy, and a real practical joker, too.

Denny Zimmerman used to follow along right behind Flemke wherever he went, like Eddie was his teacher. Which, of course, he was. But Denny wanted to be the best there ever was; you could see that kind of desire in him. He learned everything he could, and he prepared himself to go on to bigger and better things, which for him was the open-wheel cars and the Indy 500. He was willing to work to get there, and he did get there.

Red Foote was a quiet guy who just drove his heart out. In fact, he drove for me one year. Right at the tail end of that Eastern Bandits peri-

Rene Charland was an Eastern Bandits star and a four-time NASCAR National Sportsman Champion. He remains one of stock car racing's all-time characters. (John Grady photo)

Red Foote was, in Junie Donlavey's estimation, "a quiet guy who just drove his heart out." Here's Red, warming up at Norwood Arena in 1961. *(Paul Conley photo, Bruce Cohen Collection)*

od, he drove our coupe. He was such a nice guy, and it was perfect having him drive for us. Of course, he went on to move down here and marry a Richmond girl. He comes by here sometimes even now, and it's just like we're back in the old days.

But you know something? Even then, you could tell that Eddie was the leader of the pack. You could see that.

We never thought one bit about them being the enemy, or anything like that, just because they were from up North. See, we'd had a taste of that situation ourselves. I remember going up to Langhorne and Trenton to run some big races, so we understood what it was like to leave home and go far away to race. We were always treated very well up there, and I'd like to think we showed them the same courtesy.

But, oh, that Eddie Flemke was tough to beat as soon as he came down here. He specialized in running on those short tracks, and making his car handle. He just had that little extra touch as a chassis man that meant a whole lot. One thing I remember is that after Eddie set his car up, he would walk over to the right-rear tire, turn around facing away from it, then crouch down and pick up that corner of the car by hand. By the way it came up, he'd know if he had just the right amount of bite in that car.

His cars, and the cars those other Northern boys ran, were so much better than ours on pavement. Down here, our cars had been the same for a long time. They were basically dirt cars, and we just built 'em with a lot of horsepower. The driver would go like hell on the straightaway and throw it into the corner, almost broadsliding. Eddie was used to running those little paved quarter-mile tracks up North, so handling was what he worked on the most. He had conquered the method for setting up those cars to run on pavement, and it showed up right away

It's the summer of 1963, in the late innings of the Bandits era, and Flemke has won at Maryland's Marlboro Raceway. Again. *(Bob Williams photo, Larry Jendras Jr. Collection)*

when he first came here to Southside. Pretty soon, it showed up everywhere else he went in this area.

Of course, he was also a terrific driver. Flemke was a *heady* driver, very smart. Back then, they used to line up the starting field according to the points, with the high-point man starting in the back, so the fast guys really had to come through a lot of traffic. And Eddie could do that. You could see him planning his moves, and it was really something to watch him come up through that pack. Oh, he was terrific.

And here's something else about Eddie: There were a lot of nights when he could have run away with the race, and even lapped the field, but he wouldn't do that. He'd make his way to the front, and once he got the lead he'd run just a little bit ahead. He always made it look like the second-place guy had a chance to catch him. Of course, he was doing that to put on a good show for the fans. The man up there in the grandstands doesn't want to see a runaway; he wants to see a good race, and Eddie thought about that stuff more than most people did. So at the end of the night, the fans were happy because they had seen a good race, the promoter was happy because the fans were happy, and Eddie was happy because he won the feature. We all knew he was just playing around, and yet it didn't bother us because we knew *why* he was doing it.

But no matter what you say about him as a chassis man or as a driver, the best thing about Eddie Flemke was that he was so willing to help his competitors. Sometimes it was like he worked on their cars as much as he worked on his own. And whatever they wanted to know, he told 'em. I mean, he gave 'em all the information he had, whatever they wanted to know. He didn't shy away from anything. He helped everybody down here. It's just like I said about Rene Charland: Even if you had never met Eddie, as soon as you talked to him, you felt like you knew him, and you were his friend.

We all studied his chassis, because, I'll tell you, that man had some good ideas on those cars. He had that split front spring, and some other little tricks. But what I'm saying is, you could walk right up and say, "Eddie, how do you make that work?" And he would show you.

Things don't always happen that way. No, sir, some people don't want to help you, don't want to tell you anything. And it was a little bit strange to have a guy like Eddie, an *outsider*, so willing to help you any way he could. I mean, he could have whipped us all pretty easy, and whipped us for a *long* time, if he had kept those secrets to himself. But he didn't. Pretty soon, everybody was copying his cars and his ideas, and that didn't seem to bother Eddie one bit.

I do remember one funny story. When he first came down here, South Boston was still dirt, so we'd go there on Saturday nights and he would go to Manassas. I guess Manassas must have rained out or something on this one particular Saturday, because Eddie was looking for a place to go racing. So we took him to South Boston, and he just had a terrible time. We helped him as much as we could, just like he always helped us, but he had an asphalt car and it just wouldn't run on that dirt track. So after all those nights when we had to watch him whip us, now *we* got to whip *him* one time, Yes, we kinda turned the tables on him that night. But that was all right with him; we all laughed together about that.

I'm telling you, they didn't make but one Eddie Flemke. He was just a fine guy, good to be with at the track or if you were just hanging around. See, sometimes if the race rained out, or if he came down here a day early because those guys had such a long trip, we would socialize a little bit, maybe go out to eat. I really enjoyed being with him.

After those Eastern Bandits days were over and he stopped coming down here on a regular basis, I still kinda kept up on what he was doing. He was winning a lot of races up North, so I'd see his name in the newspapers. And we'd see him when we went up to run at Trenton, or the old big track at Nazareth, Pennsylvania, or even up at Beltsville, Maryland. That was always fun, because it was just like a family reunion.

You know, Eddie has been gone for a long time now, but when I get talking about him like this, it's like he just walked into this office yesterday and sat right down in that chair. And it's like that for a lot of us around here when it comes to Eddie.

We never got over him.

PART THREE

At the Top

There was something very telling about Friday, September 18, 1964, and the grid for the 500-lap Grand National (now Nextel Cup) race at the Old Dominion Speedway in Manassas, VA. In those days, some Grand National fields were sparse—this one consisted of just 20 cars—and it was common for promoters to encourage locally popular short-track stars to fill out the field.

In 1964, it would have been harder to name a bigger Manassas star than Ed Flemke. Though a Yankee, he was loved by area fans. He had followed his incredible 17-win season there in 1962 with a '63 campaign that saw him winning throughout Virginia and North Carolina, not to mention up into Maryland and New Jersey, all fertile states for anyone promoting a Manassas GN show.

Yet Flemke was nowhere to be found. Denny Zimmerman was there—he qualified 10th in a '62 Ford, then dropped out with oil pressure problems—but Flemke was several hundred miles north, running his coupe. The glory days of the Eastern Bandits were in the rear-view mirror. Towing from Connecticut to Dixie on a regular basis no longer made sense, and Flemke was nothing if not sensible.

Let Zimmerman, a kid with dreams, chase the Grand National guys around Manassas. Flemke was a modified guy, and he was looking elsewhere.

Steady Eddie had a brand new bag.

Back home, there were things going on. Norwood was a Saturday-night hot spot in the mid-'60s, boasting stars like Flemke, Bill Slater, Leo Cleary, Ernie Gahan, Bugs Stevens, Fats Caruso, and upstarts Don MacTavish and Pete Hamilton. New York had Albany-Saratoga in Malta on Friday nights, and Utica-Rome on Sundays. Flemke piled up the miles on the Massachusetts Turnpike and the New York Thruway, usually with his children, Paula and Eddie Jr., as back seat drivers. Then were often trailed through the tollbooths by Connecticut journeymen Elton Hill and Don Moon. And sometimes Flemke would stay in New York all weekend, skipping the run back to Norwood in favor of a dash up I-87 to Plattsburgh.

Steady Eddie, working on a modified. In other words, right at home. *(Carolyn Flemke Collection)*

As the years rolled along, things continued to go in Flemke's direction. The Stafford Speedway, then owned by Mal Barlow, was paved in 1967; later, under Jack Arute, it emerged as NASCAR's modified flagship. And in the early '70s, a handful of tracks—among them Seekonk Speedway in Massachusetts, Monadnock Speedway in New Hampshire, and Thompson Speedway in Connecticut, plus good old Waterford and Plainville—had great success with open-competition small-block events. Flemke turned their payoff windows into his own personal ATM machines.

The ten seasons between 1964 and '73 were incredibly productive for Ed Flemke. And with modified racing experiencing a popularity boom, his legend was solidified. He had won in the jalopies, won at all the United tracks, won throughout the South. Now he was winning all over New England, and all over New York.

Steady Eddie Flemke was at the top.

Just another work night: Flemke and car owner Bob Judkins celebrate a 1967 All Star League score at Islip Speedway. *(Carolyn Flemke Collection)*

Recounting all his accomplishments in that period is impossible. But here's a sampling which offers a glimpse at the easy, breezy way Flemke bounced from track to track, running at the front and having the time of his life.

1964: On his true home turf, Flemke captured the Plainville Stadium opener over George Lombardo, Lou Toro, Sparky Belmont, and Ernie Olson ... Norwood gave Eddie four wins, two in his own "cent-sign" coupe and two in John Stygar's "dollar-sign" ... Flemke and Stygar also took a 100-lapper at Seekonk, beating this collection of all-New England talent: Bugs Stevens, Bobby Sprague, Fats Caruso, Billy Greco, George Summers, and Danny Galullo ... Though no longer visiting New Jersey on a regular basis, Flemke won a Fort Dix 100 over Rene Charland and Pee Wee Griffin ... Steady Eddie's biggest score of '64 came on Labor Day, when he swept both 200-lap halves of the New Yorker 400 at Utica-Rome. In the first segment, he beat Fred Harbach, Caruso, Charland, and Lou Lazzaro. When they re-racked the field, Flemke topped Robbie Kotary, Charland, Bill Wimble, and Lazzaro. He was certainly the man of the year at Utica, setting records for most wins in a season (11) and most consecutive wins (five) that stand to this day.

1965: Reacquainting himself with I-95, Flemke hauled to Maryland for a pair of NASCAR events at the half-mile track in Beltsville. Though the track had a short history, it hosted some of the best coupe racers from both sides of the Mason-Dixon line. "Beltsville," says Dennis Zimmerman, "was a central place for all of us to get together." Though Flemke never won there, his Bandit résumé made him a huge attraction . . . Eddie won a second straight Plainville opener over Jap Membrino, Galullo, Johnny Manafort, and Olson . . . At the new United-sanctioned Albany-Saratoga Speedway, Flemke won a 100-lapper, beating Frank Mathalia, Billy Harmon, Elton Hill, and Galullo in front of a standing-room-only crowd . . . It was also at Malta that Flemke suffered his worst injury in years, breaking his leg in a violent crash. But there was a bright side to that wreck: it cement-ed his relationship with a young Massachusetts driver named Pete Hamilton, whom Flemke had begun to mentor after noticing the young-ster at Norwood. Hamilton spent several weeks in Connecticut helping his hobbled friend rebuild the "cent-sign."

1966: A quiet season by Flemke's standards. He drove his NASCAR sportsman car to victory in the Mid-Season Championship at Vermont's Catamount Stadium, and was declared the overall victor in Thompson's season-ending Twin 50 program, having finished closely behind race win-ners Sal Dee and Bugs Stevens. Oh, yeah, and Flemke also won twice at Utica-Rome, and at Albany-Saratoga in its first year as a NASCAR track. Some quiet season . . . Off the track, Eddie wed his second wife, Carolyn, with the reception held at the Malta, NY, hotel of Len and Margaret Bosley, owners of the L&R Speed Shop and weekend hosts to so many traveling modified racers.

1967: A legendary modified team is formed when Flemke steps into the #2X coupe owned by Bob Judkins of Meriden, CT. Their honeymoon sea-son included a 100-lap victory in the first modified main of Stafford's paved era. Flemke topped Hamilton, Dick Watson, Bob Santos, and Bill Slater . . . At Utica-Rome, Flemke won four races, three of them 100-lap-pers . . . When the touring All Star League stopped at Islip, Flemke beat Jerry Cook, Bill Wimble, Fred Harbach and Frankie Schneider . . . In Connecticut, Steady Eddie was a sports-page darling, sharing space in the dailies with stick-and-ball stars. One newspaper story claimed he "shuns points, trophies and publicity, and drives for the money." Another declared that "promoters are starting to beg for his services." When Flemke ran the Trenton 200 and then hopped a private plane bound for Utica-Rome's Sunday-evening show, the press pointed out that "the track owner and NASCAR were footing the expenses" . . . Come autumn, Flemke and

Judkins *really* hit their stride. In October, Eddie beat Leo Cleary and Slater to win the Catamount 200, billed as "Vermont's richest stock car race," then drove the #2X to a Twin 50 sweep at Thompson. He beat Hop Harrington and Watson in the opener, and Bugs Stevens and Harrington in the nightcap. Back at Thompson for the Veterans Day 100, Flemke won over Gene Bergin, Sal Dee, Fats Caruso, Fred DeSarro and Don MacTavish ... Success in racing, Flemke told reporters, was mostly a matter of having "a good relationship with your owner and mechanics and Lady Luck" ... His protégé, Pete Hamilton, had some grand success of his own, winning NASCAR's national sportsman championship.

1968: Steady Eddie got hot before the weather got warm, winning the openers at Norwood, Stafford and Thompson ... He and Judkins stood in victory lane more than 20 times, including six at Stafford (prompting a bounty) and four at Thompson. There were also 100-lap triumphs at Catamount, Plattsburgh, and Albany-Saratoga. One victory at Islip, though, was particularly spectacular; Flemke lined up 15th, and Judkins figured this was too far back to hope for much in a 25-lap feature. Instead, he saw his #2X take the lead for keeps on lap 18 ... In addition to all those wins, Flemke notched at least 18 second-place finishes (one to Ray Hendrick in Beltsville's Indian Summer Classic) and 10 thirds, accounting for close to 50 podium finishes ... Here's a great week: Eddie became a father again one Friday, when Carolyn presented him a daughter, Kristy Jo; finished second the next night at Norwood; won at Thompson on Sunday; and won at Stafford the following Friday, after which writer Pete Zanardi dubbed him "a proud new papa" ... Zanardi also witnessed an interesting Flemke moment upon arriving at Oxford, ME, where he'd gone to watch Grand National rookie Pete Hamilton. "The car was out practicing," Zanardi recalls, "but it wasn't Pete driving. They'd put Eddie in the car because Eddie knew Oxford, and Eddie knew chassis setups. As soon as he got back to the pits, he and Pete would huddle. I'm sure this was Eddie telling

Pete what he could get away with, and what he couldn't: 'You can't go past *this* point, and you've got to turn in at *that* point.' Here's Peter, whose career has been lifted out of the coupes and into the Grand Nationals, and yet Eddie's still lending him a hand."

1969: A topsy-turvy season, but a good one. Bobby Judkins had taken a shine to the rich purses—$1,000 to win, a real haul in '69—at New York's Fonda Speedway, a Saturday-night dirt track. Flemke, who never felt comfortable on the clay, wasn't interested. He ran the #2X on Fridays and Sundays, winning at Albany-Saratoga and Thompson, while the great Kenny Shoemaker drove the car to a pair of Fonda victories. Not about to sit still on Saturdays, Flemke took a ride in the sharp blue #79 coupe of Massachusetts owners Dave Welch and Greg Mills, winning at both Norwood and Stafford. When Judkins began to speak of a Fonda return in 1970, Flemke, who hated climbing into the mud-spattered #2X on Sundays, saw the writing on the wall and began ride-shopping. He and Judkins went their separate ways . . . temporarily, as we shall see.

1970: Flemke's season opened in a strange way, celebrating someone else's victory. But this was no ordinary someone, and no ordinary victory: Hamilton, driving for Petty Enterprises' team car, had won the Daytona 500. Pete interrupted the traditional post-race interview to have Flemke brought into the press box. "He put his arm around me," Eddie later recounted to Pete Zanardi, "and told all the press how important I was in his career. I think that was the greatest thrill of my career." . . . Come spring, Eddie produced a few thrills for new Stafford owner Jack Arute. Driving a coupe fielded by Arute and Flemke's old 1950s bosses, Ray and Richie Garuti, Flemke won the Stafford opener and later added two more wins there, including a 100-lapper. He also steered the Garuti & Arute #14 to three Thompson wins . . . The G&A team rarely raced outside Connecticut, so Flemke padded his schedule by running some events for his latest protégé, Richie Evans. During his salad days, Evans had often leaned on Flemke. "Eddie helped Richie a lot with the chassis," says long-time Evans crewman Wilbur Jones. So, hit by a NASCAR suspension for running non-sanctioned races, Evans put Flemke in the seat at Albany-Saratoga and Utica-Rome. In a race that has become part of modified lore, Flemke totally dominated Utica's New Yorker 400. Upon arriving at the track, Evans was informed by NASCAR stewards that he wasn't welcome in the pits, so he set up shop in the parking lot. Flemke, amused, waved his pit pass to the guard every time he drove through the gate to practice, qualify or race. He led every lap of the 400, waltzing home ahead of Robbie Kotary, Dick Fowler, Gene Mangino, and Maynard Troyer.

1971: For Flemke, more great mentoring news. Denny Zimmerman, Eddie's young shadow in the Eastern Bandits era, finally made it to the Indianapolis 500. He finished eighth, and was named Rookie of the Year. Friends in Glastonbury, CT, Denny's hometown, threw a party in his honor. "What I will never forget about that night," says Pete Zanardi, who was among the organizers, "is Eddie Flemke showing up with Pete Hamilton." . . . Steady Eddie was hot at Malta, winning three features including the Don MacTavish Memorial 100 . . . On the Fourth of July, Flemke and the crimson #09 coupe of veteran car owner Art Barry breezed to a 200-lap victory at Fulton, NY.

1972: All was right with the world. Flemke and Judkins were together again. The previous fall, Bobby's new Pinto modified had set NASCAR

Flemke was modified racing's E.F. Hutton: When he spoke, everybody listened. That's Denny Giroux in the car, while others tuning in to this early 1970s Stafford conversation include John Stygar (on nerf bar), Richie Garuti (leaning on car), Flemke crewmen and brothers Eddie (standing at right) and John Asklar (crouching at right) and Chick Zipadelli (foreground, back to camera). Yes, Zipadelli is the father of Greg Zipadelli, champion Nextel Cup crew chief. (*Mike Adaskaveg photo*)

Flemke with a very young Geoff Bodine at the 1973 Spring Sizzler. Bodine was driving the Vigliarolo #34 which Flemke had steered the previous year. *(Tim Christopher photo, Val LeSieur Collection)*

alight, winning the Labor Day 200 at Stafford with Gene Bergin, but in early '72 that car was sold to Long Islander Frank Vigliarolo. Judkins got busy building a second-generation Pinto for Flemke, but it wasn't ready when the season opened. Eddie hitched a ride with Vigliarolo, and was on his way to winning the first Spring Sizzler at Stafford when the water pump failed. Fred DeSarro, aboard Len Boehler's #3 coupe, got the laurels. Flemke won subsequent Stafford starts with the Vigliarolo #34, then climbed into the new Judkins #2X and kept on winning . . . Among Steady Eddie's victories that season: the 50-lap Waterford opener, the TelePrompTer 50 at Monadnock, an open-comp event in Quebec, plus a Stafford 100 and Albany-Saratoga's Permatex 200 on consecutive nights . . . In a Labor Day weekend 200 at Oswego, NY, Flemke stuck the nose of the #2X under leader Jim Shampine off the final corner, but lapped cars spoiled their drag race to the checkers. Shampine won, while Flemke spun across the line to finish second . . . Dazzled by some traffic moves he'd seen in Flemke's four Albany-Saratoga wins, one writer declared that "Harry Houdini is still alive and well."

1973: Flemke avenged his '72 Spring Sizzler loss by winning the race's second edition in the Judkins #2X. Interestingly, the runner-up was Fred DeSarro, who'd scooped the Sizzler loot a year earlier . . . That same month, Ed Flemke Jr. made his driving debut at Riverside Park . . . Come summer, Steady Eddie won another TelePrompTer 50 at Monadnock, beating Bobby Santos and Gene Bergin . . . Though not his biggest trophy, a July 7th win in a 30-lap Stafford show may have been Flemke's favorite. He had taken the lead from Ron Bouchard, but his engine stumbled on a restart

and Bouchard regained the top spot. Eddie went back on the attack, and as he and Bouchard fought for the lead, Bugs Stevens, Fred DeSarro and young Canadian Denny Giroux closed in. Soon the five leaders were swapping positions, exploiting every gap. Stafford fans were accustomed to close action; led by Flemke, the best shoes staged (yes, that's the right word) some amazing heat races weekly. But this was not a drill. This was for a feature win, and the intensity was palpable. Flemke stole the lead in the closing laps, and at the checkers he edged Stevens, Bouchard, DeSarro and Giroux. Columnist Herb Dodge, who had been around and was not prone to hyperbole, exulted, "What can you say when you have just seen what may be the greatest modified feature of all time?" Flemke, too, seemed to sense how special the moment was. Thirty years before NASCAR's Nextel Cup drivers would turn "donuts" into an annoying post-race cliché, he mashed the throttle, cut the wheel, and spun the #2X around and around in the Stafford infield, to wild applause. Has any modified night ever had a better closing scene?

Flemke once told an interviewer that when everything was going his way—when the engine was strong, when the chassis was dialed in—his attitude toward his opponents was, "Well, fellas, come and get me."

Gosh, how often Steady Eddie must have muttered that silent challenge in those 10 magic seasons from 1964 through 1973.

"Watching Flemke drive a race car was like watching a ballet"

An eyewitness—and "lenswitness"—view of Steady Eddie's modified mastery

by JOHN GRADY

John Grady has been shooting photographs at New York's short tracks for so many years that calling him a fixture doesn't do him justice; see, most of the fixtures haven't been around as long! Johnny was there when jalopies became modifieds, when coupes give way to Pintos and Vegas, when the once-strong paved tracks at Albany-Saratoga and Utica-Rome were covered with clay. His photo collection is a trip through history, and he takes great joy in the smiles it produces. "These days, there is a big market for nostalgia," Grady says. "I sell a lot of pictures of Richie Evans, Bugsy Stevens, Freddy DeSarro, Pete Corey, and, of course, Eddie Flemke. People ask me, 'John, how long are you going to keep doing this?' I tell 'em, 'You'll find me at the speedway when I'm 100 years old.' Take that to the bank."

John Grady

HERE'S SOMETHING I WILL NEVER FORGET: It's a Sunday afternoon at the Utica-Rome Speedway in the mid-'60s, and I'm in the pits, camera in hand, as always. The drivers are getting geared up, the mechanics are getting the cars ready. I'm standing with Wild Bill Henry, who drove the #28 coupe and was a fixture in New York for years and years. Bill and I are talking, and he happens to look up toward the highway, Route 5, at exactly the same time a ramp truck appears with Eddie Flemke's car on the back of it. And as that truck pulls into the parking lot, Wild Bill Henry exclaims, "Oh, shit. We all just moved back one spot in the payoff line."

And, really, that's how it was with Flemke in those days. He was the man to beat. It didn't matter what track you went to, and for a while it didn't seem to matter what he was driving: the "dollar-sign," the "cent-sign," the "percent-sign," the #14, the #28, the Judkins #2X, whatever. He could have been driving a baby carriage, and he'd *still* be the guy everybody kept an eye on.

Now, in those days there were some big names around here: Lou Lazzaro, Bill Wimble, Sonney Seamon, Rene Charland, Ernie Gahan, Jerry Cook. But, like Bill Henry said, Flemke was the guy. He was absolutely at the top of his game in that period.

By then, I had already known Eddie for years. I'd watched him and photographed him quite a bit in the old days of the United Stock Car Racing Club, Harvey Tattersall's group. The first time I saw Eddie was at Menands, New York, the old Empire Speedway, in probably 1952 or '53. He was actually driving in a convertible class that Harvey experimented with for a while; Dick Dixon and a lot of the United guys raced in that division. Well, I happened to be at one of these races, and I noticed that Eddie Flemke was in one of those convertibles, starting way in the back. I had heard of Flemke, and I knew he had won a lot of races, but I thought to myself, "He's starting too far back to be a factor in this thing." Well, I was wrong. *Whoosh*, here he came. He passed everybody on the track, and he did it so smoothly. He came out of nowhere to win that race, like a bolt of lightning.

At that time, I wasn't shooting pictures. I was just out of college, and I had gotten that good ol' government job: drafted into the military. It wasn't until after I got out of the Army that I really started picking up the camera and chasing those race cars around. Now, 50 years later, I'm still in the game.

I saw a *lot* of Eddie Flemke. In fact, I probably photographed Eddie in more different cars over the years than anybody else ever did.

When he first started coming to the New York modified tracks on a regular basis—first Utica-Rome, then Plattsburgh and Albany-Saratoga—he was certainly a very big name. He had done the Eastern Bandits thing for a few years, and of course before that he had won a lot of races in New England, so everybody knew who Eddie Flemke was. But they looked at him in a strange way; I wouldn't say they were suspicious of him or anything like that, but they didn't exactly warm up to him at first because he wasn't the kind of guy who instantly warmed up to *them*. He would just show up, with no big hoopla, and get the job done, and then he was gone. So I think it took a little while for everybody around here—racers, fans, everybody—to figure him out. But once they saw what he could do on the track, that won them over. His driving was the thing that converted them all, and of course he became very popular. I can still remember Jack Burgess and the other announcers calling him "the little leadfoot from Southington, Connecticut."

As time went on, you could see the level of respect people had for the man. They didn't get in his way, and I don't just mean on the race track. Even in the pits, people would move out of his way when he walked. *That's* respect.

Eddie was good at every paved track there was, but I especially enjoyed watching him at Albany-Saratoga. I think it's because I was there right from the time they built that place, and it was fun to watch him figure out this new track, which he certainly did. Now, I did see him at Stafford as well, and he certainly had a special hook at that place, too, but I watched him so much more at Albany-Saratoga and I just appreciated how enjoyable it was to see him run there. Utica-Rome was another place where he was just outstanding; that was a small, tight track, and a driver really had to know how to work traffic to do well there. And Eddie could do that with a level of finesse that I have never seen in any other race driver. He would lay back for a couple laps, let everything settle down, and then he'd charge. He was obviously aggressive, because you had to be aggressive to come from the back, but he was *passively* aggressive. He avoided contact as much as he could. So many guys, you'd watch them come through the field and give every car a little kiss, bumping it out of the way, but I don't recall Eddie ever knocking a guy out of a spot on purpose. He earned his way past, and I think that got him a lot of respect.

It was such a joy to watch him size up the other guy and then, as soon as that other guy slipped just a bit, he'd strike. I used to call him "Flemke, the U-boat commander," because he always went *underneath* the other guy, like he was in a German submarine.

John Grady's connection with Flemke goes way back to the old United convertible division. Here's Steady Eddie in a Dick Dixon ride. *(Shany Lorenzet photo, Dick Berggren Collection)*

He really seemed to interact with the car. I could always tell if Eddie was driving hard or not. If he was leaning forward, he was really pushing it; if he was leaning back, relaxed, he had everything under control. Watching Flemke drive a race car was like watching a ballet. He had every move choreographed.

I watched that man win a lot of races, I know that.

Of course, I was also there when things were not so good. When he broke his leg at Albany-Saratoga in 1965, I thought that crash had killed him. He hit the wall so hard coming out of the fourth turn; actually, it was more like he was *driven* into the wall, because he was on the outside, on the gas, and I think another car just pushed him up. I was taking pictures in turn two, and I *heard* it. It was one of those crashes that you know is bad, just because of the way it sounds. Anyway, that hit really knocked the wind out of him, and when I got over there he was *not* moving. I remember Michael Connery, another guy who used to take pictures there, saying, "My God, I think he's dead." He wasn't the only one, because the whole track got really quiet. But Eddie eventually caught his breath, and they got him out of the car, and when I looked at the wreckage later I noticed that his roll cage was made mostly of exhaust-pipe tubing. Not the smartest thing to do, but of course it made the car nice and light.

And then there was the infamous "French Barbecue," Rene Charland's big fire. This was at the end of May in 1966, the first year that NASCAR sanctioned Albany-Saratoga. I remember that whole evening so clearly. I was walking through the pits, and I saw Rene climb in and out of his car. Well, just to be a joker and because we were always friendly, I climbed into Rene's car. I said, "Here, Charland, I'll show you how to do this." That was all in fun, and we all laughed, but something strange happened when I tried to climb out of that car: I got my foot caught down by the pedals, and somebody had to help me get untangled. Anyway, I went off to shoot pictures, and Rene got ready for warm-ups.

Now, remember, firesuits were still optional. That night, Rene came to the track dressed in a white shirt and black pants, and that's what he wore in the warm-ups and the heat race. Then, right before the feature, he put on his firesuit. Who knows why, but thank God he did.

Elton Hill, a good driver from Connecticut who kind of followed Flemke to the New York tracks, was running toward the front, but Eddie and Charland were coming. Eddie got past Elton first, and the cars were all bunched up as usual, and Elton's car rode over Eddie's wheel. They got tangled, and Charland, who was right behind this, spun and hit the wall. The next thing we all heard was this horrible *Whoosh!* That was Rene's car, bursting into flames. It was as if a firebomb had exploded, and of course Rene was in there, trying to get unstrapped and get out. What I didn't realize was that Rene had gotten his foot caught, the same way I had. That car had an electric fuel pump, so the fire was being fed and it just kept getting bigger and more fierce.

Everything got very quiet. The cars had all stopped, and the spectators were stunned. And then, through the silence, you could hear this awful scream. It was Rene's wife, who happened to be sitting beside the announcer. Her screams were picked up by the microphone and the public address system. We're all thinking, "Good God, this man is going to burn to death," and over it all you could hear this poor woman. It was a terrible, terrible scene. I mean, that's the most shaken up I've ever been at a race track.

What happened next, I can still see as clearly as if it happened yesterday. Here comes Flemke—not wearing a firesuit, just dark pants and a white shirt—running toward that car and *right into the fire*. He reached into the window—got halfway into the car—and he helped Rene get everything sorted out, and then he just pulled him out. Now, Rene was a good-sized guy, and what did Eddie weigh, 125 pounds, soaking wet?

Miles Nelson and I—Miles used to own cars driven by Don Moon, and he would sneak out to the infield to watch the races—may have been the only true witnesses to Eddie's act. I mean, a lot of people were *there*, and they could certainly hear the screams from Rene's wife, but they were on the other side of the fire and the smoke and they couldn't have seen what Eddie did.

You know, that car just kept on burning. The firemen would knock down the flames, and just like that it would start up again. I'm telling you, that fire burned for 15 minutes. So you can imagine how important it was for a driver trapped inside to get that kind of help.

Rene was burned pretty badly—his hands got a lot of it—but maybe the worst part was that he had inhaled some of that smoke and flames. He told me later that while all this was happening, he kept thinking:

This Albany-Saratoga fire, dubbed the "French Barbecue," might indeed have cooked Rene Charland had Flemke not come to the rescue. *(John Grady photo)*

"Fireball Roberts, Fireball Roberts, don't breathe, don't breathe, Fireball Roberts." Because, don't forget, it had only been a couple of years at that point since Roberts had died after being involved in a very similar sort of fire at Charlotte. Of course, Rene recovered and he raced for many more years, but he did have to sit out for quite a while after that wreck at Albany-Saratoga.

Eddie, somehow, was not burned at all; or, if he was, it was something superficial that he never told anybody about. That was amazing to me, because when he dove so deeply into that car, I wasn't sure he'd be able to get out.

To this day, that remains the bravest thing I've seen in my whole life. Now, Eddie was such an unassuming guy, so he always said, "Oh, anybody would have done the same thing." But I know this: *I* didn't go running over there. Nobody did, except Flemke.

He was such a cool, calm individual, unlike so many drivers. Dick Nephew, who came from way up in Moores Forks, NY, and had won a NASCAR sportsman championship, was a very jumpy guy. Somebody would set off a firecracker, and Nephew would leap right out of his shoes. So, naturally, you'd have Rene Charland dropping firecrackers right behind Nephew just to scare the hell out of him. Well, this one particular night, somebody—probably Rene again, because Rene was always pulling these kinds of tricks—tried the same thing with Eddie, but they used an M-80. Not a little firecracker, mind you, but an M-80, and it was laying on the ground right behind Eddie with the fuse burning. *Boom!* And Flemke didn't even *flinch*. I said to myself, "This is a man with steady nerves." He proved that again one night at Stafford, when they had a big fireworks display just before the feature and, in the middle of all this noise, I saw Eddie sleeping in his car!

His true greatness, I think, was found in the way he helped so many upcoming drivers: Pete Hamilton, Denny Zimmerman, Richie Evans. You know, everybody talks about the way Eddie helped Richie Evans, but I was there to see it. I remember Richie starting out in the hobby division at Utica-Rome, and, let me tell you, this wild young man from Westernville looked like the worst driver God had ever put on the face of the Earth. Obviously, he wasn't the worst driver, but he may have had the worst *car*, and he was also completely inexperienced. But Flemke certainly spotted something, and he began to talk to Richie. It was never any big, formal deal, but if you walked through the pits after the races you'd always see the two of them talking.

And it wasn't just Richie. I remember when Brian Ross was just getting started. Brian went on to win a lot of races, but in the beginning he struggled, like everybody does. Well, we were at Malta one night, and Brian was having a tough time getting his car figured out, so he asked Eddie to try it out. Eddie took a couple of laps, pulled into the pits, and said to Brian, "Get rid of this thing." Brian said, "What do you mean?

John Grady says, "Eddie may have been the only person Richie Evans listened to at times, but the point is, he did listen." Here's Richie, hanging onto Flemke's every word. *(Mike Adaskaveg photo)*

What can I do to fix it?" Eddie told him, "Don't bother. Just get rid of this car." And, you know, that's what Brian did. He got rid of that car, and his next one was better.

I remember Flemke helping Jean-Guy Chartrand, when Chartrand was driving the Hemi-Cuda. And, you know, another guy Eddie got along with, and certainly helped as well, was Lou Lazzaro. Louie and Eddie were somewhat similar, because they were both very shy. Lazzaro might have been a tough-looking guy, and he certainly had the heart of a lion, but deep down he was a pussycat, as was Eddie.

You know, people are always talking about how tough race drivers are, and especially about how tough race drivers *used to be*. Well, I don't agree. Certainly, no good race driver is a pushover, and they all have a tendency to get hot at each other once in a while, but I've always found them to be very decent, caring people.

Show me a race driver, and I'll show you a little boy. Now, you might have to look hard to find that little boy in some of them, because they try to *act* tough, but he's in there. And there was certainly a little boy inside Eddie Flemke.

Maybe I'm playing Joe Psychiatrist, but I found Eddie to be a very complex individual. He was bright, *very* bright, and he had a great sense of humor, and he was also such a friendly guy. And yet he was certainly an introvert; he kept to himself. I know there were exceptions, but generally you had to be *around* Eddie for quite some time—months, years—before he truly accepted you. You had to give him his space, and you almost had to prove yourself to him, and eventually something in his expression would sort of say, "All right, you can come closer."

Flemke's laughing, so you can bet the wise guy with the camera said something to loosen him up! *(John Grady photo)*

That's something I noticed when I started shooting pictures of him. He was sort of indifferent to me, and then one day, for whatever reason, I noticed that he started smiling more, posing more. It was as if I had been around long enough, and I'd taken enough pictures of him, that now I was accepted. Maybe part of that was because I always used my head, and tried to read a guy's body language to see if he was, or wasn't, in the mood to be photographed. I do that with Brett Hearn today, and I do it with Tony Stewart, and I did it with Flemke back then. If I think they're in that *zone*, I leave them alone. That's just me. But, you know, once I felt like I was accepted by Eddie, I could always get him to smile. If I went to shoot him sitting in his car and he didn't seem to be in a good mood, I'd say, "Goddam it, Eddie, look professional," or "Try to look as good as you can." He'd always smile at that, and I'd get a great shot.

There's so much about Eddie I didn't know, and I still don't know, but we certainly did get to be quite friendly over the years. In fact, for a long time at Albany-Saratoga we had our own little system of "cheating." See, Eddie always wanted to know what was going on behind him, and so Miles Nelson, standing in the infield, would give him these hand signals. Well, eventually Miles stopped going to those tracks, so I sort of took over. Eddie knew where I stood in the infield every week—I was always on the same dirt mound, a perfect spot to shoot from—so he'd look over and I'd kind of fill him in on what was going on. This happened under green, under yellow, it didn't matter. If he seemed to have everybody covered, I'd hold my hands out, palms down, like saying, "You're fine. Play it cool." Or I'd twirl my finger, as if to say, "Pick it up. Somebody's catching you." The next lap, I'd tell him who it was. For example, I'd hold up four fingers if Lazzaro was behind him, or maybe

I'd mouth the words "Pete Hamilton." I was basically giving him more information than he could get from his rear-view mirror.

The funny thing was, most of the time it wasn't that Eddie was trying to find an advantage; it was the opposite. He didn't want to be a runaway winner, and he was actually trying to make the race *better*. If the guy behind him was someone he trusted, he'd back off a bit and give the fans a good show.

And, you know, this might sound strange, but Eddie and I never talked about this. We never discussed it. It was just something we did. Every week he'd look for those signals, and every week I'd give him those signals, and that was that. It was just a given: I'll do *this*, and you do *that*. And, knowing Eddie, I think the fact that he never mentioned it was his strange way of telling me he appreciated it.

You know, I've asked this question of a lot of guys: "Who was the best driver you ever raced against?" I'm always very curious about that. Well, one day I asked Charland, and he said, "Why would you even ask that? It was Eddie. It was *always* Eddie." And I could see how genuine he was when he said it. I've heard Ernie Gahan say the same thing, and Buddy Krebs, and Danny Galullo, and on and on.

I have to agree. To me, if we're talking about asphalt modified drivers, Eddie was the finest, the best. I believe that. I always say that Eddie and Pete Corey are my twins: Corey was the best I saw on dirt, and Flemke was the best I saw on asphalt.

Several years ago, *Area Auto Racing News* conducted a poll, and they asked something like 50 people—media people, mostly—to rank the 25 best pavement modified drivers of all time. I was told they ended up with 49 first-place votes for Richie Evans, and one for Eddie. Well, that Flemke vote was mine.

Now, of course, Richie had all those NASCAR championships and all those big wins, and you cannot take away what he accomplished and how good he was. So, naturally, some people who knew how I'd voted told me I was crazy. I said, "No, I have my own firsthand opinion."

See, here's how I explain it. First of all, Eddie really *was* the greatest asphalt driver I ever watched. Now, maybe there was somebody out in Arizona or California who was just as good, but I never saw him. From my standpoint, Eddie was simply the best. He was a great mechanic, a great tactician, and above all he was a great driver. So I was just being honest.

Secondly, I know how much *Richie* respected Eddie. I remember talking with Richie about that; he told me, several times, "Eddie is the Man." But, more importantly, I remembered the times when I would see them in the pits, and the way Richie would stand there and *listen* to him. Now, Eddie may have been the *only* person Richie Evans listened to at times, but the point is, he did listen to Eddie because of that respect.

So when it was time for me to fill out this ballot, I said to myself: If Richie Evans and Eddie Flemke were alive and standing in this room, and I asked them both to name the greatest driver, I know Richie would have immediately pointed to Flemke. I *know* that.

There's a wonderful story about that from Albany-Saratoga. We were there for some big daytime race, and they were running time trials. For some reason—I guess I was busy talking to someone—I didn't realize that time trials were getting underway, so instead of getting out to the infield I was stuck in the pits. Well, Richie took his laps, and as he came back to the pits we all heard the announcer saying, "It's a new track record!" Naturally, everybody around his car was happy, jumping up and down. Well, that brand-new record lasted less than a minute, because the next guy out was Flemke. Eddie set fast time, and when I looked at Richie he said, "Hey, you're not gonna beat *that* guy."

So, in my mind, that's that. Eddie Flemke was number one.

He was also someone I completely admired and loved. After he had stopped driving, we both happened to be at Lebanon Valley for a big DIRT modified race. I was there shooting pictures, and Eddie was there as a spectator. I walked up to him and said, "Mr. Flemke, I want to say something to you."

He said, "What's that, John?"

Now, it wasn't at all unusual for us to bump into each other, and we would always share a joke. But on this night, I was completely serious. I told him, "Eddie, I've known you for years and years, and I've taken a lot of pictures of you, and we've had some laughs. But all that aside, I just want you to know how much I appreciate having watched you race. You had such a distinguished career, and you will always have my respect. Thank you for all those wonderful nights."

I stuck out my hand to shake his, but Eddie wrapped his arms around me and he got very emotional. He said, "John, that means so much to me." He hugged me, and he would not let go; it was almost like three separate hugs. This goes back to what I said earlier about him being so complex. Here was this incredible racer, this driving machine, and he's giving me a big embrace. It really was a very touching moment.

Then I wandered off to take my pictures and he wandered off to do his own thing, and I know we both had tears in our eyes. And, you know, that was the last time I ever saw Eddie, because he died the following spring. When I think about that, I'm always glad I got the chance to tell him how I felt.

"When a student is truly ready, the teacher will appear"

Flemke's mentoring pays dividends, from Utica-Rome to Daytona

by PETE HAMILTON

Pete Hamilton had a Roman-candle racing career: it didn't last long, but its pyrotechnic bursts were breathtaking. Consider his coming-of-age sweep of twin modified/ sportsman features at Thompson in 1965, his NASCAR sportsman championship in '67, his Cup series rookie title in '68, and his 1970 Daytona 500 victory. Eager and likable, Hamilton attracted a string of sharp advisors, from Norwood Arena regulars Bob Bacchiochi and Bobby Melnick, to travel-savvy Eddie Flemke and Rene Charland, to his Daytona teammate and boss, Richard Petty. When a nagging neck injury ended his Cup career at age 30, Hamilton took business tips from another mentor, ex-Norwood hotshoe Jack Malone, and began developing commercial real estate outside Atlanta. These days, Pete and his wife Susie spend most of their days in the Florida Keys, where Malone is among his neighbors and closest friends. "Geez," Hamilton marvels, "I've had some good teachers."

Pete Hamilton

WHY ME? Why Pete Hamilton? That's a good question. There were a lot of young kids racing at all these different tracks in the 1960s, kids Eddie Flemke could have taken under his wing, but he took me. And I don't know why that was, I really don't.

I do know this: I was incredibly lucky at several points in my racing life, and because my career has been over for a period of time I'm now able to look back and see that. There was not a great deal of plotting and planning and figuring on my part, and so it's almost as if at times God was doing for me things I could not do for myself. He put me in the right places at the right times, and with the right people. And, certainly, Eddie was one of those right people.

It's 1965, and Pete Hamilton has just won a Norwood Arena feature with the Ray Stonkus #9. *(R.A. Silvia Collection)*

There's an old saying that when a student is truly ready, the teacher will appear. Maybe that's the best way to explain it. I was willing to shut up and listen; I was ready to learn. See, the problem with most of us race drivers, including me, is that we can all have big mouths, and, worse than that, big egos. But I was just so damn impressed with Eddie Flemke that I was willing to shut up and listen.

The first time I ever encountered Eddie in any important way was up at Utica-Rome, way back in 1965. I had raced against Eddie quite a bit at Norwood Arena, and I was so amazed at the things he could do, but I hadn't really traveled much. But Ray Stonkus and I had a car— Ray's Flyin' #9 coupe, which in hindsight was my first really good race car—and early in the season we made our first trip to Utica-Rome. Now, Utica was basically a flat quarter-mile oval, a very tough place to get around because it was so short and so tight. I was having my troubles there that day, and Eddie absolutely took pity on me. He came over and told me a few things about the track and about my car, and he helped me immensely. In fact, the things he began to teach me that day taught me about racing everywhere, and I mean *everywhere*.

Think about this: I raced at tracks that ranged in size from places like Utica-Rome Speedway to Talladega, and I know the question people are going to ask is, "How can there possibly be anything that relates from one of those two tracks to the other one?" Well, I'm telling you, there is, or at least there *was*, and Eddie pointed it out to me that day in '65. He showed me how to square a corner, which is a driver's term that's not completely accurate, because you're not actually squaring it, but it's a technique for getting a car around which in those days could help you anywhere you went.

He taught me that you always wanted the front end to push just a little bit. To make the car work, you would go in a little bit wide, kind of throw the car at the corner, and make that hook a little bit earlier than the next guy. The result, if you did this right, was that you were on the gas before the next guy was, and you could *stay* on the gas because the rear end was under you, nice and stable. And that changed *everything* for me.

Now, it was still a few years before I did anything really worth paying attention to, but the process of Eddie Flemke teaching me this technique started that very night at Utica-Rome. And it really was a process; over the course of the next few months, and actually the next few seasons, there were nights when Eddie would drive my car in practice, and I would drive his car, and then we would compare notes. That's how generous Eddie Flemke was with me. This usually happened at Albany-Saratoga on Friday nights. The two of us were often in different places on Saturday nights, one of us at Norwood and the other at Plattsburgh, but on Fridays we were always at Albany-Saratoga, and that's where Eddie really worked hard on my head. And, eventually, I came to understand that technique of his, which was a matter of having just enough push in the car to let you throw the car at the corner, turn it early, and get back on the gas first. And the guy who gets back on the gas first wins the race, every time. Getting off the corner, Eddie preached, is ten times more important than getting into the corner.

What made this even more important was the fact that in those days, NASCAR ran the modifieds and the sportsman cars together, and almost all of my racing—and Eddie's, too, in this particular period—was done with sportsman cars. The cars themselves were the same in both divisions, but the sportsman cars were limited to small-block engines and carburetors, while the modifieds ran big-block engines and fuel injection. So we didn't have much horsepower to play with, but Eddie's little trick solved that problem. He closed up the tire stagger across the back, which gave it that nice little push, and you could really *drive* that sucker off the corner. Even at places like Stafford or Thompson, we could hold our own. The big-block cars had more horsepower, but our cars had lighter engines and we handled better, so it made for a pretty even show. I mean, I can still remember Gene Bergin and Bugsy Stevens flying by me with their modifieds at the end of the straightaway, but when we got to the next corner they'd slide up just a bit from carrying all that extra speed and I'd jump back underneath 'em. I won my share of races with those sportsman cars, and Eddie did, too, and that was simply because we out-handled the modifieds. I might have only had a 327-cubic-inch small block and a carburetor against your 400-and-whatever-inch monster with injectors, but I was on the gas, driving off the corner, while you were sliding around and spinning your wheels.

It took a while for me to understand how to make that "Flemke turn," throwing it into the corner, but Eddie stayed after me. He'd say, "You're just going to have to learn that." And I *did* learn it. It scared the hell out of Ray Stonkus for a while, because he'd say, "Goddam it, Pete, you look like you're going to spin that thing out." But before long I figured out how to get the thing turned and jump on the gas, and I'd be gone.

I'm not sure I realized right away that Eddie was taking me under his wing this way, but there came a point when it dawned on me that I could go to this man with any question I had, and he was not afraid to tell me the truth. There were plenty of other older guys—winning veterans—who were not so free with their information; they would rather keep their secrets than pass them along to some young punk. So as this occurred to me, our relationship was more a matter of me going to Eddie than Eddie coming to me. I might even have become a bit of a pain in the ass to him, because in that period, right at the beginning of my traveling days, I asked a *lot* of questions.

Again, I go back to the fact that I was so lucky in all of this. When I hooked up with Eddie, the only thing I wanted to do in life was race, and I was a young, healthy, single guy who didn't have anything to stop him from doing that. I was sharing an apartment in West Roxbury, Massachusetts—right outside Boston—with Butch Walsh, who went on to be a very successful midget racer. That apartment was a story in itself; it cost us next to nothing, but it had no heat, which was a ridiculous situation in Boston in the winter. But, anyway, I was hungry, so hungry that I was willing to say, "Help me. I know nothing. *Please* help me." And here came Eddie, who was willing to say, "Come on, kid, chase around the country with me for a while." On top of that, it just so happened that right off the bat Eddie and I got along very well personally, which helped.

In this time, he was definitely as big a name as there was in modified racing. But what I liked was that it was hard to separate the Eddie Flemke you saw in the race car from the Eddie Flemke you saw walking around in the pits, or the Eddie Flemke you rode with in one of his beat-up station wagons, towing his car 10 hours each way to a race in

Flemke-owned cars, like this "percent-sign" coupe, featured no frills. Says Pete Hamilton, "That man never had much money to work with." (John Grady photo)

Richmond or someplace like that. He was the same guy in any situation, and that appealed to me.

Eddie had what I'd call a *method* for racing, and his method was bigger than just the setup of his car, and bigger than just his style, and bigger than the individual little lessons he taught and the little things he said. His method was a combination of all these things, and a genuine love of both driving the race car and working on that thing and making it better, lighter, faster than the next fellow's car. It was a way of life, a *lifestyle*, and I really caught on to that. I enjoyed that life a great deal.

I'm not sure today's short-track racers even *know* about that life. Sure, some of these drivers still work on their own cars, but do they live like we did? We built all our race cars, and those cars meant the whole world to us. I mean, people may not understand this because of how many races Eddie won, but that man never had much money to work with. When he had his own cars—the "dollar-sign," the "cent-sign," the "percent-sign"—he had *no* money. He rarely had new parts, so everything was rebuilt and refurbished, and of course he tweaked everything using his own ideas. Eddie's secret had nothing to do to with fancy cars or lots of equipment or new tires or big engines or money. His secret was that he knew how to make the *whole* more important than all those *parts*. He simply knew how to get a helluva lot out of very little. In hindsight, I think I loved the fact that he almost seemed to be getting away with something; he'd take what he had, and maybe he'd borrow a wheel from Rene Charland and a tire from Leo Cleary, and he'd beat some other guy who had rolled in with a beautiful car and a nice trailer.

There was nothing that man wouldn't do to go racing.

It was also in '65 that Eddie got clipped at Albany-Saratoga and had a big crash which broke his leg, and he was on the sidelines for a while.

That set up another situation that changed everything for me. He was in a bad spot, because he needed to get his car back together so it'd be ready when he healed up. I said, "Look, Eddie, I'll come down and help you. We'll tear apart the wrecked car and salvage what we can, and we'll get a new frame, and we'll get you going again." I packed up my gear, and stayed with him for several weeks. Again, this all goes back to luck and timing: I didn't have anything in my life besides racing, so I was free to do this. I left Boston, and just headed to Connecticut. I would sneak away on the weekends to drive Ray's car, but basically I just lived with Eddie for a while and I became his legs. Eddie wasn't helpless —he could still weld, and work on some things—but he definitely needed that extra person in the shop to do the things he couldn't do.

Our days were pretty interesting. Eddie never did care about getting out of bed too early, so we might not get to the shop before ten or eleven o'clock in the morning, but we'd always work late into the night. And he also had some sort of involvement in a service station—I believe it was Rocky Germani's place, in New Britain—so we spent some time there, too. But most of our days and evenings were spent at his little race shop, not far away from the service station. Now, it wasn't exactly a wonderful fabrication shop by any stretch of the imagination, but it was everything you needed in those days. We'd work until we were tired, or until we had done all we could do with what we had that day, and then we'd head home.

And, you know, even then we weren't finished. It turned out that Eddie and I were both big Cheerios fans, so no matter how late we worked in the garage, we'd get back home, pour ourselves some Cheerios, and sit there talking racing while we ate our cereal. I mean, we would talk race cars 24/7, which was fine with me. See, at that stage of the game, all I wanted to do was work on race cars, drive race cars, and talk about race cars. We would have these long discussions about tire stagger, and how the setups would differ from small tracks like Malta or Utica-Rome to longer tracks like Stafford or Thompson. And he told me so many other things that stuck with me, just these little *sayings* that he had. He'd say things like, "If you want to be a race driver, you need to have a little larceny in your heart." Now, that's just a funny little line, but it obviously stuck with me because 40 years later I still remember him saying it.

During this time, Eddie became a lot more *human* to me. He was still a great driver, of course, and still a man I looked up to so much, but once you're with somebody as much as Eddie and I were together, you can't help but see the non-racing side of the person. For example, it's funny to think back on this, but I remember being taken aback when I saw Eddie being soft and romantic with his girlfriend Carolyn, who he eventually married. I was flabbergasted! I don't know why that bothered me, because I was single and I liked girls as much as the next guy did, so why wouldn't Eddie? But that's how naïve and one-dimensional I was at the time: I never contemplated the idea that my racing hero, my mentor, could actually be *involved* in something like that! In time, I got over it, and I began to see this other side of Eddie; I got to know his kids, Eddie Jr. and Paula, who would often come to the races with us, and also Carolyn's children, Laurie and Timmy. And, looking back, it was really wonderful to see that side of him. The more human he became, the better it was for me. But, like I said, it definitely was a bit of a shock.

All this time, we were putting together a new car for him. As I remember it, John Stygar came by quite often and helped, too. We got ourselves a frame out of the junkyard, probably a '54 Chevy, and cut it apart until all we had were the two rails; then we joined the rails by making new cross-members. Eddie and I gas-welded the roll cage together using EMT, which stands for Electrical Mechanical Tubing, basically conduit pipe. That stuff was pretty much half the weight of the good steel tubing we *should* have used, so we ended up with a car that was not necessarily too safe but was definitely nice and light. That was a real advantage, because in those days the officials *never* weighed the cars.

Well, the way I thought then was, if that sort of a car is good enough for Eddie Flemke, it's *damn* sure good enough for Pete Hamilton. And so Ray Stonkus and I began incorporating a lot of what I'd learned, and putting those ideas into our car. We won several races with that Flying #9, including both ends of a twin-50s doubleheader at Thompson at the very end of 1965. In fact, that success at Thompson, you could say, was kind of the moment that put me on everybody's radar. It told people that I was coming.

For 1966, I got a ride in the Worcester Sand & Gravel #69, driving for Matteo Trotto, and Ray came along with me. That was a pretty well-

This Worcester Sand & Gravel #69, a Flemke-inspired flyweight coupe, carried Pete Hamilton to the 1967 NASCAR national sportsman title. That's New York legend Bill Wimble alongside. *(John Grady photo)*

known ride because Fats Caruso had driven the #69 before me, and the whole situation was a step up because it meant we were certainly better funded than we had been with Ray's car. Ray built a new car for Worcester Sand, again using all the lightweight tricks I had picked up from Eddie, and we ended up with a nice little coupe that was a little bit different from Eddie's but still similar in a lot of ways. But the biggest thing that worked in my favor was that in '66, I was with Eddie pretty much every weekend. I finished in the top 10 in the NASCAR sportsman standings that year—Don MacTavish won the championship—and that was simply a result of me chasing Eddie around. Following Eddie from track to track meant that I raced an awful lot, and the points accumulated, so we ended up pretty good. Our normal circuit that year was Catamount Stadium in Vermont on Thursday nights, Albany-Saratoga on Friday nights, Plattsburgh or Norwood on Saturday nights, and Thompson on Sunday afternoons. Mac raced even more, because he was chasing points, but that was pretty much the weekly deal for guys like Eddie, Bugsy Stevens, and myself. If we were really pressing things, we'd also try to run Utica-Rome on Sunday nights. Those Thompson-to-Utica runs, which some guys did often but I only did once in a while, were just insane. That's three and a half hours even in good conditions, and we'd go flying up the Mass Pike and the New York Thruway in these old trucks just to try to make the feature. Then, after you ran the race and got paid, you'd realize that you were four hours from home.

Now, 1967 was even crazier. I was fortunate enough to win the NASCAR sportsman title that year, and I believe I went to something like 120 or 121 different events. We got rained out something like fifteen times, which means I actually competed in over 100 features. Our operation was based in Needham—at Jack Malone's complex, which everybody called "Gasoline Alley"—but we traveled so much that we were almost never there. A lot of different people helped that year, but the guy who went to all those races with me was Dick Trabish, a mechanic friend of mine from Needham. And at the end of that season, Dickie said to me, "I love you, Pete Hamilton, but I don't care if I *ever* go to another race."

I'm telling you, chasing points in those days was a hard, hard thing. We raced everywhere from Oxford, Maine, to Hialeah, Florida. In between, I ran Trenton, Langhorne, Malta, Catamount, Plattsburgh, Martinsville, Norwood, Stafford, Thompson, Islip, Utica-Rome, everywhere. We even ran a late model car at strange places like Baton Rouge, Lousiana, and Macon, Georgia, and Jeffco Speedway outside Atlanta, because those races counted toward the NASCAR sportsman championship, as did the 300-mile late model race at Daytona, which started the season.

Speaking of Daytona, it was Eddie Flemke who brought me there for the very first time, in 1966. By then, we had gotten to know each other pretty well, and I piled into Eddie's station wagon with a couple of his buddies and drove down there. First we spent some time down near Miami, at his sister Betty's place, and then we went up to Daytona for the races. That was interesting for me, because MacTavish ran the late model race that year, which put a thought in my mind: "If he can do this, I can do this." After all, Mac had been a Norwood Arena kid, just like me. And the following year, 1967, I did run Daytona for the first time, which was a hold-your-breath deal because the car was absolutely awful. It belonged to Rocky Hinton, who later gave me my first ride in a Cup car, but it wasn't Rocky's fault that the car was so bad. We just did-n't know any better, and that thing sat as high off the ground as a buggy. But what I remember is that when the race ended, Eddie walked over to me and said, "What do you think, kid?" I told him, "Eddie, get me the hell out of this place. I never, ever want to run here again." But I did continue to race at Daytona, of course, and Eddie was usually somewhere close by.

When Don MacTavish got killed at Daytona during the sportsman race in '69, Eddie was one of the people who came to me and gave me encouraging words. I was running in my first Daytona 500 the next day, and Mac had been a good friend, so that was a very difficult time. There were several people who talked to me—including Eddie, Jack Malone, and interestingly, Richard Petty—and reminded me, basically, that, "Hey, this is what we do, what we *choose* to do, what we love to do."

The ride of Pete Hamilton's lifetime came with Petty Enterprises in 1970, aboard this Plymouth Superbird. *(Bones Bourcier Collection)*

Victory Lane after the 1970 Daytona 500: New England's very own Pete Hamilton clutches the trophy, and the trophy girl. *(Bones Bourcier Collection)*

There's no way to put into words how helpful that was to me in that moment.

And, of course, Eddie was there in 1970 when I won the Daytona 500 in the Petty Enterprises car, and he was even with me in the press box during the interviews later. It's kind of a blur to me now, the way all that happened and how he ended up there. I mean, that was such a big day, and the memories all run together. But, as I recall it, one of the reporters mentioned to me that Eddie Flemke was outside waiting for me, and I just said, "Bring him in." That was a wonderful moment for

On a promotional visit to Albany-Saratoga in the spring of '70, just months after his Daytona score, Hamilton spends some quality time with his modified mentor. *(John Grady photo)*

me, and I guess it was for Eddie, too, because he later mentioned it in some stories I read. I was always glad about that, because it told me that Eddie positively *knew* he made me a better race driver, and that makes me happy. In my eyes, he's still on a pedestal, and there is no way I'll ever feel that I reached the level he reached in racing. Yes, I had the Daytona 500 win and some other success in the Cup cars while Eddie stayed at that modified/sportsman level, but in my eyes I never quite caught up to him.

You know, a lot of people remember Eddie mostly for being this great thinker, and he was certainly that. And as he got older, he certainly became more cerebral, as we all do. But I really want to make this point clear: The biggest thing Eddie had going for him is that he was truly amazing in the cockpit. I do not want that thought to be lost. I mean, this was a man who could make race cars do some cute things, things you wouldn't believe they could do. I go back to those nights at Albany-Saratoga when we'd take each other's cars out in practice. I had a car that was basically identical to his, but I couldn't make his car do what *he* made it do, and yet he could jump in my car and make it do whatever tricks he wanted it to. God gave him a wonderful bit of eye-hand-ass coordination, a wonderful *feel*, and he made the most of it.

Racing against him was always a double-edged thing for me. See, it was a great chance to learn something, but it also meant there was a very good chance I wasn't going to win that night. He beat me a helluva lot more than I ever beat him, that's for sure.

To this day, I can't think of Eddie Flemke without smiling, and I'll tell you why. At any track you run, however big or small, there's always a pause while the car takes its set; it's that instant just before you get back on the gas. Well, Eddie and I were side-by-side in a lot of those moments, very often with him on the outside, and so many times I'd catch him looking over at me. He'd give me that little grin of his, and maybe he'd playfully give me the finger or he'd show me a little hand signal, saying, "Come on, let's go. We're going to the front." But there was always that little snicker, and that will never leave me.

So, we get back to the same question: Why me? I guess I'll never know why he took me under his wing, but I'm so glad he did. He had a great way of communicating, and his message to me was clear: "Get your ass in gear, boy." And it worked.

I know I keep saying this, but it's true: Eddie changed everything for me.

"From the very beginning, I was an Eddie Flemke fan"

A stock car racing lifer reflects on his boyhood hero

by ROBIN PEMBERTON

Robin Pemberton is NASCAR's Vice President of Competition, quite a career leap from his childhood responsibilities at Dunster's Restaurant. In between came mechanic/crew chief jobs at Petty Enterprises, DiGard Racing, Roush Racing, Sabco Racing and Penske Racing South, as well as a stint as Ford Racing's field manager. In Pemberton's case, you can take the boy out of the bullrings, but you can't take the bullrings out of the boy. "Greg Narducci remains one of my best friends," Robin says, "and I run into Pete Hamilton and Rene Charland occasionally. To them, I'm still that kid from the restaurant. I still see Eddie Flemke Jr. when I can get to a modified race, and when Ron Bouchard was still running a Cup car I reintroduced myself to Eddie's daughter Paula at Michigan. I love the idea that in this great big country, I can still cross paths with those people."

Robin Pemberton

MY MOM AND DAD owned a restaurant, Dunster's, just down the street from Albany-Saratoga Speedway, maybe a mile away. The restaurant sat on the corner of Routes 9 and 67, just off I-87, the Northway. It was a nice little family place with the usual stuff: hamburgers, hot dogs, steaks, seafood, milkshakes, handmade ice cream, just good ol' comfort food.

The race track opened in 1965, but while it was still being built, Larry Mendelsohn, one of the original partners, would come to the restaurant with his wife for lunch. My dad knew everybody—people used to call him "the Mayor of Malta"—and so he got to be pretty friendly with the Mendelsohns. They'd come in soaking wet from working in the rain, wearing these muddy boots, and through them our family got interested in this whole racing thing. So this must have been in '64. I was born in 1956, so I would have been, what, eight years old?

Now, my grandmother, Belle Dunster, had grown up in Amsterdam, New York. As a young woman she had gone to Fonda Speedway, so the fact that they were building this new track in Malta kinda sparked the race fan inside her. Yeah, my whole family was very excited about the track being built. In fact, it was a big thing for *everybody*. Back then, it was a really rural area; Ballston, where I went to high school, was five or ten miles away, and it was about the same distance in another direction to Saratoga Springs. So Malta was, like, in the middle of nowhere. There were plenty of motels up and down the road, because we were sort of at the bottom end of the "resorty" area of the Adirondacks, but there wasn't a whole lot going on locally until the speedway was built.

Me and my brother Randy—he was three years younger than me— were hooked right from the beginning. A lot of Friday nights, we'd get Mom to drop us off at the gate. Then we'd sit there, watch the races, and try to get back to the restaurant in time to see the drivers stop in to eat on the way home, because my parents would keep it open 'til midnight or whatever it took. And every one of the top drivers from Albany-Saratoga would come in there, it seemed like.

From the very beginning, I was an Eddie Flemke fan. I guess my initial attraction to him was kind of silly; Eddie's coupe had a "cent-sign" on the door instead of a number, and that made it *different*. It wasn't Bill Wimble's #33 or Kenny Shoemaker's #24, and I guess I just thought that was pretty cool. But as time went on, the number didn't have anything

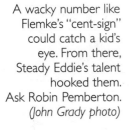

A wacky number like Flemke's "cent-sign" could catch a kid's eye. From there, Steady Eddie's talent hooked them. Ask Robin Pemberton. *(John Grady photo)*

In 1967 and '68, there was no tougher driver and car on the Eastern New York NASCAR modified circuit than Flemke and the Judkins coupe. *(John Grady photo)*

to do with why I liked him. He jumped out of that "cent-sign" and into the Bobby Judkins #2X, and I was still a Flemke fan. I mean, I was a card-carrying member of the Ed Flemke Fan Club, had a Flemke T-shirt, the whole works. I remember really wanting one of those cool jackets they had—those two-tone, red and white #2X jackets—but that was a little too top-shelf, a little bit out of my reach at the time. Now, Randy was a big, big Flemke fan, too, but he strayed a bit, because for while he really got into rooting for Hank Stevens. But for me, it was always Eddie.

He was such a successful guy, and obviously such a great driver. Pulling for him back then was like a Cup fan pulling for Jeff Gordon today, or pulling for Rusty Wallace in his heyday. Eddie was not too long out of that Eastern Bandits phase, which meant he had raced everywhere, and at the time when I first saw him he was winning a lot of races, so he was as big a star as there was in that period of modified racing. Richie Evans was coming along, but he wasn't at the top yet, and I guess Geoff Bodine was just getting started, so at the top you had Eddie, Wimble, Rene Charland, Shoemaker, the point-chasing guys like Jerry Cook, Bugsy Stevens and Freddy DeSarro, people like that. But I remember being impressed with Eddie's mannerisms, and the type of person he was. He was always nice and polite to me, and nice and polite to everybody else, too. I guess I was pretty lucky, because he was my hero and yet I got to see that personal side of him.

What really helped that situation was the L&R Speed Shop. Margaret and Len Bosley owned L&R, which was right across the street from the restaurant. They built a small motel right there on the property, six or eight rooms, and it was always filled with racers. Eddie used to stay

Joe Lesik, a behind-the-scenes force in the building of both Utica-Rome and Albany-Saratoga, visits with Flemke. (John Grady photo)

there, and so did Rene Charland, Pete Hamilton, all kinds of really good guys. See, in those days there was a pretty good NASCAR modified circuit going in that region: Catamount, over in Vermont, ran on Thursday nights, Albany-Saratoga ran Fridays, Plattsburgh ran Saturdays, and Utica-Rome ran Sundays. And, don't forget, you also had the old All-Star League passing through there just about every week. So that Malta area was a really convenient base for these guys, especially because the Bosleys were so good about letting people work on their cars there. I remember Richie Evans working on his car at L&R and then winning a big Schaefer Beer-sponsored race at Malta. I guess he got a keg of beer as part of the winnings, so he and his guys dragged it back over to Bosley's to finish it off.

L&R Speed Shop was where it was at, man, where everything was happening. Hell, for a long time in the '60s, Don MacTavish worked there; in fact, he dated my aunt for a while, although, knowing MacTavish, I'm sure that just put her among the other hundred girls he was dating.

Every weekend, all summer long, these great racers would stay at the motel, they'd work on their cars at L&R, and they'd eat their meals—breakfast, lunch and dinner—at my family's restaurant. And Eddie was certainly part of that group. For me, that was so cool: Here was my guy, in my restaurant. Incredible.

Our house was right there on the property, so when Eddie would show up for breakfast on a Saturday morning, my mom would either call or come get me. All she had to say was "Eddie's here," and I'd be off running. And he was so good with my brother and me; we'd sit and eat with him, ask all kinds of questions, and he would take the time to talk with us. I mean, there really wasn't anybody from that racing crowd who *wasn't* good with kids, but I definitely remember Eddie being especially nice to us.

You know, I can't answer the question of *why* he was so good as a racer. I was too young, I'm sure, to process all that stuff and understand it. Obviously, he was an incredibly talented driver, which definitely helps. But, looking back on it with the hindsight of having been involved with race cars for so long myself, I'm sure all those afternoons he spent at places like the L&R Speed Shop were a big part of it, too. I mean, I know *everybody* worked on their own stuff back then, but people like Eddie and Pete Hamilton and Don MacTavish seemed to be different. It was like they *lived* it. They'd work on their car, yes, but even if they stepped back to lean on something and smoke a cigarette, you could see them just *staring* at that car, *thinking* about it. So I don't think it was just the idea that he worked on his own stuff that made Eddie so good, but it was the *way* he worked on it.

And maybe what I liked most—the thing that made him the most *cool*—was that it wasn't at all unusual to see him work on somebody else's stuff. I can remember watching Eddie rebuild an engine on Len and Margaret's picnic table, and then you'd find out later that it had come out of some other guy's car.

Man, that was just an *unbelievable* era. I mean, everybody who grows up in racing probably has his own unbelievable era, a period that really gets under his skin. My two youngest brothers, Ryan and Roman, grew up after Albany-Saratoga was dirt, so I'm sure they thought Kenny Brightbill and Jack Johnson were the coolest. But as far as I'm concerned, that period in asphalt modified racing in my area was definitely something special. I mean, you can just rattle off the great racers who made an appearance at Malta—Bugsy Stevens, Freddy DeSarro, Jean-Guy Chartrand, Denis Giroux, Ron Narducci—and a lot of the best guys ran there every week. When those guys pulled their haulers into the restaurant parking lot, the tires on the race cars were still warm and the engines were still creaking and crackling, cooling down. I still remember the way those cars *smelled* sitting there. And then to be able to interact with all these heroes on a regular basis was just amazing. Those things stuck in my mind, and they've been there forever.

I honestly think that whole situation, and those people, were what drove me to spend my whole life in racing. I mean, obviously I liked *cars*, but it was the *people* that made the sport seem so special.

Really, they were the ticket to everything that came later for me.

Everything in racing changes, of course, and as the '70s rolled in it seemed like the really hot modified scene started to shift toward New

England, and a little bit away from New York. Guys like Eddie and Bugsy and Freddy were sticking closer to home—Stafford, Thompson—and they weren't coming into my back yard so much. And, I'll tell you, I *missed* those guys. All of a sudden, I'd find myself really looking forward to the All Star races or the other big events that might attract 'em back.

At home, we had a split-rail fence out in front of the house. If I wasn't working at the restaurant on a race night, I'd sit on that fence and watch for the race teams to come, because from that spot you could see, way off in the distance, the ramp trucks come off I-87. If I saw somebody different—Freddy Harbach from Long Island, or maybe one of those New England guys—that meant one of two things: either there was a big show at Albany-Saratoga, or maybe there was bad weather at their home track, so they headed to Malta. And of course, if I saw that Judkins truck with the #2X on the back, it was extra cool because it meant Eddie was going to be there.

But, yeah, things had changed. By then, my life had started to change a bit, too.

I had already gotten to know all the young local guys who were really into racing—Steve Hmiel, Brian Ross, people like that—and I got to be really good friends with Greg Narducci, Ron's son. In the very early 1970s, I was able to travel to a lot of different tracks with the Narducci family. Ron had kinda taken over working summers at L&R after Don MacTavish got killed, so we'd ride with Greg's grandmother, or we'd pile into the truck with Ron. Looking back, I guess I used the restaurant as *bait*. I mean, it was an easy decision for me to trade a hot dog for a ride to the races. I'm not sure *Dad* would have supported that idea, but, hey, for me it was a no-brainer.

So I started going to the different races, and then, along with Greg and his brother, Ronnie Jr., I began helping with the cars and tried to be a little bit of a mechanic. I was able to measure tires and check different things; it wasn't much, but it certainly was enough to get my interest going. Now, this whole time I was still working at the restaurant, so it was hard to get too deep into being part of a race team. But, like I said, at least I was *involved*. And that was really a cool change for me.

I had another big change when the Cup guys came up to run at Malta in 1970. In those days, the smaller Cup teams didn't even have full crews, so they always found volunteer help. The Narducci team, me included, ended up helping on a pit crew; I should remember who it was, but I'm not exactly sure, although I think it was Dave Marcis. Anyway, I was in the infield for that race, working on a car.

Here's how different things were then: Richard Petty and his team actually stayed at Margaret and Len Bosley's hotel. That was a neat deal for me, because Pete Hamilton was driving for them that year. He had won the Daytona 500 in a Petty car, but he was only running a partial schedule so he wasn't in the Malta event, which was a huge disap-

pointment for us. But he came up for the race anyway, and they made a big deal out of him being there, which was cool.

I remember being blown away by the fact that in this Cup stuff, especially with the bigger teams like Petty Enterprises, you actually had people making a real *living* working on race cars. They wore uniforms, and they worked with nice tools, and they traveled with a truck and a trailer and a team station wagon.

And, you know, seeing those full-bodied cars caught my interest, too, because that was something new, something different. I started really following late model racing; I remember being really into those old Chrysler Kit Kars because the Pettys had been involved in producing them, and paying attention to how Joey Kourafas did with the Kit Kar he ran on the old NASCAR North circuit. I ended up hitting a lot of those races with Len and Margaret Bosley and their son, Steve, and eventually Steve built and raced a late model, a Nova, while he was still a teenager. I traveled with those guys quite a bit in the mid-'70s— Thunder Road, Oxford Plains, all those places—and just had a ball. Along the way, I became a certified welder.

I ended up moving South, or *trying* to move South, in 1976 or '77. I found a job at Mike Laughlin's car-building shop, so I packed up all my stuff and moved to Greenville, South Carolina. Lasted two or three days. I didn't like it, and I didn't have enough money, and was homesick, so I headed back to New York. A couple years later, Steve Hmiel—who worked a little bit for the Pettys before moving home to do a season with Jerry Cook and then went *back* South—called and told me that Petty Enterprises was starting a second team for Kyle. Steve said, "Man, if you want a job down here, now is the time." I made some phone calls, and I ended up talking to Richard, who either actually remembered me as the young kid from the restaurant up by Albany-Saratoga Speedway, or was at least nice enough to not let me believe he *didn't* remember. Either way, I got the job.

It paid $2.65 an hour, and I've made my living in racing ever since, with teams, with manufacturers, and with NASCAR.

But, you know, I still think about those Malta days, and, honestly, I

Come the Pinto days, Flemke visited New York less frequently. The good news was, he still showed up for the big Albany-Saratoga specials, often alongside All Star competitors like New Jersey's Buzzie Reutimann and Massachusetts hero Ollie Silva. *(Mike Adaskaveg photos)*

wouldn't trade that experience for *anything*. I mean, everybody's got something that trips their trigger. At some point, every surfer dude went to the beach, saw some guy riding a wave, and said, "Wow!" Every stick-and-ball athlete had that moment when he got into a game and realized that he had what it took. And I'm incredibly fortunate that I was at that place, and at that time, when I could realize that there was something I loved about the smells of those cars, and the action, and the people. That was just plain *luck*, the idea that we'd have this restaurant and they'd build a race track right down the street, and all these cool guys would come and race there. Guys like Eddie Flemke.

I can picture Eddie sitting in that restaurant, just like it was yesterday. I can still see that crooked smile he had as he sat there with the people who were his friends. Those guys from that era were a pretty good bunch of practical jokers, and on a Friday night after the races the place would be busy and kinda loud, and everybody would be laughing. These were people who were doing something they loved, and that left a deep impression on me. I remember all those faces, and particularly Eddie's. Seeing Eddie smile was just a wonderful thing, and, in my mind, it still is.

"In my eyes, he never did anything wrong"

Steady Eddie Flemke, father and family man

by PAULA BOUCHARD

Paula Bouchard, the eldest child of Ed Flemke and Christine Bowen, spent much of her young life traveling from speedway to speedway with her father and her kid brother, Eddie Jr. Back when short-track racers were just getting used to seeing women in the pits, teenaged Paula raised eyebrows by occasionally hot-lapping dad's modifieds. In 1983 she married Ron Bouchard, having met the standout Massachusetts driver—where else?—at a race track. These days she helps guide the business activities of husband Ron, who gives her great credit for the success of his ever-expanding collection of automobile dealerships. In addition to four children from Ronnie's previous marriage, the couple has one son, Chad, currently attending college in Florida. Though his Bouchard/Flemke racing bloodline would seem stout enough to keep any potential rival on the trailer, Chad prefers golf, which is just fine with his mom.

Paula Bouchard

YOU KNOW, I never really thought of my father as a race car driver. Yes, he did drive race cars, and he did win an awful lot, but there was also a real guy there, a real person. To his kids, he was someone who did what a father does: teach us right from wrong. My father had so much wisdom, so much analytical sense—I think my brother Eddie has a lot of that, too, but I didn't inherit any—and he taught us a lot of, you know, life lessons. He loved us a lot, and any time he could help us experience something besides racing, he would do that, even though racing was so much of our lives.

I guess I started going to race tracks when I was just a baby, a couple weeks old. My mother told me later how she used to put me in my lit-

Looking after daughter: Ed Flemke and a bundled-up Paula on a wintry New Britain day, at the dawn of the 1960s. *(Marge Dombrowski Collection)*

tle bucket—the little thing that a baby's carried in—and bring me to the track. I'm sure it was the same with my brother Eddie; he's only 14 months younger than me, and we were always together growing up.

I always knew that my father was different, or that he *did* something different from the other fathers. Racing was not as popular as it is today, so the kids I hung around with thought we were weird. All the other fathers were firemen, or mechanics, or they worked in factories. My dad raced. So from the time I was real little, and right up through high school, I was just different, and that was because of racing. I had school friends and racing friends, and I did different things with *these* friends and *those* friends.

Eddie and I were very young when my parents separated. I guess I was probably five or six. We lived with our mom; we stayed in New Britain for a little while, and then we moved to Middletown. But we were always allowed to go to the races with our father on the weekends, as long as we got all our chores done, and there was a very long page of chores! And if any of those chores was *not* done, that would be our punishment: "You can't go with your father." Which, you know, was the worst thing that could ever happen to me and Eddie. We loved being with him, and we loved the races, and to go with our father on the weekend was everything.

We would pack our clothes in a paper grocery bag, and off we'd go.

We would either ride in the truck with him, or ride with somebody who followed him. I'm sure that all depended on how many guys were there to help him. I remember John Stygar going with us a lot. On a long trip, it might be a whole station-wagon full. I liked it best when it was just my father and us kids, going from track to track. Sometimes we stayed in hotels, and sometimes we slept in the car, in a rest area or wherever. If we had stayed in the car, as soon as we got to the next race track he'd bring us over to the mens' room and the ladies' room, and he would make us change our clothes, brush our teeth and wash up. He made sure we did all that.

Of course, then he'd have to find somebody to watch us. They didn't let the wives and kids in the pits—which my father didn't believe in anyway, having women in the pits—so he'd ask Lenny Boehler's wife, or someone else he knew, to watch us. Back then, it was so different; everybody was like a family. He'd would make sure we were set, and had someone to sit with, and he'd give us each some money for the night. Then he'd go sign in, and he'd go off to the pits.

When it was time for him to come onto the track to race, he'd park next to the fence and we'd run over there, screaming, "Dad! Dad!" But in the grandstands, we'd always behave; my father was very strict about that. He had all his rules about how you were supposed to act at the races. You never wanted him to hear that his kids had been bad. I used to wear all these rabbits' feet for good luck; I think they sold them at Utica-Rome and Malta, and I'd buy them and hang 'em around my neck.

The cars I remember most, as a child, are the "cent-sign," the "percent-sign," the "dollar-sign," and the "Gray Ghost" car. I guess it's because those were his cars, the cars he worked on the most. As far as drivers, I remember Bill Slater, Gene Bergin, Johnny Thompson, Leo Cleary, all those guys who were around his age. To me, they were good, but my father was always the best. If anybody said anything bad about him, I'd want to fight them. In fact, my brother Eddie would kick 'em in the butt, and we'd run!

We usually didn't hang around too long after the races, although that depended on what kind of night he had. Obviously, if he won he'd probably stick around a while longer, because there are things the winner has to do. But other than that, he didn't drink and party, so there was nothing to hang around for. He'd stay around long enough to talk to any fans who stopped to see him, but then we were off and running. Usually, all of us would go from the track to a diner—my father, us kids, the crew, and whatever buddies he had—and he would buy everybody supper. He would open up the glove compartment when we got to the restaurant, and it would be full of money. *Full.* The promoters used to pay off in cash, and he would just stuff it right into the glove compartment.

The only time we definitely wouldn't stop to eat would be if it was a Sunday night and we were somewhere like Utica-Rome, because that was a four-and-a-half hour ride and he was usually the only driver, and he had to get us kids home. See, another one of the rules about us going away with him was that if we didn't go to school the next day, we weren't allowed to go with him the following weekend. So after Utica, he'd be like, "We're out of here," because he had a long journey ahead.

I'm sure we were too young to realize this at the time, but looking back I can see that my father tried hard, *very* hard, to have a normal relationship with his children. I'll tell you a little story about that. Eddie and I were different as kids. I would always listen to my parents and obey, and if my father would just *talk* to me, I would melt. But Eddie, he was the little rebel. Everything with him was racing; he would draw pictures of race cars on his bed sheets, detailed drawings with numbers and everything. My parents would ask me to inspect his room, and he'd say, "Don't look underneath the bed. That's where I hid everything." Oh, he was bad. And he was always in trouble at school, constantly. My mother said to my father, "Eddie, I can't take this anymore. I can't control this boy. He needs to live with you for a while." So that's what happened. But my father lived in Manchester by then, and yet he would drive Eddie from Manchester to Middletown every day—that's like 25 miles each way, and you've got to go through Hartford—so he could go to summer school. That was my father's commitment: This kid needs to go to summer school, so I'm going to take him.

It was even harder for him on weekends. He'd go out of his way to pick us up on Fridays, and then on Sunday nights, after Utica-Rome, he would go out of his way again to drive us all the way back to Middletown. By then, he was so exhausted—after racing all weekend, working on the cars, and driving home—that sometimes he would actually fall asleep in our driveway for a while before he went home himself.

Racing takes so much time, and so much energy, but he really made an effort to be there for us as a father. He had so many things to do, but he always made time to do the dad things. Like, I remember the World's Fair being in New York City in the mid-'60s. If there was a race down that way, he'd say, "Kids, we may not have all day to stay there, but we have three hours, so we're going to the World's Fair." We went to Freedomland, which was a big amusement park in the Bronx, and we went to Palisades Park, another old amusement park in New Jersey. We couldn't spend the whole day there, but we would go, and Eddie and I would take it all in. I remember my father saying, "Okay, kids, we're going to Manhattan, and you're going to see the Empire State Building." Naturally, because he was on his way to a race, we didn't have time to park the car and take the tour, so he pulled up in front of the building and said, "Okay, look up! This is the Empire State Building! Here it is!" We loved that.

Daddy's little girl, all grown up. Paula takes a break on Dad's rear bumper at Thompson Speedway in 1977. *(Mike Adaskaveg photo)*

When my dad married his second wife, Carolyn, she'd already had two kids of her own, Laurie and Timmy, who were just a little younger than Eddie and I. Not so long after that, together they had our little sister Kristy. Meanwhile, my mother remarried, too, and she and her husband, Paul, had our little brother Kenny, who also had a loving relationship with my father. Sounds confusing, I know, but we were kind of like one big family, and somehow everything worked out well. You know how you hear so much about how after a divorce, no one ever talks to each other, and this one hates that one, and stuff like that? Well, it was never that way for us. Everybody got along very well: Carolyn, my father, my mother, my stepfather, they all got along. Among us kids, me and Eddie and Laurie and Timmy got along really well, and as Kristy and Kenny got older, they fit right in, too.

Carolyn was a great stepmom, and she did a good job looking after all of us when we were together. They moved to Southington, and my father loved it when everybody came over to that house and sat by the fireplace. I think we all did. Carolyn and my father and my mother, everybody must have done a very good job, because even with all of us around, I don't remember any animosity, none at all.

I'm sure our lives were complicated by my father's racing, but we didn't really think about it. If you had a big personal event and he had a race scheduled, you didn't say, "Oh my god, he's not coming to my graduation," or, "Oh my god, he's not going to be home for my birthday." You knew he was going racing, and that was that. Like, my birthday is in early February, and he always went to Daytona, so depending upon when the race was, he might not be around. If he hadn't left yet, he'd come by and wish me a happy birthday; if he couldn't do that, he would call. My graduation? I don't think he was there. My mother and my stepfather were there, but I don't think my father could come. But that's what I mean: It was not a big deal.

Besides, when you really look at it, racing was a great way for a family to stay close. Even as we got to be 16 or 17 years old, we always wanted to go to the races, always wanted to be with our father. And it was nice for him, too: His kids were with him, and I'm sure that was a relief to him. They were not left home, and they were not out getting in trouble. It was a great thing, a real family thing.

I know I was a big tomboy, which always made my father smile. When we were little, he ran a gas station in Cromwell, and behind it there was a dirt go-kart track. We raced there all the time, and I used to beat all the boys. Oh, my father loved that. Then, as we grew up, I was the oldest, so I got to do things first. Like, I remember him teaching me how to drive when I was just a girl. We would be leaving Malta, and we'd get on the New York Thruway. Well, he'd scoot way, way over to the left side, and he'd let me steer while he worked the brake and the gas. That's how I learned how to drive! I was probably ten years old, but I was my father's little hero because I could steer.

My first car was a 1960-something Cougar my father bought from Bobby Karvonen, who was also a modified driver. It was a wreck from Bobby's junkyard. It cost $99.99, and then my father gave me the extra penny. He brought it back to the shop and took it all apart, and he made me participate. That was part of it, you know: "This is your car, so you're going to help." It was a four-speed, and he taught me to drive a stick-shift. To show me how to drive in the winter, he would take that car and get it stuck way deep in the snow, on purpose, and make me drive it out. He'd sit there and tell me what I was doing right, and what I was doing wrong. He even taught me how to spin out; he'd spin the car out, tell me how to get out of it, and then have me do it. That was just to teach us what to do in case we needed it. I liked cars, and that was unusual for a girl. I remember Ronnie Rocco—who went to school with me, and who later drove modifieds for a long time—calling me a "gearhead."

Whenever I was driving and I got a little too adventurous, cruising along a little too fast, my father would say, "Pull into this parking lot."

Down front, it's Eddie Jr. and sister Paula with stepsister Laurie Olender. Flanking Steady Eddie are crewmen Eddie Asklar and Ken Bouchard. It's Victory Lane after the 1977 Thompson 300. *(Mike Adaskaveg photo)*

Then he'd say, "Slow this goddamn thing down. You can't be driving like this." Of course, he was the one who taught me to drive fast, but he would always say, "You need to be responsible about what you do."

I'd say he was a strict father. Like, the way I remember it, I had to be 16 years old before I could get my ears pierced. My mother says no, it was 13, but I swear I was 16. And I remember the first time I put on makeup; it was not a lot of makeup, but when he saw me, he said, "You get in the bathroom and you wash your face, *now*." If I wore a skirt, he'd say, "Okay, now kneel on the floor. If that skirt doesn't hit the floor, that's a little too short!"

And he was very serious about manners. If we went with him to a restaurant, and we ordered a cheeseburger, fries, and a Coke without saying "please," he'd say, "Nope." Then it was like, "OK, next?" And the next one of us to order would be *sure* to say "please." He'd say, "You know the proper way. You know your manners." He was very, very strict about it. I always thought he was too harsh about that, but in later life

I've gotten compliments on my own son Chad, what great manners he has, so my father must have done a good job passing that along to me. He'd say, "Good manners are cheap, good manners are respectful, and it's easy to say 'please' and 'thank you.'" And I think that's so true.

I'm sure my father was happy to see that both Eddie and I loved racing enough to stay in it, Eddie through driving and building cars and me through being involved with Ronnie. Of course, first he had to get over the big shock of Ronnie and I being together. I'm sure part of that was because Ronnie was someone he raced with, a competitor. But, you know, my father had eyes behind his head when it came to that situation. By the time we got to the point where I was going to go tell him about it, he had already figured the whole thing out. And for a while, he wasn't happy about it. I'm sure it's because I was still young and hadn't dated a lot of people, and Ronnie had been married and had four kids. He'd ask me if I knew what I was getting myself into, and he'd get mad at me. Finally, my brother Eddie said to him, "Dad, you know how important she is in your life, so before you lose her, you need to get over this." And once he accepted that this was a serious thing, it all worked out well. Very well, in fact.

He was so proud of Ronnie and what he did in racing, especially once we started doing the Winston Cup stuff. Whenever I talked with my father on the phone, before long I'd hear, "Okay, what about Ronnie? How'd he do this weekend?" Yes, he was very, very proud of him, and so happy, I think, that I continued on in racing, because he loved it so much.

My father died at the end of March in 1984, and for a long time I had a very sick, lost feeling inside of me. Then seven months later, I found out I was pregnant with our son Chad, and that helped me to cope with it. This sounds very strange, I know, but it's the honest truth: When I learned I was pregnant that October, I said to myself, "Okay, the Good Lord took my father, but now he's given me this baby." I mean, my father was the most precious thing in my life; I'd always said that if anything ever happened to him, I'd kill myself, because that's how intense my love was for him. And that lost feeling was so bad, until I got pregnant. So in my mind, I decided, "Well, maybe God took him and gave me Chad," and I was able to see things that way.

I was never big on going to the grave to visit my father. I know some people get something out of that—my brother Eddie goes, and he leaves flags, flowers—but for me it was always too difficult. Well, when my son was born, I said, "Chad, I'm going to take you to see your grandfather." So I brought him there, and it was very hard for me. And as soon as we left the cemetery, there was the most horrendous downpour, with all this thunder and lightning. I told myself, "This is my father's way of telling me he knows it makes me way too sad to come here, and that it's okay." And I never went back again.

After Paula Flemke and Ron Bouchard were married in 1983, the couple hosted an informal reception in Massachusetts. Here's the father of the bride, checking in with his daughter. *(Marge Dombrowski photo)*

I don't go to very many races today, or racing-related things. I'm not sure I can explain why, but it's sort of like this: After Ronnie quit Winston Cup, I said, "Well, that's the way my life was when we did that. I met wonderful people and established great friendships, and memories that I will always cherish, but it's not the way my life is now." Chad was only three years old when Ronnie got out of racing, so being a mother to him was a new way of life for me, and one of the best things I've ever experienced. Also, being home allowed us to spend more time with Ronnie's other children—Gene, Robbie, Michelle and Tracy—who I'm sure missed their father when he was so busy with the Cup schedule. So my life was very full without racing, and I feel like it still is.

Ronnie still goes sometimes, but while he's at the track he's always busy. There are people he wants to talk to, and people who want to talk to him. And forget about me watching my brother race; that makes me too nervous, too afraid. That's strange, because I could always watch Ronnie and my father race together, and it would not bother me at all. But it's different with Eddie, because growing up I was always his little protector, like his mother. I can't do it. So I don't go very much.

But even so, I still run into people who want to talk about my father. It's always been that way. When Ronnie first went Cup racing, I was around so many guys—Robin Pemberton, Steve Hmiel, a lot of crewmen, even people like Dale Earnhardt, Richard Petty, and Bobby Allison—who knew my father, and liked to talk about him. And even now, through the automotive business, it happens. Ronnie and I will be somewhere, and we'll meet a rep from a company; the guy will say, "You know, I used to go to such-and-such track, and I followed Ron Bouchard." So they'll talk about racing, and Ronnie will say, "Well, do you remember Eddie Flemke? That's Paula's dad." And the guy will say, "Oh, of *course* I remember Eddie Flemke." That's always nice.

I'm very proud of that. I mean, my father has been gone all these years, and his legend still lives on. People still think of him, and they remember all those races.

But, like I said, that's not what I think about the most. I know he was a great race driver, but he was more than that to me. He was always —how do I say this?—he was the most important, most loved person in my whole life. He was just perfect to me. In my eyes, he never did anything wrong . . . except he left us too early.

"The way I looked at it, I had the best driver there was"

Steady Eddie's winning ways, through a car owner's eyes

by BOB JUDKINS

Bob Judkins has owned race cars for over 40 years, these days fielding a Florida modified when the spirit moves him. His place in the New England Auto Racing Hall of Fame was assured when Gene Bergin and a new Judkins #2X, carrying the first NASCAR-legal compact body, led every lap of the 1971 Stafford 200, thus sparking the Pinto Revolution. But just as notable was the 1967-69 stretch when Bobby's coupe, with Ed Flemke in the saddle, won almost anywhere it went. He and Flemke, Judkins acknowledges, seem forever linked: "Eddie drove for a lot of owners, and I had a lot of drivers, but people still connect us. Even now, in Florida, people walk up to my car and say, 'Does this #2X have anything to do with the #2X that won all those races up North with Flemke?' I guess we made a good impression."

Bob Judkins

I'M SURE MOST PEOPLE think about Eddie and I from the years when he drove for me, but I knew him long before that. When I first moved to Connecticut from Maine and was just getting involved in racing—in, oh, '52 or '53—I met him through Jerry Wheeler. Jerry was a friend of mine, and later on he ended up being my first driver. Anyway, Eddie had been winning a bunch of races at Plainville, and Jerry said, "I want you to come and watch this guy drive." So I went and saw him, and of course he went like a rocket. And then I met him, and he was just this little fellow.

You know, if you looked at Eddie you'd notice that his eyes were slightly misaligned; they didn't both look straight ahead. I saw that when I first met him, and I said to Jerry, "Maybe that's why he's so good. He can see things in every direction."

From that point, I started to follow Eddie's career a little bit. He was already a winning driver, jumping around to all the different tracks around Connecticut. I'd stop and see him when he worked at the dairy in New Britain and kept his car there. Later on he had another shop—actually, it was Bert Brooks's shop—and I'd stop there, too. I was working at Garvey Welding in New Britain, which was lucky for Eddie because he was building a car and needed a welder. He said to me, "Hey, what are you doing at lunchtime?" So every day while he built that thing, I'd go over to his garage at lunchtime and help him weld up his car. That's when I really got to know him.

I started building my own car in 1962. At that point I was working for a construction company, and because I was so busy it took me a few years to actually build it. It was a Ford coupe, and I ran it mostly at Plainville. Like I said, Jerry Wheeler was my first driver, but Eddie ended up driving that car, too. I guess he had wrecked his own car someplace, so he asked if he could drive mine and we won a few races together. Once he went back to his regular ride, I hired Tony Mordino—Tony and I won, like, seven or eight races in a row at Plainville—and then I had Billy Harmon for a while. And every now and then, Eddie and Gene Bergin drove it a little bit. Fats Caruso drove that car, too, and we did some winning together.

Then I built another car, a '36 Chevy, which turned out to be a really good one. This was just before the 1967 season, and that's when Eddie and I really hooked up. When we'd raced together before, I never looked at it like we were a team, because he only ran my car now and then. In '67, we were *really* a team. I had a gas station by then, and he'd stop by at least two or three times a week. Eddie wasn't an early riser, but come late morning or early afternoon he'd come bopping in. I remember he'd always have a cup of coffee, and one for me, too.

In that period, Eddie was a big name. He had done a lot of racing down South, and won a bunch of races in New York. He had won *everywhere*. So it was a big thing for me to have him in my car on a regular basis. Let's face it, everybody wanted him. The way I looked at it, I had the best driver there was.

At the track, Eddie never said much, but he was always thinking. When he wasn't racing or practicing, he'd be right there at the fence, watching the competition. He saw where they were good, and where they weren't. He'd put all that information together in his mind, and come feature time he'd go right past those guys, *zing-zing-zing*, like it was nothing. I mean, Eddie could start 18th—because of the handicapping system, we always started in the back—and he'd drive to the front and make it look as easy as you or me driving down the Berlin Turnpike. He was amazing. *Amazing*. He made the right moves, and he made them

Ed Flemke and Bob Judkins in 1973. They repeated this scene on scores of occasions. *(Mike Adaskaveg photo)*

at the right time. Now, he worked hard at what he did, but he had to have so much natural ability to do that.

He could be a hard guy to read sometimes. When we first got together, he'd look a little bit slow in the warm-ups, so I'd say, "Eddie, what's wrong with the car?"

He'd shrug his shoulders and say, "Oh, there's nothing wrong. We're all right."

I'd say, "Are you sure? You weren't going for *beans*."

"Don't worry," he'd tell me. "We're fine."

Sure enough, he'd go out there and win the feature.

That happened all the time, and it drove me crazy for a while. Then one day Eddie said, "Bobby, there's no sense putting all our cards on the table in practice. If I show 'em what we've really got, you'll see every toolbox in this pit area open up. Let's just keep a low profile."

From that point on, I never worried again when I saw him laying back in practice. Whatever he wanted to do was fine with me.

Geez, we ran a *lot* of races back in the late '60s. The All Star League raced on Tuesday nights and Wednesday nights, all over the place. On Thursdays, we'd run up at Catamount. Then you had Stafford on Fridays and Norwood Arena on Saturdays. On Sundays, we'd go to Utica-Rome. That was pretty much a normal week. But, don't forget, there were all kinds of tracks running big modified shows back then, and we'd hit all of 'em: Malta, Plattsburgh, Lee, Oxford Plains, you name it.

And there were several times when we'd run Thompson on Sunday afternoon, then rush like hell to make Utica-Rome that night. That's almost a four-hour drive, but they'd hold up the consolation race at Utica if they knew we were coming. More than once, I watched Eddie start last in that Utica-Rome consi and win it, then start at the tail of the feature and win that, too.

I don't know how the hell we did all that racing, but somehow we did. I remember my coupe getting totaled in an All Star race at Lee, and I worked for two days without sleep so we could make it to Stafford. And one day back when I was still towing my trailer with a car, I was riding in the passenger seat—I can't remember who was driving—and I turned my head to look back for some reason. Well, the trailer was *gone*. It had fallen off. We backtracked until we found the trailer off the road, with its tongue stuck in the dirt. We hooked it back up, and off we went.

Eddie was ready to go racing, *all the time*. I remember getting that coupe ready for a big race at Trenton, a Sunday show, and he wanted to stop and run Islip the night before. I didn't like that idea. We had done a lot of work to get ready for Trenton, and that little bullring at Islip was a great place to get wrecked. But he said, "Don't worry about it. We'll be fine." So he talked me into it. We went to Islip and started in the back of the pack, and Eddie drove to the front and won the feature. Never put a scratch on the car. I couldn't believe it. I just shook my head, loaded up, and off we went to Trenton.

You know, Eddie was an easy guy to work with. Believe me, not all the top drivers are that way. There were nights when Gene Bergin climbed out of my car, threw his helmet and kicked the door. Gene was a great driver, but when things went wrong, oh, he could be *wicked*. Eddie was the exact opposite. I mean, we never had a single problem, and he never complained. If we had a bad night, he just accepted that. You can't win 'em all, and he knew that.

Now, sometimes he might get a little bit stubborn about an adjustment he wanted. He had his ideas and I had mine, and that doesn't always work well between a driver and a mechanic. But the good thing about our relationship was, I'd listen to his ideas and he'd listen to mine. Then we'd hash it out and decide which way we were going to go, or maybe we'd compromise if we couldn't make up our minds.

I have to say, most of the time we went with his ideas, and they usually worked. Of course, the way Eddie was, even if his idea was wrong, he'd make up the difference on the track, just so he could show you he'd been right. And that was fine with me; I never cared about being right or wrong, as long as he was happy and we ran good.

I'll tell you a funny story. There were a couple times when he'd ask me to make a change—say, turn a bolt in the left rear—when I *knew* that car was good just like it was. So I'd crawl under the car and tap the wrench against the frame a few times, make some noise, but I'd never

Flemke and the #2x at Norwood Arena in 1968. The scarring on the tail was a souvenir from a pit fire at Trenton. *(Lawlor Family Collection)*

even touch the bolt. He'd run a few practice laps and say, "Yup, that's better." I never told him the truth. It's important to keep a driver happy, because it's a psychological thing. And, let's face it, as good as he was, you pretty much knew that 99 percent of the time he made the right decisions about that stuff. Eddie always did know how to turn the bolts.

As a car owner, I liked the fact that he was so good at missing the accidents. Once in a while we'd get bent up, but not too often. The other thing I liked was, unless we were late for Utica-Rome or something like that, we very seldom had to run a consi. He always qualified through the heat, so that meant you had one less chance of getting crashed.

He drove that coupe for me through 1969, and we won dozens of races. The only reason we split up was that I started to do some dirt racing at Fonda Speedway on Saturday nights. Fonda paid $1,000 to win, good money in 1969, so I went there with Kenny Shoemaker and we won a couple of races. Eddie still drove for me on Fridays at Stafford and Sundays at Thompson, and he'd run for other people on Saturday nights at Norwood or wherever. Oh, he used to *hate* it when I'd show up at Thompson with the Fonda mud still on the car. In 1970, Stafford switched to Saturday nights. I told Eddie I wanted to keep running Fonda, so he ended up getting into the Garuti & Arute car at Stafford, and he drove a bunch of other cars elsewhere; in fact, he drove a second car for Richie Evans quite a bit in New York.

Eddie and I were still friends, so I always kept an eye on how he did. He ran really well in the Garuti car—that #14 coupe, with the aluminum block—and he won with Richie's car, too. I stayed at Fonda for about half a season, and then I gave it up. I came back to the pavement, and in 1971 I built my first Pinto, which Gene Bergin drove. Gene and I won the Stafford 200 at the end of the year, which was a big deal because it was the first win in NASCAR for a Pinto-bodied modified car. Then, in '73, Eddie and I got back together and he drove my second Pinto.

Actually, Eddie did end up driving that first Pinto, too, but it wasn't the #2X at the time. I sold that car to Frank Vigliarolo just before the '72 season, and I said to Frank, "Hey, if you need a driver, I think Eddie Flemke is available." Frank jumped at that, and in fact they almost won the first Spring Sizzler. They lost the water pump with 10 laps to go, leading.

My second Pinto—which *did* win the Sizzler in 1973, with Eddie— was just a little bit smaller than that first one, and that was because of Eddie. He kept saying, "Make *this* smaller, make *that* smaller." He said it was because he didn't need a lot of room; I think maybe he wanted it small so I couldn't put anybody else in it! We ran that Pinto for two seasons and had a lot of success, especially in '73.

Toward the end of 1974, we split up again. See, the Race of Champions at Trenton was coming up, and Eddie didn't want to go. He didn't think we'd run good there. Honestly, we hadn't been running

A historic car, but in disguise: the first-ever NASCAR-legal Pinto mod, after its early-'72 sale to Frank Vigliarolo. That's Flemke in the seat. *(Lawlor Family Collection)*

very well in the second half of that season, but I thought we'd be all right at Trenton. Eddie didn't like the big tracks—he'd tell you that himself—so I figured *that's* why he didn't want to go. Meanwhile, Gene Bergin had been calling me, telling me he'd drive if Eddie didn't want to. Now, Gene always went really good at Trenton, so I called Eddie one last time to make sure he didn't want to go. He said again that he didn't think the car would run good there. He said, "I don't think it matters whether you go there with me or Gene. It's the car. Go ahead, but I think you're making a mistake."

Well, Eddie was right. We *didn't* run good at Trenton.

And you know something? Just because Eddie didn't like the big tracks, that doesn't mean he didn't run good when he went to those places. We did some races together on the three-quarter-mile track at Pocono, and he was fine there. He did a good job in my car at Langhorne, too, even though we always had problems. And in '73 at Trenton, Eddie passed Roger Treichler for second on the last lap. I can still see them coming down the frontstretch: Richie Evans won, Eddie was second, and Treichler was third. So Eddie could definitely get the job done at those places. He just didn't like 'em.

Anyway, Eddie and I never did get back together after '74. He found a couple of other rides, and I kept Bergin in my car. It's kind of funny that I had Eddie, then Gene, then Eddie again, and then Gene again, but that's just the way it worked out. Before too long, Eddie hooked up with Bill Thornton and I hooked up with Ronnie Bouchard, and both of those turned out to be regular situations.

Bobby Judkins on the job, getting his Pinto ready for the fight. *(Mike Adaskaveg photo)*

So even though we went our separate ways twice, Eddie and I never really had a break-up, not the way some teams do. There were never any hard feelings, never a time when we weren't friendly. Both times, it was just a case of one of us wanting to do something and the other one wanting to do something different, and we understood that. He'd still stop and see me at the gas station—always bringing the coffee—and when he had his shops in Manchester and East Hartford I'd stop there and see him.

He was a good friend. You know, Eddie ended up giving me the best dog I ever had, a German shepherd named Major. He belonged to Eddie first, but I guess he kept barking in the yard at home or something, so Eddie said, "I've got just the dog for you." I told him I couldn't have a dog that was mean, because I had customers walking in and out of the gas station all day. He said, "No, this dog isn't mean at all."

So he showed up with this big shepherd—weighed about 110 pounds—and I said, "Eddie, I don't know about this." He told me not to

Flemke and Judkins in 1972, with Eddie Jr. and young Kristy Jo Flemke joining in the festivities. *(Mike Adaskaveg photo)*

worry, told me it was a good dog, told me, "Bobby, this dog isn't going to give you any trouble." He chained him to a car outside my station, and the dog seemed fine. Eddie stayed for a bit, and then he went home. Well, just a few minutes later a customer came in and walked past the dog, and Major came right after him like he was going to eat him up. The only thing that saved the guy's life was that Major's chain was too short.

I called Eddie and said, "Come get this dog. He's gonna kill somebody!"

Eddie said, "Bobby, that dog is harmless."

When it came time for me to go home that night, I said, "How the hell am I gonna feed this thing? I ain't going *near* him." I put some food into a dish, walked over until I was just out of reach, put the dish on the ground, and kicked it over to him. I did that for several days, and the whole time I kept hearing from Eddie what a great dog this was.

Maybe a week later, I was working late on my race car. That dog was

A light pre-race moment between Flemke and Frank Ferrara, whose Ferrara Speed & Sport was one of the Judkins team's backers. *(Mike Adaskaveg photo)*

going crazy, wanting to get off that chain. By that time, I was so disgusted with him that I just snuck up and turned him loose. I said, "Hey, whatever happens, happens. If he wants to run away, or run across the Turnpike, I don't care. I've *had* it." Well, that dog ran around for a few minutes, and then he came right back to me. And when he came back, he was just the nicest, calmest dog you ever saw. I couldn't *believe* how different he was, how friendly. The whole problem was, he just didn't like that chain. The next day I left him untied, and kept a close eye on him; whenever anybody walked by, he'd just lie there and look at 'em. I never chained up Major again, and he turned out to be the greatest dog in the world. I had him for 18 years. Eddie loved that dog, and taught him all kinds of tricks. In fact, he loved dogs, period. *Loved* 'em.

He was such a good guy. I'd love to be able to sit with him again, and just talk. We had so many fun times.

When we were together, we won all over the place: Thompson, Stafford, Norwood Arena, Utica-Rome, Albany-Saratoga, Plattsburgh, Catamount, Waterford, Westboro, Monadnock, Islip, Old Bridge . . . just about everywhere we went.

You want to know the best thing about owning a race car? It's having a guy like Eddie behind the wheel, and seeing him take it up through traffic, all the way to the front. Whenever I'd see that, I'd always say, "I don't know why anybody wants to *drive* these things. It can't be more fun than standing here and watching this!"

PART FOUR

Father Figure

Everything Ed Flemke had done—all that winning, all that mentoring—helped establish the position he held by the mid-1970s. Certainly, it was a position of honor. Smart people in the business, Flemke included, have always insisted that no man is bigger than the sport, and that is true enough. But as he pushed past his 25th year in the cockpit, Flemke was as influential a figure as modified racing had.

He was more than just the ex-jalopy king, more than just the former leader of the Eastern Bandits, more than just the guy who had won, well, everywhere. He was a titanic presence, history strolling around in Nomex.

Right from the time he'd gotten fast, the announcers had called him Steady Eddie, and it fit, because the man was as dependable as the sun. But as his hair —graying for years—turned a distinguished silver, there were other sobriquets: Flemke was The Boss, or, to those who knew him best, Pops.

On one level, that last nickname was literal, because he and his son were now sharing track space. After starting out at Riverside Park in '73, Eddie Jr. had branched out to Stafford and Thompson. But on a whole different level, a figurative one, Pops was the perfect handle. Flemke had become modified racing's father figure.

Behind the wheel, he was still going strong. "I haven't even thought about retiring," he told Jackie Arute in 1974. And, really, why would he have? That summer he won at Stafford and Thompson, as usual, and decimated an open-comp field at Plainville. Up at Monadnock, he won the Yankee 100 over four of that period's prominent names: Leo Cleary, Ollie Silva, Brian Ross, and Gene Bergin.

But off the track, there had developed what writer Pete Zanardi called "the Flemke mystique." A generation of modified people had grown up with Flemke having always been on top, and to them he was a monument. Younger drivers watched his every move: Pete Fiandaca, who raced against Flemke often, says, "Even getting towed into the pits, that guy could look so cool. It was the way

Pete Fiandaca, part of a generation of racers who'd watched Flemke on track and off, says, "Eddie had style." The two are shown together at Waterford in 1979. *(Steve Kennedy photo, Val LeSieur Collection)*

he sat, with the helmet already off and the hand out the window, holding the cigarette. Eddie had *style*."

That mystique was not confined to the pit area. It was felt in the press boxes, too. Flemke was certainly the elder statesman of his division, and thus a necessary go-to guy for journalists. The feeling amongst the modified media was: If you need a story, go see a quote machine like Bugs Stevens; if you already have a story, but it needs the stamp of authority, find Flemke.

Steady Eddie also carried lots of clout in speedway front offices. He'd always had an interest in the business end of the sport; photographer John Grady remembers a much younger Flemke debating rules and purses with promotional giants like Harvey Tattersall and Larry Mendelsohn. But the longer he raced, the more closely he examined the complex relationship between competitors, promoters and fans.

And, being Flemke, he was never afraid to speak his mind about what he called "the show." Though he was a racing purist, he knew that to the paying customer a night at the track was entertainment. He understood, as clearly as any short-track hero ever has, the importance of tracks doing well and fans going home happy. Always, his motto was: We're in this together. Stevens, a promoter's racer if there ever was one, remembers Eddie telling him, "You know, Bugs, this game is our bread and butter. Let's help those guys promote the races, because that will promote us."

But more than anyplace, his mystique was felt in the grandstands. For better than 20 years there had been a devout legion of Flemke followers; yet as the years passed and he became such a ubiquitous figure—forever in the front pack, forever in the racing papers, forever *there*—even fans of other drivers seemed pleased when Steady Eddie did well. Jackie Arute, Stafford's promoter at the time, says, "Even if they rooted for Bugsy or Ron Bouchard first and foremost, nobody didn't like Eddie Flemke."

He was winning, he was aging gracefully, he was held in considerable esteem. The mid-1970s were shaping up to be a special time for Pops.

One of the toughest small-block combos of the mid-1970s was Steady Eddie and the blue #7 Pinto owned by his old Bandits partner John Stygar. *(John Grady photo)*

Sadly, things soon took a turn for the worse. Or, more correctly, a pair of turns for the worse, in the form of two violent crashes that, coincidentally or not, marked the beginning of the end of Steady Eddie's time at the top. The wrecks happened just 11 months apart, and on both occasions—the first in the 1974 Stafford 200, the second in a 1975 Star Speedway open—he suffered fractured vertebrae. One broken back in a lifetime is serious; two in less than a year is major trauma, especially when the injured party is in his mid-40s.

After the first crash, Flemke rebounded well. Driving a pale blue #7 Pinto owned by Bandits-era cohort John Stygar, he grabbed the 1975 Blast-Off at Waterford (over upstart Ron Cote and perennial Speedbowl champ Dick Dunn); beat Don Moon and Stan Greger to win a Plainville 100 (a reporter crowed that "Flemke drove the last laps with his hand out the window, resting on the roof"); and led the Thompson points for much of the season. And as part of a new NASCAR team fielded by Manchester Sand & Gravel boss Bill Thornton, Flemke won a Stafford feature and lost another only because of a controversial disqualification promoter Arute still regrets.

But behind the smiles he mustered for the victory photos, there was pain. Flemke was the kind of proud man who kept his troubles private, but those closest to him saw grimaces when he climbed into his race cars (and, it should be pointed out, modified interiors were getting tighter all the time). They noticed that his walk had stiffened, particularly when he thought no one was looking.

The Star wreck only made things worse. That one put Flemke in a back brace (although few outside his inner circle knew about it) and kept him out of the first-ever Thompson 300, which in the autumn of '75 drew more than 100 small-block modifieds. Two years earlier, a healthy Flemke would have been among the favorites to win the thing. Now, busted up again, he served as the 300's Grand Marshal.

As 1976 progressed, there began to spread the first chatter about Flemke being in some sort of a slump. Though still competitive—he passed Geoff Bodine to win the Thompson Icebreaker, one of seven victories that year—he was clearly not the consistent on-track threat he'd always been. If you were in the Flemke camp, you chalked that up to the months lost to hurt and misery. If you weren't, you probably figured that the torch had been passed to the modified generation after Flemke's. Its standouts included Bodine, who had arrived from New York to pilot Dick Armstrong's high-dollar Pintos; Richie Evans, who had matured into a NASCAR champion; and Ron Bouchard, who, in addition to winning all over the place, was dating Flemke's daughter, Paula (much to Eddie's initial dismay).

Soon there were whispers, and even the occasional printed hint, that maybe Steady Eddie Flemke's time had come and gone. The cruel phrase "over the hill" was used more than once. There was some logic, however cold, in that assumption. Think about it: While today it is common to see drivers winning as they close in on age 50—Mike Stefanik, who in 2006 clinched his seventh NASCAR Modified Tour title at age 48, credits healthier lifestyles—Flemke was in uncharted waters when, at 46, he won Stafford's final weekly show of 1976. The general feeling was: A really good guy might still win at that age, but he isn't going to win *big*.

And then came the autumn of '77. It had been a frustrating year for Flemke, who battled NASCAR just to get his radical new modified on track, and then struggled to perfect it. Prior to September, the only bright spot had been a July victory at Thompson. Imagine the joy, then, when—in the space of 13 days—Flemke and the Manchester Sand & Gravel #10 won two of modified racing's biggest events, the Labor Day 200 at Stafford and the Thompson 300.

There were some twists of fate in play at Thompson, as you will read, but absolutely none at Stafford. On that Monday, Flemke was simply the class of the field, beating—and, he claimed, toying with—those who chased him home: Bodine, Maynard Troyer, Evans, Bobby Santos, and Fred DeSarro.

In victory lane, there was suffering on his face, but redemption in his words. "I'm 47 years old and proud to say it," Flemke told *Manchester Journal-Inquirer* columnist Mike Adaskaveg. He added, "If anybody says Bodine, Evans, or Troyer could have caught me if the race was longer, they're wrong. I'll go back on the track right now, and beat them again."

Alas, those were the last of the great days. The next season, 1978, was a disaster. Brutal crashes at New Smyrna, FL, Seekonk, and Stafford couldn't have done Flemke's battered body any good. But what probably hurt worse was the fact that, for the first time in 30 years, Steady Eddie went without a win.

Steady Eddie's last great victory came in the 1977 Thompson 300, where car owner Bill Thornton and starter Dick Brooks greeted him in Victory Lane. (Mike Adaskaveg photo)

A sad day for legends: In March of '79, both the now-unsponsored Flemke and the great Virginian Ray Hendrick, alongside in Billy Corazzo's #12, missed the qualifying cut at Martinsville. *(Mike Adaskaveg photo)*

When Bill Thornton opted out of racing at the close of that year, more than a few folks thought Flemke might hang it up, too. But Ronnie Bouchard points out, "Racing wasn't just Eddie's job. In a lot of ways, it was his whole *life*. How do you walk away from something that is your whole life?" Flemke didn't have that answer. He chose instead to run his own team, using a car he'd picked up from Thornton.

It was an optimistic move, given both his age and the spiraling cost of racing. Modifieds had long since outgrown the corner gas station, and change was constant. New suspension technologies and offset chassis designs arrived, and rules meant to equalize big-block and small-block engines seemed to cost everybody money. The era belonged to teams with strong budgets, tire deals, and the personal attention of major engine builders. All Flemke had going for him were those 30 years—three decades of driving, tinkering, refining—but, as the '70s melted away, all that experience wasn't enough. His results in 1979 were mixed, leaning toward depressing. Though Eddie had 14 top-five finishes in 37 starts, mostly at Stafford, Thompson, and Riverside Park, he also missed the qualifying cut for March's Dogwood 500 at Martinsville, a tough blow.

But there was one glorious night that summer, on July 7th to be exact, when all was good again, and Steady Eddie Flemke stood with checkered flag in hand. It happened at Riverside, and it turned out to be the last vic-

Steady Eddie looks over his self-owned #10 at Monadnock in 1979. In the foreground is crewman Jeff Zarrella, who graduated from the Flemke camp to become a Nextel Cup and Busch Series tire specialist. *(Val LeSieur Collection)*

tory of Flemke's incredible career. Lest you draw the conclusion that maybe he was cherry-picking against a weak field, check this out: Hot on Flemke's tail were Reggie Ruggiero in the Mario Fiore #44, Ray Miller aboard Mike Greci's #01, and Stan Greger in the Billy Simons #9, three of the hottest driver/car combos in Riverside's modern era.

It was another highlight in a life full of them, and a night of relief for a 48-year-old legend and his 70-year-old back. But soon, things were back on a downturn. Despite a new car and a handful of fine runs, 1980 was another winless season.

At Flemke's side through all these ups and downs was Eddie Jr., whose own driving was on hold. "There was no way both of us could race," Junior recalls, "and I was realistic about that. I said, 'If one of us is going to do this, who is the obvious choice?'" And the son had made another sacrifice, turning down an offer to work in the Atlanta car-building business of an old family friend, one Pete Hamilton. "My father begged me to go, because he thought it would be a great move for me," Junior recalls. "But he was coming toward the end of his career, and I said, 'I can't leave my dad right now.'"

To subsidize their own racing, father and son—working out of a rented shop in East Hartford—launched a car-building enterprise of their own. It blossomed into a chassis fabrication business called Race Works (today a

At the close of the '70s, Flemke returned to his old Saturday-night stomping grounds, Riverside Park. He was welcomed back by the Park's top shoes, including, from left to right, Bob Polverari, Ron Wyckoff and Ray Miller. *(Mike Adaskaveg photo)*

partnership between Eddie Jr. and NASCAR Modified Tour mega-winner Reggie Ruggiero). Among the early buyers were stalwart owners Dick Barney and Tony Ferrante, Wall Stadium regular Harry Reed, Bay Staters Butch Walsh and Jean Michaud, and local racer Ray McTeague.

As the workload increased, the natural question for the elder Flemke was whether he was ready to transition fully from driver to constructor.

In early 1981 he insisted he still had some racing left to do, and spoke of building himself a new ride. But that car never materialized, and Flemke devoted that season to cutting and grinding on weekdays, and advising customers on weekends.

He did make a one-off Stafford start for Tony Ferrante, and later steered a Dick Barney car in the '81 Thompson 300 as a fill-in for injured driver Tony Siscone. But things did not go well; Barney's son, Robert, remembers Flemke climbing out of the car mid-race. Maybe Steady Eddie simply got tired. Maybe his aching bones, having been lulled into thinking they'd never be abused by another long race, rebelled. In any event, he surrendered the reins to S.J. Evonsion, whose own ride had fallen out. It was Flemke's last race in New England, a territory he once ruled.

He competed just once more, in a 1982 feature at Wall Stadium. It was basically a test drive, done to help customer Harry Reed. But it gave Reed's #7A a certain place in history, as the last modified driven by a man who had wheeled so many famous ones: the Garuti #14, the "dollar-sign," the Judkins #2X, the Welch-Mills #79, the Evans #61, the Art Barry #09, and all the rest.

There was no ceremony surrounding the race—much less the fanfare that heralded the last modified rides of Bugs Stevens in 1987 or George Summers in '83—because no one, Flemke included, realized its significance. But 34 years after he'd won that first heat at Cherry Park, Eddie Flemke had removed his helmet for good.

Last ride of a legend: Steady Eddie drove his final race in 1982, test-hopping the Wall Stadium ride of chassis customer Harry Reed. *(Pete Lawlor photo)*

He was still a pit-area fixture, still a busybody. The chassis operation kept Flemke energized. Dick Barney says, "In those days, modifieds were developing really fast, so we'd always talk about things. 'How can we do *this* better? How can we do *that* better?'"

Bob Potter, grand champion of the Waterford Speedbowl, had a spanking new Race Works ride for 1983. "I won the title that year," Potter told Pete Zanardi. "We helped each other; I learned stuff from Eddie, and Eddie learned stuff from me because I was driving the car. Holy mackerel, that was an awesome car. I could run around the bottom like you wouldn't believe."

Flemke had plenty of opportunity to watch Potter that season. He'd accepted an invitation from the Waterford brass to serve as a steward, charged with cleaning up the rough driving which had become the Speedbowl's unwanted trademark. Potter says Flemke wielded a velvet hammer: "He stressed that if you have respect for the other guy, the other guy will have respect for you." The result? "We got to the point where even two yellows a night was unheard of," Potter recalls.

The steward's role represented a chance for Flemke to continue doing on Saturday nights what he had done forever: serving as that father figure. And at the shop, it was almost a full-time gig. Without a race car of his own to fuss with, he found himself holding court over coffee almost daily. His audiences were as wide-eyed and eager as Flemke himself had been as a young man at Jake's Garage. The Boss gave them what they came for.

"It was incredible, all those guys who would hang around my father's garage, just listening to him," says Paula Bouchard. "These were kids 17, 18, 19 years old, who would drive a half-hour just to be with him. And I think he helped them all, in one way or another."

That was Pops. Driving, building, officiating, or just shooting the breeze, Steady Eddie Flemke led the standings in respect.

"Any promoter who ever encountered Eddie Flemke misses that man"

A front-office view of a big-picture star

by JACK ARUTE JR.

Jack Arute Jr. is known nationally for his broadcasting work, having covered auto racing, football, and assorted other sports for a variety of outlets, including ABC-TV, ESPN, and MRN radio. But to folks from his native New England, where friends still call him Jackie in deference to his late father, he will always be connected with his family's Stafford Motor Speedway. There, Jackie played a number of roles, from promoter to announcer to fill-in flagman. He was just a kid when, in the 1950s, he first encountered Eddie Flemke, who was then steering the hulking coupes of Kensington, CT, brothers Ray and Richie Garuti. "Ray's Garage was right over the hill," Arute recalls. "I could ride my bicycle there." According to Arute, "Growing up, Eddie was my hero. I mean, if the argument came down to God or Eddie Flemke, I was going with Flemke every time."

Jack Arute Jr.

JUST THE OTHER DAY, I was looking at a couple of old quotes attributed to Eddie Flemke. The first was something he said to Ken Squier, who was promoting races at the old Catamount Stadium up in Vermont when the NASCAR modifieds used to run there. It's probably from 1968 or '69. Eddie told Ken, "We're partners. You risk your money, I risk my life." The second quote came from the *Journal-Inquirer* newspaper in Connecticut, in a 1979 column by Mike Adaskaveg. They were talking about the relationship between the tracks and the racers, and Eddie said, "If the crowds are good, we should be considered in the purse. If the crowds are bad, it should be our duty to improve the show and improve the crowds. The race tracks work for us, and we work for them. No dog-eat-dog stuff."

Boy, when I think about that man, those two quotes hit the nail on the head. Because Eddie always understood that it really *was* a partnership. OK, he may have been a little melodramatic with the stuff about putting his life on the line, but he's making his point: "You do your end, and I'll do my end, and we'll both be better off."

He thought like a good promoter would think; he thought about the show. Everybody from that era remembers the nights when he and Bugsy Stevens and Freddy DeSarro and Ronnie Bouchard would put on those great shows in the heat races. Eddie was the ringleader in that, but those guys all played a role. That was them doing *their* part. Now, they didn't do it magnanimously; they expected the promoter to do *his* part, too. And just like the drivers will tell you that Eddie was behind the idea of putting on those great shows, he was also probably the most outspoken guy when it came time to tell a promoter, "Hey, now it's your turn to step up."

Sometimes I think Eddie had that mindset because back when he started, the purses were generally based on a percentage of the gate, so keeping the crowd entertained *this* week might mean more money in his pocket *next* week. And you know, I'm pretty sure he would have preferred that system—40 percent of the gate—right up until he stopped racing. He told me more than once that calculating the payoff based on the receipts was the fairest, most equitable way to do things. "That way," he said, "if it rains on you, it rains on us, too." And, obviously, if it was sunny for us, that would be good for the racers. Of course, the current structure of posted purses was an outgrowth of having some less-than-reputable promoters who tilted the numbers in their own favor. But maybe that's something that needs to be reexamined in short-track racing; a good night would be a good night for *everybody*, and that would go a long way toward making the competitors and the track owners into the kind of partners Eddie talked about.

But what made Eddie so unique, from the promoter's point of view, was that he took an honest look at the big picture. He took into account your whole *season*, not just your good nights. Using Stafford as an example, he didn't just look at the Spring Sizzler and say, "Oh, you guys had a standing-room-only crowd." He also looked at those nights when it was raining everywhere except at the track, and the stands were just about empty.

He was so good at seeing both sides. Back then, Bob Johnson was one of the top modified owners—he and Ronnie Bouchard won so many races together—and we had our share of problems with Bob at Stafford. No matter what happened, he was going to point out something we had done wrong. Eddie, on the other hand, would point out that same problem, but his approach was to come to us and say, "You really ought to take a look at this. If you do it differently, it could make the whole show go better." And, you know, I'm sure this wasn't just a

Stafford thing; I'm pretty certain Eddie had that same sort of relationship with Larry Mendelsohn, Harvey Tattersall, and so many other promoters long before my dad got into the race track business in 1970.

You know, I can't look back on those years without thinking about Seymour the Clown, and here again is a lesson about Eddie.

Early on in our promotional days we'd had some terrific races, but when it came to the overall show we were lacking something. We weren't sure what, but *something*. Well, Butch Farone, who worked at Arute Brothers Construction, was a guy whose family had been involved in racing at Plainville Stadium, and he had done some work as a clown, just knocking around locally. I thought it'd be a great idea to make him part of the show at Stafford, so we had him come up. Mike Joy and I were announcing, and we named him "Seymour the Clown," the idea being that you could "see more" at Stafford.

The kids loved it, but to a lot of the other guys in the front office—my dad, my uncle Chuck, and Bill Slater, who was our race director—this was *not* a good idea. I'd hear things like, "Jesus, this is supposed to be a *race track*." I'd hear my dad saying, "Well, what time does the freakin' circus start?" And it didn't go over much better with most of the competitors. We all know how serious a driver can be just before a race. Depending on his situation, he's thinking, "I've got to do a good job tonight" . . . "My car owner's mad at me" . . . "I hope this car runs right tonight" . . . "I hope I don't screw up." And now he's got some guy in greasepaint and a red wig busting his balls in front of the whole crowd. That can get a little bit tense. So between the fact that the racers didn't like it and the fact that some people thought it was slowing down the show, it was looking like Seymour the Clown was going to be about a three-week experiment gone wrong.

Well, that didn't happen. The idea began to catch on, and in my mind the guys who were most responsible for that—in addition to

In costume, and out: Seymour the Clown plants one on Flemke, while Butch "Seymour" Farone confers with Steady Eddie and Bugsy Stevens. Jackie Arute credits Stevens and Flemke for helping boost Seymour's appeal at Stafford and elsewhere. *(Mike Adaskaveg photos)*

Butch Farone, of course—were Eddie Flemke and Bugsy Stevens. They saw the potential in the whole Seymour thing, and they understood that what was good for the crowd was ultimately good for them. They *got* that. So they started participating in all the hijinks; Bugsy and Seymour might have a squirt-gun fight, or Eddie might climb into his car and chase Seymour around the infield. Before long, you had other drivers getting involved. Suddenly, you could see the fans getting interested in this *interaction*, and I mean fans young and old.

Now, what made "Shrek" a great movie? It's the idea that kids loved it for one reason and adults loved it for another reason, but they both loved it. Same with Seymour; the kids loved to poke his red nose on the midway and they loved the lollipops he handed out, but without Bugsy and Eddie the whole thing would have gotten old very quickly for the adults. Instead, Seymour became something of a New England icon, and to me it all went back to those two guys seeing the value of what was happening.

And, you know, the two drivers who will always be most connected to Stafford, in my mind, are Bugsy and Eddie. With Bugsy, there's a lot involved in that; he was so colorful, and he had won those three NASCAR National Modified titles, and he had such a huge personality. But Eddie was kind of like our *rock*. Now, obviously, he's someone my family thought a lot of anyway, because he was driving for us when my dad bought the track. But there's more to it than that.

For one thing, he was probably the first star of the pavement era at Stafford. Remember, when Eddie won that first race on the asphalt in 1967, Bugsy hadn't won his championships yet, Ronnie Bouchard was still a kid at Seekonk, Richie Evans was just getting his feet wet, and nobody had ever heard of Geoff Bodine. Eddie, meanwhile, had already been through his days down South with the Eastern Bandits, and he had done a lot of winning all over the Northeast. He was a big, big name. So he's the first Stafford star on the pavement, and you could even make the argument that he might have been the longest Stafford star, period, going all the way back to the dirt days. Other winners came and went; Eddie was there for so long, and he always ran up front. He had some big years at Stafford, and even when Bugsy and Ronnie and Bodine had their dominant seasons later on, Eddie was right there with 'em. He still did some winning.

My father was big on all these sayings. And one of them was, "You can have the nicest hardware store in the world, but if you don't have the right product on the shelves, you've got nothing." To a promoter, the racers are the shelf product, and we had a good one because, in addition to those other guys, we always had Eddie.

Like I said, he was our rock, a solid part of that whole Stafford program, on the track and behind the scenes. Yes, we certainly appreciated what Bugsy meant, and we certainly appreciated what Ronnie meant—

Jackie Arute interviews Flemke after a 1974 score at Stafford. *(Mike Adaskaveg photo)*

and, later on, Geoff and Richie and the rest—but when the chips are down, you always count on the guy you know best. In our case, based on where we came from, that was Eddie Flemke. Because of that, we leaned on him quite a bit. We'd ask him to do a radio show for us, or maybe make an appearance somewhere. I don't think he ever enjoyed that stuff the way some guys do, but he'd always come through. You never heard him say, "Geez, I was just on WCTX last week," or anything like that. It was more like, "All right, what time do you need me?" And when Stafford ran on Saturday nights, I can't even guess how many Sunday mornings Eddie spent in the kitchen of our family home in New Britain, talking with my father about every little detail of how the show went. Again, we're back to that partnership thing.

Now, I should point out—and I'm smiling as I say this—that Eddie could be as stubborn as any racer you'll ever meet. There were days when if you said the sky was blue, Eddie would come over five minutes later and say, "I've been thinking about this, and I think the sky is *black*." Then he'd proceed to tell you why he was right and you were wrong. And he wasn't always the best person to go to when you had to make a decision, because it's always easier to find the guy you *know* is going to reinforce what you're already thinking. It was suicide to do that with Eddie, because he not only told you what he honestly thought, he also told you what *other people* were going to think. And he did all this

in a way that made you hear him out. It was as if he was saying, "I've got no control over whether you're going to heed my advice, but at least I'm not going to wake up one day and wish I'd told you this." If he sensed that you didn't get his point, he'd take another run at you the next day, or the next week.

So he wasn't always easy to deal with. There were times when I'd have rather had my arm amputated than deal with Eddie after a difficult night; he'd walk into the office, and I was never sure if I was mentally strong enough to discuss things on the level I knew he'd take the discussion to.

Eddie taught me—the hard way—that every racing situation needs to be looked at on its own, that it isn't good policy to rely on simple black-and-white answers. This was in his early days of driving the Manchester Sand & Gravel #10 for Bill Thornton. Eddie got caught up in a big wreck early in the feature; it tore off the bumper and a piece of lead, and did some other damage. Well, he went to the back of the pack, battled his way through, and won the race. The problem was, we always had the top five weigh in before the winner went to victory lane, and Eddie's car came up, like, three pounds light. The culprit, of course, was that crash. Boy, this was a sticky situation. Thornton was a close friend of my dad's, and of course my family and I thought the world of Eddie. On the other hand, the rule said you had to weigh a certain amount after the race, *period*. So we disqualified him. I was the promoter, and it was my decision.

Now, Eddie and I had a bad time over that one. He told me, "Sometimes you've got to look at the intent, not the action." I insisted that a rule was a rule. And you know something? I was *wrong*. He hadn't cheated, and that one race wasn't the end of the world. In consideration of all the things Eddie had done over the years as a showman—

hell, just for the show he put on *that night*—I should have gone the other way. He had taken his medicine after the wreck by restarting at the tail, and he put on a heck of a show, and we should have given him the win. But I was just too caught up in sticking to my guns. I think Eddie took to his grave the idea that I did him wrong that night, and that has always bothered me. Hell, I'd known him since I was five years old. So that was certainly a tough spot for us.

But you know something? Even when you were dealing with Eddie in those difficult moments, you knew you could *trust* him. And when it comes right down to it, when you're a promoter, that's all you really want from a star driver: someone you can trust. You want a guy with whom you can have that sort of partnership Eddie talked about. See, in this business, every so often you're going to be bare-ass naked, metaphorically speaking; you're going to be in a position where you're very vulnerable. And you hope that the guy on the other side of the equation is not going to look at your situation only from his perspective. You hope that he'll also try to see *your* side.

Eddie Flemke was that kind of trustworthy.

In 1976, we ran a show we called "Modified Madness," basically an anything-goes race for modifieds. It was a radical concept for that time, and it was *my* show. My father didn't want anything to do with it, and nobody else at the track did, either. So even though I thought it was a great idea, I was starting to doubt it. Well, I went to Eddie, and ran it past him. I don't think he was sold on it—meaning I don't think he was too crazy about the format—but it was like he put on his promotional hat and he could see that it might be appealing. And he said, "Jackie, what's the worst that can happen?" He reduced it to those terms, and when I looked at it that way, I decided it was worth the risk. The rest is history: Evans and Maynard Troyer showed up with supermodified wings and blew everybody away, and it's a night people still talk about. It's part of New England lore, and it's another one of those things Eddie touched in his own small way.

Since Eddie's been gone, we've never found anyone who's come close to replacing him. We had some terrific drivers at Stafford—*great* drivers —and a lot of them had *some* of those qualities that made Eddie special. But none of them had *all* those qualities. In fact, I don't think I've seen a guy like that anywhere, even when I've covered the Indy Cars and the Cup cars on TV. There was a consistency to the man, through good times and bad, that was very rare. Now, I'll admit that when it comes to Eddie Flemke, my opinions are certainly shaded by the relationship we had. But I think I'm also able to be objective, and I mean it when I say that I've never encountered another guy like him.

I miss him so much, both personally and professionally. From a personal standpoint, the best way I can say it is that—as of right now, today —I've had two great losses in my life: my father, and Eddie Flemke.

Whatever I've made of myself, I owe 90 percent of the credit to those two guys. And from a professional standpoint, I know I'd still be beating a path to Eddie's door, to ask him about the little bit of promoting I still do. Any promoter who ever encountered Eddie Flemke misses that man, or at least what he represented.

It's sad to say, but that kind of racer almost doesn't exist anymore. And I'll tell you a little story to illustrate that point.

There was a time in the mid-'70s when Dave Monaco, who raced at Stafford for several years, was just starting to get going pretty decent. He showed up with a nice new modified, started up front in his heat race, and walked away with it. I mean, he beat Eddie and Bugsy by maybe a dozen car lengths. Well, as soon as they all got back to the pits, Dave had some visitors: Eddie and Bugsy. I got this story straight from Dave. He said they told him, "Kid, we don't race that way. You were going to win the heat, no matter what; even if we caught you, we were going to let you have it. But as long as you're in a qualified spot, the heat race doesn't mean anything. So from now on, don't stink up our show."

Now, think about that. They didn't say "Stafford's show" or "Arute's show." It was "*our* show." That says so much about the way those guys thought. By the time the heat races rolled around, Eddie already had his homework done, so now he had a chance to play—and to him, running that closely with a guy like Bugsy was playing—and a chance to get the crowd buzzing.

Fast-forward to just a few years ago. There's a driver who was coming up through the ranks at Stafford, and who has since gone on to win races on the NASCAR Modified Tour. He's a bright guy and a great driver, and I *like* him; I'm not throwing him under the bus when I tell this story, just using him as a way of juxtaposing the way drivers think today with the way Flemke thought. Back when this guy was running with us on Friday nights, he went out and just about lapped the field in a meaningless SK Modified heat race. Well, I walked over to him and told him about the days when Eddie, Freddy, Bugsy and those guys would dice around and have the crowd up on its feet. And this driver said to me, "You don't understand. My fans want to see me *dominate*." I walked away thinking, "Kid, *you're* the one who doesn't understand . . ."

That was an epiphany for me. That brief moment drove home the point that today's racers, generally speaking, just don't understand the entertainment involved in what they do.

A lot of guys talk the talk, but Eddie walked the walk. When Ed Flemke strapped into a car and pulled out onto the track, you *knew* he was going to give your fans their money's worth.

"Let's give 'em a show"

Precision driving and packed grandstands went hand-in-hand

by RON BOUCHARD

Ron Bouchard authored one of New England racing's most brilliant careers. After cutting his teeth aboard his father's cutdowns at rough-and-tumble joints like Hudson and The Pines Speedway, he moved to Seekonk and rattled off four straight "Class A" track titles as a teenager. NASCAR modifieds came next, and in those cars Bouchard was simply stunning. Driving for Bob Johnson, Marvin Rifchin, Bob Judkins, and Dick Armstrong, Ronnie won modified championships at Stafford and Thompson, and his major victories included Martinsville's Cardinal 500 and the Thompson 300. Bouchard's crowning achievement, certainly, was his 1981 Talladega 500 victory, which came in only his 11th Winston Cup start. Not surprisingly, he was a charter inductee in the New England Auto Racing Hall of Fame, the youngest member of that glorious first class. He is married to the former Paula Flemke, the daughter of his late friend and rival, Ed Flemke.

Ron Bouchard

EDDIE FLEMKE was a great race driver, but he was also a great showman. People still talk about how interesting those weekly modified races used to be, and how we all used to put on those exciting shows in the heat races. Well, all that that goes back to Eddie. He was the instigator of all that, no doubt about it.

Eddie would wander over to look at the line-up board early in the night, and if you happened to be in his heat race he'd come up to you in the pits and remind you: "Once we get up front and into a qualified spot, let's give 'em a show. If you need to run hard for a few laps to see how your car is handling, do that, but then back off. If I'm leading, I'll do the same thing. Let's dice it out." That happened everywhere we ran: Stafford, Thompson, Seekonk, Malta, it didn't matter.

145

He got everybody to play along. In the beginning, I remember doing it mostly with Freddy DeSarro, Bugsy Stevens and Eddie. As the years went along, a lot of other drivers got involved, too: my brother Kenny, Bob Polverari, Ray Miller, Richie Evans once he started coming to New England every week, and guys like that.

Now, it's not like we planned out *everything*. We didn't say, "All right, I'll run the top, and you run the bottom, and maybe we can put this other guy in the middle." The fast guys always started in the back, which meant you didn't know who was going to get to the front first, so you couldn't figure out all the details. But, most of the time, whoever busted through the pack first would wait for the next good guy to come along, and then you'd start mixing it up. You'd move up a lane and let a guy get under you, and then you might go back by him on the next lap. Or you might just jump to the outside of him and run two-wide for a while. You could take a quick peek up into the grandstands and see everybody going crazy, rooting for their guy.

And you know something? The people in the stands never knew. *Never knew*. Yeah, maybe if you looked at a stopwatch you'd have seen that we slowed down a little bit, because that's what happens when you run side-by-side all the way around the track. But we didn't slow down *much*. It's not like we had the whole field stacked up or anything.

There was one night at Stafford when Bugsy, Kenny, and I ran most of an entire heat race three-abreast. Bill France Jr. was there, the president of NASCAR, and from what they told us he was as excited as the fans were. As I remember it, Kenny and I got up front first and diced around a little bit, waiting for Bugsy. When he caught us, he jumped to the bottom, Kenny took the top, and I ran the middle. And the funny thing about doing that with Bugsy was, I'd look over at him and he'd actually be smiling behind the wheel! That was just so enjoyable for us, and it was *really* enjoyable for the crowd, much better than if one of us had just run as hard as he could once he got up front.

Now, just because we were playing, that didn't mean it was easy. Don't forget, when you start doing some of the things we did, you've got pretty much the whole race track used up. And because we were constantly side-by-side and swapping around, we were *always* close together, so you still had to be careful. Like I said, even if we backed off a little, we were still going fast. So you really had to trust the other guy, and I think that trust came easy because we all knew each other so well. I mean, I raced against guys like Eddie and Bugsy three or four nights a week, every week. We really understood each other's styles, and on top of that we had friendships, and we obviously raced with a lot of respect for the other guy. When it came time to run the feature, we were *fierce* competitors, but at the same time there was always that trust. We're talking about drivers you never had to worry about, even on the last lap of a big show. I've run a lot of close races with Eddie, going for the win,

It's a kid-versus-veteran battle as Ronnie Bouchard leads Flemke down the Stafford homestretch. *(Mike Adaskaveg photo)*

and I don't remember him ever touching me. Same with Bugsy, same with Richie. If any of those guys happened to run into you a little bit, you never gave it a second thought because you *knew* they hadn't done it on purpose. And you know, in all the years we played around in those heat races—season after season, track after track—I don't remember anybody getting into another guy by mistake, at least not to the point where somebody crashed.

Eddie felt so strongly about putting on a good show that if somebody went out there and ran away with a heat race, he'd have a fit. He'd say, "Listen, boys, these heat races don't mean a thing, and they don't *pay* a thing. You're going to start in the same place in that feature whether you win the heat or run third or fourth. But you see all those people in that grandstand? We need to think about them."

I know, because he said that to me. See, when I first started running Stafford and Thompson and places like that, I was, what, a 22-year-old kid? I wanted to win *everything*, and if I could win it by a mile I was *going* to win it by a mile. But Eddie straightened me out quick, and the way he said it made perfect sense. He told me, "Son, we need the people in those grandstands to go home happy and excited. They couldn't have seen too much in your heat race that was exciting to them." I understood what he meant, and from then on it was like I was part of the gang.

That was a special time for me, jumping up to the NASCAR tracks and running against the big guys. I had come out of Seekonk, and before that Hudson and The Pines. I had raced with a lot of really good drivers, guys like Georgie Summers and Deke Astle and others. But moving up to Stafford and Thompson meant running with all these guys I'd always heard about: Eddie, Bugsy, Freddy, Leo Cleary, Bobby Santos, guys like that. In those days, if you could go to the NASCAR tracks and be competitive with them, boy, that was like jumping into Winston Cup and running right with Dale Earnhardt and Darrell Waltrip.

As I remember it, Eddie was the easiest of all those guys for me to get to know. He liked helping people, and he never felt threatened by the new kid on the block. My first race at Stafford was an open-competition race in 1971; I went there with my Seekonk car, a Camaro with a little wing on the back and a 327 cubic-inch Chevy engine, and I'm sure it really stood out because all those guys were running big blocks and coupes. Anyway, we ran really well. I came up through the pack and caught up to Freddy, who was leading, and ran alongside him for a while. But I ended up running the brakes right off the damn thing, because with that little motor I had to run so hard into the corner just to keep up. I ended up finishing third, but I'll tell you, that one race helped me so much. It made a lot of people recognize me, and that led to rides with Dick Armstrong and Bob Johnson, and driving for Bob really turned out to be my big break in the modifieds.

I'm not sure if it was at that first race or the next one, but I remember Eddie coming over and helping me at one of my earliest Stafford races. He knew me, or at least knew who I was, and he said, "Son, this is what you've gotta do to run good here . . ."

From that point on, he would always make it a point to stop and talk, especially if he saw we were having trouble with the car. He just liked to help people, so it wasn't only me. Eddie was that way with *everybody*. He always had a good word to say, and that was so important to a young guy just coming in.

On the race track, he was a tough, tough competitor. Eddie had his own style; he loved to make his car handle on the bottom, and he was good at that, and he really made it work for him. Of course, he'd get up there on the outside if he had to, but he liked to have that car working so good down low that he could kick the stones right out of the infield.

And what really made an impression on me, early on, was that he never ran any harder than he had to. I can remember this like it was yesterday: I'd be running along in Bob Johnson's car, just flying, and as I was catching Eddie I'd tell myself, "I'm gonna jump right up beside him and go on by." Because, man, I *loved* to run the outside. Well, I'd get that left front tire up by his door and I'd be there for a lap or two, then I'd start falling back to his right rear, and pretty soon I was all the way back to his rear bumper again. After he did that to me a few times, I realized that Eddie had only been running as quick as he needed to run to keep the lead, and when somebody caught him he'd just run a little harder.

He was the master at running his own pace, staying on the bottom, and not worrying about what you were doing. If you wanted to jump up and try to pass him, that was fine with him. He'd just pick it up and pull away again, or, even worse, he'd just *leave* you out there. There was a night at Stafford when the two of us were out front, with him leading,

and I was running so good I thought passing him was going to be easy. Well, I jump up beside him, and that son of a gun picks up the pace just a little bit and now we're battling side by side. I keep on trying to get the lead, because I *know* I'm really going good, but as I'm looking in the mirror I can see everybody else—Bugsy, Freddy, all the other good cars—reeling us in. Pretty soon they're all lined up down low, right on Eddie's bumper. Now, instead of passing him for the lead, I'm fighting like hell not to get shuffled back to fifth or sixth. Eddie won, and I ended up finishing second with my tongue hanging out from working so hard.

That man had a great career. *Great* career. I mean, he won a zillion races, and no one knows for sure how many. He was one of those guys who was so good that, if there were three races on a given weekend, you just knew Eddie was going to win at least one of 'em.

We raced an awful lot together, but of course he was a good bit older than me. I guess you could say his best days came before *my* best days. We had a few seasons there in the early '70s where things kind of overlapped and we were both really competitive, but by the time I was really winning a lot—with Johnson and later with Bobby Judkins—Eddie's career was kind of going the other way. I'm not saying he slowed down, but he was racing a lot less and he wasn't winning as much. Instead of a lot of victories, he had a lot of top-fives and top-tens. That's just something you see in all kinds of racing; there's always a new group of guys coming in to take your place. But I really wish I could have raced with Eddie for a longer period when we were both on top of our game. You *enjoy* racing with a driver like him.

You know, very seldom did you ever see that guy get mad. Even if you rubbed him on the race track, he was OK with that as long as he knew it was just hard racing. The only time I saw him really lose his

Ron Bouchard says, "I loved the outside. Eddie liked to have his car working so good down low that he could kick the stones right out of the infield." Here's Ronnie up high and Eddie down low at Thompson in 1977. *(Mike Adaskaveg photo)*

What Steady Eddie angrily suspected might be a "fling" between daughter Paula and Ron Bouchard turned out to be anything but. They are shown here at Thompson in 1976 . . .

temper was at Thompson. I was running decent, but not great, and I'm sitting second, just hanging on. Eddie's leading in the Manchester Sand & Gravel car. Along comes that ol' #1 Pinto, Geoff Bodine, who was really fast in that period. Well, Geoffrey gets inside me in the corner and gives me his usual shot to the nerf bar, and grinds his way past me. Now he's chasing down Eddie. Pretty soon he's looking underneath Eddie, but Eddie's holding him off, lap after lap, using the momentum you get up top at Thompson. Geoff is faster, but Eddie's driving smart, holding his line. I'm back aways in third, watching all this.

Now it's getting close to the end of the race, and things start to get serious. We come down the front straightway, and Geoff's got his right-front tire up against Eddie's left-side nerf bar. Well, Eddie's already out against the wall, so he's turning a little to the left, trying to move Geoff over where he's supposed to be. I see that, and I back out a little bit; I can see that maybe something's going to happen. We go another lap, and down the front straightaway it's the same thing: Geoffrey's got that right-front up against Eddie, grinding away again. I'm thinking, "Well, *this* ought to be good!" I could just see Eddie getting madder and madder. He kinda nudged Geoff over, but that didn't work, and finally, just past the start-finish line, Eddie just hung a left. They bumped and got out of shape, and Eddie hooked Geoff's right-rear, and the both of them spun down the old pit road on the outside of turn one and into the sandbank. I can still see that sand flying everywhere as I went by.

Well, I come around the next time, and there's Eddie, standing right

by Geoff's window, madder than hell. I thought he was going to punch him! I raced with Eddie Flemke for years and years, and I never, *ever* saw him get that mad.

Now, he did get mad at *me* once, too, but that wasn't a racing thing; it was when he found out I was dating Paula. That definitely affected our relationship, even on the track, I think. It's so funny to look back at this now, but when Eddie first found out, I kinda watched out for him a little bit. I remember Bob Johnson, who didn't know about any of this, screaming, "What the hell is the matter with Flemke? If he runs you any higher in the turns, you'll end up out in the parking lot!" Yeah, he was a little bit upset with me for a while there. Part of that, I think, was because I had already been married and had kids. That went on for a while, and then I guess he and Paula talked, and maybe he finally understood that this wasn't just some kind of a fling. Whatever happened, from that day on things between us were terrific again. Our relationship just progressed from there, and it only got better and better. In fact, when I had the opportunity to go Winston Cup racing for Jack Beebe in 1981, I discussed it mainly with three people: Paula, my own father, and Eddie. Jack had asked me to drive for him a couple years earlier and I had refused, and now he was asking me again. I remember Eddie saying, "Son, most people don't get *one* chance like that." Yeah, Eddie had a big, big role in me deciding to take that ride.

And once I went to Winston Cup, the first call I got when I came home every week was from Eddie. We got to be very close, and I just

...and here in 2007 at their home in Fitchburg, MA. The couple married in 1983, by which time Eddie and Ronnie had what Bouchard calls a "terrific" relationship. *(Mike Adaskaveg photos)*

wish he had lived long enough to see what Paula and I were able to do, not just in racing but also in business, with the dealerships. He'd have been proud as a peacock about that, just like my dad is. And, of course, Eddie would have loved our son Chad, because he just had such a good way with kids.

Obviously, I still think of him a lot, and it's not just the racing stuff. You know, you could learn an awful lot from Eddie. If you listened to him, you could learn about life, about people. One of his best features, I think, was that he could really *read* people. Good guy. *Good guy*.

And, of course, I still think about those heat races, because those were some of the best times I had in racing. I mean, to run that close, lap after lap, with Eddie, Bugsy, Richie, Freddy and those guys, that was just amazing. Honestly, that's as much fun as I've had in a race car, ever. I don't think you'll ever see those days again. And, like I said, it all went back to Eddie Flemke.

And you know something? All that talk from Eddie really sunk in, because as I got older and I was off racing at one track while Eddie was someplace else, I'd get things going myself. At Seekonk I'd be in a heat with Georgie Summers, George Murray and guys like that, and if I got alongside them I'd just hang out there and put on a good battle.

Eddie must have been a promoter's dream, because he thought so much about the show. But, you know, part of that was also because most of his living came from racing. He worked a little bit here and there doing other things, but racing was his bread and butter. He understood how important it was to have good crowds, because good crowds meant good purses, and I don't think a lot of drivers thought that way until they met up with him. I had kinda seen that side of things already, because of Anthony Venditti at Seekonk. See, when I was still a teenager racing there, Mr. Venditti let me sell hats to the fans, and he used to say, "Now, Ronnie, you make sure you sign those hats for the people who buy them." That was a good deal for me, because we made some money doing that, but Mr. Venditti knew it was good for him, too. I was young, and I was popular because I was winning races, and he could look into the grandstands and see all those red and white polka-dotted hats. Any good promoter would like that.

But, really, Eddie was probably the first *driver* I heard talk that way, and he convinced the rest of us that what was good for the fans was good for us. It reinforced the idea that you should do things for the people who support you. In my case, I became one of those guys who would always sign autographs—I can still remember how the fans used to pass stuff through the fence at Stafford—and I'd hang around long after the races had ended, when the fans used to come down into the pits.

That kind of thing brought people to the race tracks, and kept them coming back, and that's what was important. Eddie had that figured out all along.

"Your story just wasn't finished without him"

A journalist looks back on modified racing's guru on the mount

by PETE ZANARDI

Pete Zanardi authored what may have been the first truly national feature story on Ed Flemke, a 1968 profile in Stock Car Racing *magazine. In his long tenure as a sportswriter for the* Hartford Times *and the* New Haven Register, *Zanardi's contribution to regional racing was immense. Rather than merely reporting results, he spotlighted the drivers, bringing fans inside the lives of modified heroes like Flemke, Bugs Stevens, Ron Bouchard, Richie Evans, and others. Pete's work as public relations director at the Stafford Motor Speedway played a huge role in that track's rise in the 1970s, and more recently the Waterford Speedbowl benefited from his deft PR touch. Over the years, Zanardi has written for trade publications like* Speedway Scene, Trackside *and* Racing Times, *and he still produces an occasional short-track piece for* National Speed Sport News. *Pete and his wife Jane live in Chester, CT.*

Pete Zanardi

INTERVIEWING EDDIE FLEMKE, as I recall, wasn't very easy. When you think about the guys who were in that era, a lot of them were very predictable. You could pretty much develop your story ahead of time, and then ask your questions because you knew how they were going to answer. And most of the time, they seemed to catch on, and they would sort of give you the answers they knew you wanted.

Well, you sure couldn't do that with Flemke. I mean, Eddie *gave* you nothing; you had to earn every nugget you got from the guy, and I think that was by design. I think he enjoyed the idea of making the writer work for it.

I first met Eddie in the early days of Stafford running as an asphalt track. It might not have been the first year, 1967; it was more likely in '68. I was a sportswriter for the *Hartford Times*, so I knew him at first in a purely professional way. It was later on, after the Arutes bought Stafford and I did the PR work there, that I came to have a true relationship with Eddie. But I guess we hit if off pretty well from the start, because the first story I ever wrote for a national publication was in 1968, for *Stock Car Racing* magazine, and it was about Eddie Flemke. I can remember it vividly; it was called "The Modified Man," and I remember finding it interesting that the lead photo was one of Eddie working on an engine because he was known primarily as a chassis guy. The interview was done at his house in Southington, with my wife Jane and the kids there swimming in the pool as Eddie and I talked.

By then, Eddie had already made a serious mark on the sport. He was certainly a figure of authority. And, you know, he also had a great respect for racing history. Very few of the modified guys had a feeling for what came before them; the midget guys did have that feel, and maybe Eddie was that way because of his brother George, who had been a terrific midget racer. Whatever it was, Eddie could tell you about all the old tracks, and all the old drivers. He had something close to a reverence for old midget heroes like Len Duncan and Georgie Rice, guys he had seen as a kid. The modified guys might tell you stories about what was going on when they got started, but Eddie really understood the history of what went on well *before* he began driving. That only added to his credibility.

If there was an issue in the modified division, a hot topic of any kind, you *had* to get Eddie's opinion on it. I mean, a baseball writer couldn't do a story on the great centerfielders without talking about Willie Mays, and it was impossible to do a serious story on any facet of modified racing—on tires, on rules, on anything topical—without talking about Eddie Flemke. And that held true throughout the '70s, when you had a lot of press people discovering the modifieds. There was sort of a media revolution going on back then; the daily papers and the radio sports shows were catching on, and even guys like Barry Cadigan from the *Boston Globe* were doing stories about the short tracks. So the timing was just right for those people to discover Eddie, because by then he had all this stuff sorted out in his mind. He knew the history, and he knew what was going on at the present time, and I think he also understood *his* place in the whole thing.

Now, the people who wrote columns in the trade papers might not have looked at him the same way. They tended to focus on the social side of things, so that meant that you read a lot about Bugsy Stevens and Richie Evans and the guys who raised hell and partied. They were the media darlings, and in New England you could also throw in Ronnie Bouchard, because in the early '70s he came in like a house afire and won a lot of races as a young guy. In a very short time, Ronnie became

Flemke and Bugs Stevens run the bottom, with Jerry Cook and Richie Evans upstairs at Stafford in 1973. *(Mike Adaskaveg photo)*

a real personality. Meanwhile, Eddie was the guy who won the race, got in the car and went home, and so I never got the sense that those trade paper people latched onto Eddie as much.

But for guys like Charlie Mitchell from the *Norwalk Hour* and Pete VanderVeer of the *New Haven Register* and myself, guys who wrote for the dailies and always needed that *complete* story, Eddie was a key figure. Don't get me wrong, Bugsy and Richie were very important to us, too. Those guys were always great stories, and they played a giant role, media-wise, in what was happening with modified racing. I'm not saying Eddie's contribution was greater, only that it was refreshingly different. Even then he was regarded as the sage, the guy who would look at things logically and give you an honest answer. Your story just wasn't finished without him. If you had a great story on, say, Bugsy, it was only going to be better if you could work in a Flemke quote.

By the way, it's not like we were geniuses in figuring that out. It became obvious over time, simply because every time you talked to the stars of that period—Gene Bergin, Bobby Santos, Richie, whoever—sooner or later the conversation came around to Eddie. It didn't matter what the subject was, they would all bring up Eddie's name. So you began to understand the kind of regard they had for him, and his role in things.

Looking back, it's amazing how many interviews I've done that came back somehow to Flemke. I've got a pile of tapes, long interviews done with a bunch of different guys, and I'll bet you 90 percent of those tapes include at least one story about Eddie. For example, I remember Leo Cleary telling me that when Norwood Arena first went NASCAR in

Steady Eddie makes a young fan happy, scribbling an autograph as his daughter Kristy looks on. *(Mike Adaskaveg photo)*

1960 and the coupes came in to replace the cutdowns, it was Flemke who the old cutdown drivers first paid attention to—Leo, Bobby Sprague, Freddy Schulz and those guys—as they tried to figure out those modifieds. I once interviewed Fred Rosner, the great mechanic and chassis builder, and Rosner sat there telling me about all the tricks Eddie used to play. Hell, just in the last month or so I interviewed two guys, Bob Potter and Ronnie Wyckoff, who kept referencing Flemke. That has happened in so many interviews: "I bought that car from Eddie" . . . "Flemke showed me how to do this" . . . "I followed Eddie out to that particular track."

These guys make it a point to tell you these things. They *find* ways to give you specific examples of ways Eddie helped them, or things he taught them. I can't think of any other figure in this sport who comes close, in that regard. If you talk to Ernie Gahan, if you talk to Billy Greco, if you talk to any given star of the 1960s or '70s era, it always comes back to Eddie. It could be the educated, refined Ray Miller, or it could be the crazy-ass Bugsy Stevens, it doesn't matter. You don't go more than 25 minutes into any interview with anybody from that era

without Eddie's name coming up, and from there the accolades just keep coming.

With all due respect to Bugsy, Richie, or anybody else, you didn't get the sense that people were willing to climb mountains to talk to them. Those guys were thought of very highly, and rightly so, but Eddie was the guy so many other racers talked of as their guru. They *still* look at him that way. He sits up there on that pedestal simply because of a heartfelt, honest-to-God feeling they have that he helped them succeed in one way or another.

In a strange way, it's like so many of these people validate their own status, their own place, by their association with Eddie. Maybe Leo Cleary is saying, "I *know* I'm good, because I raced with Flemke and sometimes I beat Flemke." Maybe that's the way Potter, Wyckoff and these other drivers feel, too. If that's true, it sure says a lot about Eddie. And, you know, the catch phrase for a lot of the guys on these interviews seems to be, "Eddie really took a liking to me." That is a magic phrase, and it's another way of staying associated with him; it's like saying, "My immortality is assured, because Eddie liked me." Everything was OK, everything was right, because Flemke was in their corner.

You know, I read someplace once that immortality is in the hearts and minds of those you leave behind, and Eddie is a perfect example of that. All these years later, we talk about the man he was and the driver he was, and even people who never met the guy hold him in such high esteem. Eddie is a Babe Ruth-like figure; what I mean is, I never saw Babe Ruth play baseball, but I can damn sure tell you all about him, and I suspect that the generation after me can also tell Babe Ruth stories. It's the same way with Eddie.

Of course, a lot of that is due to that mentoring quality he had. I did a story in *Stock Car Racing* way back in the 1970s, called "Eddie's Boys," about the fact that two of New England's greatest racing accomplishments—Pete Hamilton's 1970 Daytona 500 victory and Denny Zimmerman's Rookie of the Year run at Indianapolis in '71—could be traced right back to Eddie Flemke. Anybody who was involved in New England racing at that time can still tell you how proud we were on those two occasions; we'd never had anything *close* to that sort of success on the national stage. And here was a guy, a modified racer, who was widely acknowledged as being instrumental in both those moments. That whole situation solidified Eddie's status as the father figure of the division.

What also helped was that the people he mentored were happy to tell you about it. Pete and Denny never failed to talk about Eddie in all their interviews, and Richie Evans would always tip his hat to Eddie, too. I remember Richie telling me, "I am one of Flemke's guys." I distinctly recall him going out of his way to express that debt. That sort of thing tends to snowball, and that had so much to do with the image Eddie had in the '70s. I mean, if you're a guy who's helped Hamilton and Zimmerman and Evans, people are going to just naturally turn to you. And the more people turn to you, the more it gets around that you're that kind of guy, and it just keeps going.

Over the years, I did a lot of feature stories on Eddie, probably as many as anybody. There were a couple for *Stock Car Racing*, a few for the *Hartford Times*, one for *Trackside*, one for *Racing Times*, and I'm sure a couple for *Speedway Scene*. All those stories—plus the normal race coverage I did—made for a lot of interviews, and I don't remember Eddie ever saying no. Even if I just needed a quick situational quote and I had to bother him at the track, I can't remember him ever brushing me aside. I never got the sense that he didn't like the press, and he certainly wasn't *afraid* of the press, the way so many drivers seem to be.

It's fair to say that the average Flemke story was much more serious in tone than the average story on, say, Bugsy Stevens. That's because you didn't get to ask Eddie about this party or that party, or any of that social stuff. You went to Eddie for a purpose, and I think those stories reflect that. You weren't influenced, and so the stories weren't colored, by the crazy lifestyle stuff you might have tried to put into a story on Bugsy or Richie, or even guys like Santos and Sonney Seamon, two guys who could tell you all about the wild parties at places like Trenton and Martinsville. No, Eddie was a professional racer—to him, a big race was just another paycheck—and because of that you got stories that *sounded* professional.

Now, that didn't mean they weren't interesting. You could get some fascinating stuff from Eddie about his philosophies on racing, and about the dynamics of driving a car. And, you know, it says a lot for Eddie that

Standing tall: The pint-sized Flemke takes the high ground as Stafford announcer Jim Powers holds the microphone in a 1973 victory interview. *(Mike Adaskaveg photo)*

a story about him could be so interesting *without* any of that wild hell-raising stuff that helped prop up the stories on those other guys. But, like I said, he could make your job difficult, because he made you work for every single quote he gave you.

Still, he was a great one-on-one interview. Hell, he was a great one-on-one *conversation*. When he was racing out of the Manchester Sand & Gravel shop, I was living in Glastonbury, so he wasn't too far away. Well, I'd go over there sometimes, and it might last for 20 minutes or an hour and a half. One of the things I remember is that Eddie was always *sitting* on something as he spoke; it might be a bumper, or a nerf bar, or a race car tire he laid on its side, but it was almost always something lower than a common chair. Naturally, that meant that I had to sit down, too. Now, maybe I'm reading too much into this, but Eddie was a short guy

Steady Eddie with Riverside Park star Ron Wyckoff, just one of the top drivers whose life and career intersected with Flemke's over the years. *(Mike Adaskaveg photo)*

and there might have been a six- or eight-inch difference in our heights, and I honestly think this was his conscious way of bringing me down to his level, so to speak. I don't know that for sure, but Eddie was certainly that kind of a thinker. I wouldn't have put that past him.

Another thing I remember is that whenever I interviewed Eddie back then, he talked very slowly. This was back before every reporter carried around those little cassette recorders, and you actually wrote things down. So Eddie would talk slowly, almost like, number one, he wanted to be sure you understood his point, and, number two, he wanted to be sure you got it down right.

Over the years, he said some heady things. He's been quoted as saying things like, "You can't eat trophies," and "Points don't put food on the table," which are great lines. And it's Eddie who gets credited with "Dirt is for planting potatoes," which became a famous line among the asphalt modified crowd. Who knows if he really said it first? There's no way to be sure. But even if it *wasn't* Eddie, he'd have been the logical person to credit.

He did know how to play the media. There were times when he would instigate things, and he was smart enough to use this writer or that writer as his torpedo. Did he do that a lot? No, he didn't. But the point is, he was bright enough to know just how to do it. And the position he held, in our eyes, probably made it easy for him to get away with that.

I think he might have treated different writers in different ways. What I mean is, Eddie would tell you things once he trusted you, and

once he felt that you would understand the weight of what he was saying. For example, Eddie told me—and this has since been quoted elsewhere, but I know I hadn't heard or read it before—that his biggest thrill in racing was having Pete Hamilton invite him into the press box after he'd won the 1970 Daytona 500. He had been waiting outside to see Peter, and I guess somehow Peter found out Eddie was out there, and he had somebody bring him inside. And this, Eddie said, was "the greatest thrill of my career."

Now, he told me this in the late '70s, toward the end of his career. Think about that. Here's a guy who won the Spring Sizzler, the Thompson 300, the Stafford 200, the first-ever race on the asphalt at Stafford, the New Yorker 400 at Utica-Rome, a guy who was *the* Eastern Bandit . . . and his greatest joy was seeing *someone else* succeed. That's a big thing to say, and I think Eddie trusted that I'd know he was telling me something important. He trusted that I'd know what to do with it.

If Eddie was around today, I'm sure I would still be seeking him out from time to time. And, you know, because there are so many more writers covering the modifieds today, Eddie would probably have become one of the *great* sources. Because he'd be the same guy, more intuitive

Flemke with Wild Bill Slater, whom he knew as a rival, a track official, and a friend. This shot was taken at Thompson in 1976. *(Val LeSieur Collection)*

than most people you could interview. He'd still be the guy who gave you the inside look, who helped you get into the heads of the other racers. Eddie had one of those special minds; when people like that talk, they paint pictures, and you can see everything that's going on. Yeah, he would still be spending a lot of time answering our questions. We'd still be going to him, no doubt about it.

There are definitely some things I'd want to ask him, things I'm still curious about. For instance, we all know about the guys he helped, but I never got to really ask him *why* he picked the people he picked. Why Zimmerman? Why Hamilton? Why Evans?

And I'd ask him about something he said to me that ended up getting a lot of attention. He talked about the idea that the perfect battle, his dream race, would involve him and Bugsy and Gene Bergin, all three of them in equal cars. I wish I'd pressed him more about that, because he never really *explained* it. I still remember that interview. We were at the Manchester Sand & Gravel garage, and I simply asked him what he thought made an ideal competitor. Anyway, I ran that quote in a story in *Racing Times*, and I know it had an effect on those other two guys; Bugsy is well aware of what Eddie said, and so is Gene, but neither of them can really grab hold of what he meant. So it would be nice to get his whole story on that: Why did he choose those two guys? Why not Richie, or Ronnie, or Greco, or Jim Hendrickson, or Ray Hendrick? Why those two? Wouldn't it be great to have that answer?

I'd like to say that Eddie and I were really great friends, but that would be a stretch. I never had the sort of relationship with Eddie that I had with Bergin or Bugsy or Bill Slater, three guys I got very close to. I regarded Eddie as a guy I could rely on for answers, and as a guy I liked, and we were definitely friendly. But I really don't know how to size up how close we were. I know how I felt about him, but I have no way of knowing how he felt about me. I suspect Eddie kept that sort of thing to himself.

I'd like to think that he respected me as a writer, and I know I certainly appreciated his position in the game. He was one of those guys you find every so often in any sport who reach a point where you simply have to respect them from the time you show up. They don't have to *earn* it; their position was solid before you came along. That's the situation Eddie was in when I arrived, and it was justified and fortified by everybody I talked with, and everything I saw. And I just accepted it.

Like I said, he was the sage, and I knew that. We all did.

"If I needed six inches, Eddie would give me seven . . . but only seven"

Racing hard, but racing fair, was the law of their era

by GENE BERGIN

Gene Bergin is a charter member of the New England Auto Racing Hall of Fame whose versatile career encompassed modifieds, midgets, sprints, even Indy cars. A high school football hero, he followed his father, a jalopy-era car owner, into racing. Gene's first underage outing at Stafford in 1949 saw him escorted off the grounds. But he recovered nicely, winning a 1962 Riverside Park title and, in '67, the first modified championship of Stafford's paved era. Blessed with what Pete Hamilton called "a level of talent that was God-given," Bergin won on both asphalt and dirt, scoring at Thompson, Norwood, Waterford, Utica-Rome, Oxford Plains, Wall Stadium, Lakeville, Keene, Grandview, and elsewhere. In his weekday life, he worked construction and managed parking lots. "Racing was a great second job," says Bergin, now living in Florida. "I made good money driving for 40 percent, and I met so many wonderful people."

Gene Bergin

THIS IS THE WAY WE RACED: If I was outside Eddie Flemke and I absolutely needed six inches of room to survive, Eddie would give me seven. But *only* seven. And I'm sure he was saying, "Gene, if you can get it done in that seven inches, good for you." Naturally, I treated him the same way.

Now, let me tell you, none of us was going to give somebody the whole race track. That goes for Eddie, or me, or any good driver. When you're out there racing for money and for prestige, you've got to answer to your car owner and your crew, so I'd always make it as tough on the other guy as I could. I mean, Muhammad Ali didn't climb in the ring and punch only with his left hand, did he? No, you saw him use his right hand, too, because you've got to do everything you can to win. But, again, you've got to be clean about it. Fair.

163

I guess that sort of respect was handed down from one era to the next. We simply understood, from the time we each started racing, that you never tried to knock somebody out of your way, and you never tried to block. I ran some very tough race tracks over the years—from bull-rings like Riverside Park and Norwood, right up to Thompson and the bigger tracks—and I think most of the guys treated each other very well at all of them. The slower guys fought you, like they should, but not *too* much; the faster guys passed cleanly.

Of course, when you race like that, there's a lot of trust involved. If you're on the outside, going around a guy, and you see him edging out wider and wider as you get onto the straightaway, you've got to believe in that guy enough to know he's going to give you the space you need. If it was Eddie, or Bugsy Stevens or Freddy DeSarro or one of the top drivers, that was no problem. You *always* trusted them. You were safe, and you knew that.

There's the same sort of trust when you're on the bottom, getting passed. If you give that outside guy his seven inches, you've got to believe he's good enough to operate in that space, and that he's not going to bounce off the wall or get into you.

With some guys, you had to be *so* careful. You gave them as much room as they needed, just to protect yourself. That's something a driver has to learn. In my case, there were times when I'd catch a guy really fast—fast enough where he should *know* I'm obviously handling better —but when I'd jump to the outside heading into the turn, suddenly that guy would want to run as fast as I was. Now he's in over his head, and I'm in the worst spot in the world: outside of a guy who's out of control. Forget that.

Eddie always knew how far he could stretch the situation. If you were fast and you came up behind him, he gave you the room you need-ed, and if you made the pass, he was OK with that. He knew he had been beaten.

He was that kind of a driver, that kind of a man.

I can't say for sure when I first encountered Eddie, but it was prob-ably at Riverside Park in the late 1950s. By then, he was already a big-name shoe. He had come out of Plainville Stadium, along with a few other top-shelf guys like Moe Gherzi and George Lombardo. And I'll tell you, over the years I ran a lot of laps with Eddie.

We used to test each other out, especially in the warm-ups. Sometimes, the warm-ups were nothing more than a big con game. If you had the fastest car, you tried not to show it; if you weren't the fastest, maybe you'd figure out a way to psyche out whoever was the best. I remember being up at Oxford Plains with Bobby Judkins, back when he had just built his first Pinto. I was going really good, but Bugsy was just a little bit better than us. Well, Bobby jacked the car up and took the cover off the rear end, as if he was changing the gears. Of

Gene Bergin in his prime, just loaded with natural ability and pure speed. *(John Grady photo)*

course, all we were trying to do was get Bugsy and his car owner, Sonny Koszela, to think *they* needed to change gears, too.

Eddie was a master at that stuff, just an absolute master. In fact, he played all his tricks on us so many times that we had to be dumb to pay attention, but we did. I mean, there were nights when you knew he was lying to you—holding back on the track, or making you think he was tinkering with his car because it was slow—and yet you believed him. I'm telling you, a lot of people fell for Eddie Flemke's tricks over the years. I'd ask him how he was going and he'd say, "Aw, gee, Gene, it's pretty decent," downplaying things. Then he'd end up going two or three tenths faster than everybody else.

On the other hand, Eddie would never lie to you if he knew you honestly needed help. If you told him your car wasn't acting right and he suggested you try this or try that, you could trust him completely. He would never give you bad advice, or tell you anything that was going to get you in trouble.

He and I were very different drivers. Eddie was like a great dancer, just so *smooth*, so light with his touch. Me, I was totally the opposite: hard into the corner, slipping and sliding, tough on the car. Just more aggressive in general, I guess. I'd put the hammer down and go. I got my style from people like Jimmy Little and Frankie Blum. Most people today have never heard of those guys, but they were incredible race drivers; just give 'em a steering wheel and they'd go fast, whether the track was dirt or asphalt. They'd go charging into the corner and slide through it, and I just loved watching them. That, I thought, was how you were supposed to drive a race car.

Gene Bergin recalls the trust shown by the top drivers of his era. Here, Flemke runs the top at Albany-Saratoga, allowing Lou Lazzaro plenty of room …

But, as I learned, that style was good for *their* time; it wasn't as good later on. See, in every sport, things change. An NFL team today plays a much different style of football than they played in the '50s, and styles also change in racing. As the cars got better and more sophisticated, it was better to *drive* through the corner instead of sliding around it. It took me a while to figure that out.

The other thing that made us different was that Eddie was very mechanical, and I was not. He was always toying with ideas, changing suspension designs, trying to make his car go faster by improving its handling. That wasn't me. My theory was, a car can only do two things —it can push, or it can be loose—and it was my job to explain to my mechanic which of those two things the car was doing. From there, it was up to him. I couldn't say, "Let's jack in this much wedge," or "Let's add some air in that particular tire," but I could generally tell 'em what was wrong. As long as I was with the right mechanic, like a Bobby Judkins or a Beebe Zalenski, we could communicate and get the car going. I used to drive Beebe nuts with all the changes we'd make, but we won a lot of races, so I must have known what to tell him. But building an engine, or changing a carburetor, or designing a chassis? Forget it. That wasn't something I could do.

Eddie and I battled an awful lot—him passing me, me passing him —but he never, ever hit me unfairly. Oh, we'd bump, sure, and maybe one of us would give the other guy a shot in the bumper, but nothing worse than that, because we felt that wasn't the way to do things. I'll use a boxing comparison again: To me, knocking the leader out of the way is like hitting the other fighter below the belt. A fair fighter wouldn't think of doing that, just like I wouldn't think of banging Eddie Flemke

or Freddy DeSarro out of the way. You wanted the other drivers to respect you. In my mind, if you earned the respect of the fellows you were competing against, you had to be a pretty good driver and a pretty good man. Sure, there were always a few guys who raced the wrong way, a little too rough. I'd watch them banging into the other drivers, and I hated that. I'd have quit racing before I'd treat a man that way.

I could never understand the thinking of a driver who would wreck another man's vehicle just to pick up *one position*. Because, I mean, that's what it comes down to: you wrecked a man to gain a spot, whether it's for the win or whatever. What did you really accomplish? You didn't do anything that takes *talent*. All you did was crash into the other car. Plus, in my opinion you spoiled a good race, because racing is about watching drivers try to out-think each other. I like the idea of watching a driver trying to be *smarter* than the next guy, trying to set him up, maybe faking to the outside and then passing on the inside. Eddie could set you up that way; Bugsy could set you up that way. I'd like to think that if I was faster than the next guy, most of the time I could figure out a way to beat him. And if I didn't? Well, I remember something Rene Charland always said: "You got me tonight, but I'll be back next week." That was our theory. Maybe we had finished second or third, but we had finished a *fair* second or third.

Gain the respect of your competitors. That's the way to race.

Now, we all make mistakes. When you're driving in close competition, that's going to happen sometimes. I spun out Fats Caruso at Thompson once, and that was a stupid mistake. Fats was one of my dearest friends in racing—I just loved the man—and on this Sunday afternoon he had the feature won easily. I was running second, and I

...and here he does the same thing on the bottom, this time against Bugsy Stevens. It was, says Bergin, a matter of respect. *(Mike Adaskaveg photos)*

could have raced my heart out all day and never caught him. I noticed him backing off, as if to say, "Come on, Gene, get up here. We'll have some fun, and put on a show." So I closed in on him, but with a couple laps to go I got *too* close, and I hit him. He spun out, and I won the race.

Now, Fats was a tough guy, and when I saw him walking toward me in the pits later I thought he was going to wallop me. Instead, he just looked at me and walked away. That was terrible. I wish he had hit me right between the eyes, or stuck his foot in my butt, or something. I would have felt better.

I'll give you another example: We were at Trenton for the Race of Champions, and I made a mistake that ended up knocking out Ronnie Bouchard. My car was pushing every time I went into the first turn, so I had to take it a little bit easy and keep it on the bottom. Well, on this one particular lap I came into the turn the same way I had been, but there was another car in my lane going much slower than the rest of us were, and I had to move up. My front end started pushing and I got into the side of Ronnie's car, and he crashed. Now, there was never a driver who was more of a gentleman on the race track than Ronnie Bouchard; he'd try you on the outside, all night long, and if that didn't work he'd rather finish second than hit you in the bumper and knock you out of the way. And here he was, just trying to make a clean pass on the outside like he always did, and I had crashed him. It *always* bothered me to get into somebody, even if it was an accident.

It's a different kind of driver that you see today. Contact doesn't concern them. If they're ahead, they're not going to give you *two* inches, never mind six or seven. And if they're behind, some of these guys only seem to know how to pass one way, and that's on the inside. If they can't get past you on the inside, they'll just knock you out of the way. Then they'll say, "Oh, that's racing." Well, that's a bunch of bullshit.

Can you imagine what would have happened if one of us had knocked Leo Cleary out of a win and then told him, "Hey, pal, that's racing"? Leo would have answered with a left hook, and then maybe a straight right, and the conversation would have been over.

We hated the idea of unnecessary banging. I think that's partly because a lot of us came out of the days when stock cars were absolute junkers; as things improved and we finally started getting into better and better equipment, we *appreciated* what we had. The last thing we wanted to do was hurt that race car.

And, aside from that, I always worried: What if I hurt somebody? What if I did something deliberate, and the other man crashed and was injured? It's bad enough when you have an accident and someone gets hurt, and, let's face it, those things are going to happen when you're running 100 miles per hour. But if I ever crashed a man *on purpose* and anything happened to him, I wouldn't have been able to live with myself.

These were guys I knew. These were my *friends*. Sure, we would fight like hell once they threw the green flag, but when it came right down to it, these were people I cared about, and I knew they cared about me, too.

Take Eddie, for example. Here's how much he cared about me: I'm down at Old Bridge, New Jersey, and I get into a crash, break my arm, and off I go to the hospital. Meanwhile, my crew packs everything up and they go home, and I'm left there in the emergency room, waiting for a doctor to see me. Well, I sit there and sit there, and I'm getting mad, and who comes walking through the door? Eddie Flemke and his crew. That's the gospel truth; my own crew is long gone, but here's Eddie. He says, "How are you getting home?" I told him I didn't know, and he said, "Gene, don't worry about a thing. We'll wait, and you can ride back with us."

Eventually the doctor came, but all he did was tape my arm to my side so I couldn't move it, stick me with a couple of shots to take the pain away, and give me a few pills to take when the shots wore off. Eddie put me in his car, and off we went, headed for home and the Hartford Hospital. And, wouldn't you know, we were almost there when we ran out of gas on the Berlin Turnpike! We're out of gas, and I'm out of pills! It must have been four or five o'clock in the morning, but Eddie got to

Steady Eddie and Gene Bergin, two of New England's best ever, share a laugh prior to the 1981 Thompson 300, when both their careers were winding down. *(Howie Hodge photo, Val LeSieur Collection)*

a telephone and he woke up Charlie Brayton—who drove modifieds for years up at Riverside Park—and said, "Hey, Charlie, I'm out of gas on the Berlin Turnpike, and I've got Bergin in the goddam car with a broken arm. We've got to do something." Charlie came down with some gas, and Eddie got me to Hartford Hospital.

Now, I raced against Eddie for years after that. *Years*. And how in the world was I not going to treat him with respect? Like I said, he cared about me, and I cared about him. Even if he *had* banged me around on the track, I wouldn't have let it override what he had done for me.

The thing I'll always remember most about Eddie Flemke is his passion for racing. He just loved the sport, and I think he loved it more than any other person I ever knew. We went out to dinner together more than once, and the conversation was *always* about racing. I mean, I enjoyed racing, too, and I was fortunate enough to have some success along the way. But Eddie truly loved going around in circles, and he loved it most when he could do it faster than the rest of us.

I feel like the Good Lord blessed me just by letting me get to know a guy like him. Eddie treated me very well, helped me out, and was such a good friend. Even after I stopped racing, sometimes I would stop and see him when he had his shop in East Hartford, just to shoot the bull. I miss the guy, I really do, and I'll continue to miss him.

I remember reading about Eddie and his idea of the perfect race, how he said he'd put me and Bugsy in there with him because we were "fair and clean racers." Really, that's all we expected out of the guys we raced with: fairness. And, believe me, if I was out there racing with Eddie —or Bugsy, or Freddy, or Richie, or Ronnie—I had complete trust. I never, ever had one of those guys do anything foolish to me. Yes, they made it rough, like they were supposed to do, but I knew they weren't going to treat me badly.

I'm not sure why Eddie mentioned just Bugsy and me, because he could have mentioned quite a few different guys. But I'm glad he thought that way about me. And I'll tell you this: I would have hated like hell to run a match race like that against Eddie, because I'd have probably wound up behind him. But not *too* far behind!

"He sure taught me the hard way . . . but I thank him for that"

The professor, as remembered by the pupil closest to him

by ED FLEMKE JR.

Ed Flemke Jr. is a fixture in the modified division, and old-timers who remember him best as "Eddie's boy" might find it hard to fathom that Junior's career has now equaled his father's in length. Having graduated from local racing to the NASCAR Whelen Modified Tour, Eddie Jr. has put together an impressive record of 16 Tour wins (as of the end of 2006). A frequent championship contender, he finished as the series runner-up in 2004 (to Tony Hirschman) and again in 2006 (to Mike Stefanik), and fans voted him Most Popular Driver in 2002. Outside the NASCAR Tour, he has close to 20 victories in weekly competition. Eddie Jr. and fellow modified driver Reggie Ruggiero operate the Race Works fabrication shop. Interestingly, Junior isn't technically a "junior" at all; his given name is Edward Donald Flemke, while his father's full handle was Edward Arthur Flemke.

Ed Flemke Jr.

THE FIRST RACE CAR I ever had was a modified, a coupe. My friend Tony Altieri and I were partners, and we bought the car from his father and another guy. They ran it at Riverside Park and Plainville Stadium as the "Flying #2," with Danny Galullo driving, but the car had just been sitting around for a while. Tony and I had been putting together a six-cylinder car with a couple other guys, but that all sort of fell apart. Tony's father said, "Why don't you just buy our coupe?" So that's what we did.

My father helped us a little bit as we were taking it apart and then putting it back together, making sure it was safe, but he mostly kept his distance. He wanted us to do our own thing.

We had it ready for the season opener at Riverside. I'll tell you exactly when it was: April 14, 1973. Something else I remember: My father had always insisted that us kids dress well when we went to the race track, because image was important to him. And when he saw me that day, wearing corduroy pants and a decent shirt, he said, "Go change. Put on something green. Let's get that out of the way right now." I guess that was his way of telling me not to worry about superstitions, or anything like that. So I wore green to my own first race.

My dad was racing that weekend at Thompson, driving for Bobby Judkins. Actually, they were running the #2X modified against the supermodifieds. Anyway, he wasn't going to be able to spend much time with us at Riverside Park, but he did come up that afternoon. In fact, he basically set the car up before we went; Tony and I helped him, but it was definitely his setup. And when we got to the Park, he drove it first, just feeling it out. Then he put me in it, and said, "Okay, go ahead." That was it. Not, "Watch out for this." Not, "Don't do that." It was just: "Go ahead." Keep in mind, I'd only had my driver's license for, like, three months. I had never even driven a standard-shift car until the previous week. But he told me to go, so I went, with him standing there in the infield.

I made two or three laps, and then he stepped out to the edge of the track and waved me in. And I'll never forget this: He reached in, and said, "Okay, next time put it in *high* gear." We had a three-speed, and because I wasn't much of a mechanic I'd installed the shift levers upside-down. When I thought I was in third gear, I was riding around in second. I was too nervous to notice it, but of course he could hear the thing screaming. So I went back out, got it into third gear this time, and made six, eight, ten laps before he called me in again.

He sat down on the nerf bar, leaned in, and said, "Okay, I've got to go." Then he paused, and he said, "Just remember, the only person you have to impress is yourself." And he walked away.

I was like, That's it? No real advice? Not even, "Good luck, keep it in one piece"? What I supposed to do with *that*? I mean, I knew *nothing*, and he knew *everything*. Obviously, I was looking for more information.

See, I had watched my father help a lot of guys, teaching them. He loved that. In fact, he loved *audiences*, even though he was basically shy. I guess what I mean is that he loved a *captive* audience, loved being able to share what he knew with people who would listen. He was the kind of guy who would give you the shirt off his back anyway, but when he could help someone just by passing along his knowledge, he really did enjoy that.

For example, I remember him and Denny Zimmerman being so close, even though I was very young at the time. Denny used to come to my father's garage, and we'd all eat lunch together. Remember how, years ago, milk used to come in those tiny bottles? Well, Denny would

take a swig from one of those bottles, and joke around that he was practicing how he'd do it when he won the Indy 500. I know my father
thought very highly of Denny, and was very proud of him. When things
went wrong, he could get frustrated with Denny, which only meant he
cared about him. Yeah, he really liked Denny, and would do anything
he could to help him.

It was the same with Pete Hamilton. I mean, Pete even lived with us
for a while, when I was maybe nine or 10 years old. I remember Pete
swimming with us, and talking all night, and telling us stories. Pete had
so much going for him, as a positive role model; he was a good-looking
guy, well spoken, very articulate. He was animated in the way he talked,
using a lot of body language like that whole generation seemed to. And
my father just loved him.

Richie Evans was another one. Every Monday morning, whether
they'd seen each other on the weekend or not, they would be on the
phone for *hours*. You always knew it was Richie calling, because my
father would pull the phone over to a little alcove in the shop and sit
down in a chair, very serious. When other people were on the phone,
he would pace back and forth, or put his foot on the bumper of the car,
and maybe talk for couple minutes. But he thought enough of Richie

Eddie Flemke Jr., suited
up and ready on his first
night behind the wheel.
The scene is Riverside
Park, and the date is
April 14, 1973. (*John
Grady* photo)

that they'd talk for an hour, two hours, whatever. And it's funny how many times one of them would call the other one right back as soon as they hung up, because they had forgotten to say something in the first conversation. There was a tremendous bond there.

Unfortunately, my father never talked to me about why he liked those guys so much, or why he helped them. He wasn't the type of man who talked about *feelings*, or about personal stuff. He kept that inside. So I had to watch these relationships, and figure out what it all meant. I saw him take so many guys under his wing, help them build their cars, hook them up with the right people, open up his garage to them, and in some cases open up his *home* to them.

And yet with me that first night at Riverside Park, it was: "The only person you have to impress is yourself."

Happy birthday, Dad! Junior presents Pops with a pre-race cake at Stafford more than 30 years ago. *(Mike Adaskaveg photo)*

Of course, when I got home that night he was sitting in the driveway, waiting for me. He wanted to know all about what happened. I didn't qualify for the feature, so I really didn't have much to tell him, but he wanted to know *everything*, and he had some thoughts on each different thing we discussed. I was like, "Gee, I really could have used this stuff *before* I got in the car . . ."

What I didn't realize then, but I understand today, is that he wanted me to learn this stuff the hard way. To him, that was the *best* way. One of his favorite sayings was, "A lesson hard earned is a lesson well learned," meaning that you never forgot it.

I've got a good story about that. That first night, he set my car up with a push, because he knew I couldn't get in too much trouble with a push. The next week, he set it up to be loose, so I could experience what that was like. The third week, Tony and I set it up ourselves, doing what he'd told us to do. I used my dad's cigarette pack to set the wedge; at Riverside Park you needed about four inches of wedge, so you'd stand the Lucky Strike pack on its end. That night, the car was good.

The fourth week, we were on our own. Well, it may have been a little too soon for that, because we ran absolutely *horrible*. My father still wasn't at the track with us, because Stafford was a Saturday-night track back then and their season had started. Anyway, we couldn't figure out how the car had gotten so bad. We only had a limited number of things we could screw up; that coupe had the old Flemke front end, which my father had taught me the basics of, and really no adjustment at all in the rear. But this car just pushed, pushed, pushed, no matter what we tried.

Well, Monday night would be our version of "school." We kept that car at the old Rocky's Amoco in Southington. Rocky Germani and my father had been friends for years, and I worked there, pumping gas. Anyway, on Monday nights the whole crew would come to the station —all of us were just kids—and my father would show up and let us tell him what happened at the track.

After this horrible fourth week, he sat us all down and said, "Tell me what you did Saturday, and start at the very beginning."

We said, "Well, we loaded the car, put gas in the truck, and drove to the race track."

My father said, "Okay, then what?"

"Well, we unloaded the car, put the race tires on, and went out for practice."

"Then what?"

And he took us through everything, step by step: "How many laps did you run in practice?" . . . "What did you do to try to fix the push?" . . . "When that didn't work, what did you try next?"

I went through every adjustment we made. I mean, every single thing we had done, all night, and how it affected the car. Then he said, "Start at the beginning. Tell me again, everything."

We said, "Okay, we loaded up the car . . ."

My father said, "Stop right there." He walked us all around to the front of the car, and said, "Tell me everything you did when you loaded the car." He wanted every detail. We told him how we'd done it the same way we always did, putting on the loading tires and then putting these blocks of wood between the axle and the frame so the front end would be raised up enough that we didn't catch the oil pan on the truck.

He said, "Okay, now tell me everything you *didn't* do when you *un*loaded it." And we all looked down and realized that we had never taken those blocks out of the front end. We ran the whole night, and made a hundred adjustments, but the whole time we basically had a solid front end. Oh, it was aggravating to realize that we had done something that stupid.

Now, once he had noticed what we had done wrong, he could have just told us. But that was not his way. He would make us figure it out, make us sweat. And whenever that happened, it was another example of "a lesson well learned," because it taught you to do things smarter, step by step, the next time. I mean, I *know* we never forgot those blocks of wood again.

He did help us with some things he thought should have been obvious. Like, Tony and I used to always over-tighten things, so one day we showed up at the garage to find that my father had cut every one of our wrenches in half. With a short wrench, you couldn't over-muscle things. He said, "Go ahead, boys, pull on 'em all you want now!"

But most of the time, he would let us go in our own direction, and watch from a distance. In fact, even when he wasn't around, he was watching in his own way. See, I didn't realize this at the time, but that whole first season at Riverside Park, him not being there didn't mean he was in the dark about how I was doing. He had people looking out for me: other drivers, car owners, mechanics, whoever. Even Harvey Tattersall, the promoter, was in on it. They had a handicapping system that made you start at the back your first three times out. Well, on the fourth week, Harvey came over and said, "Eddie, I'm sorry, but you're just not ready to start up front. We're going to have you start in the back again tonight." I learned later that this was per my father's request. He had basically said to Harvey, "Do me a favor. Watch my kid, and don't let him start up front until you're sure he's ready." So in his own way, my father was *there*; I just didn't know it.

But I'm glad he wasn't around to watch me in person, because I'm sure I was more embarrassing than good back then. I did make a lot of mistakes—which every kid does—and at least I knew he couldn't see them. Later on, that was the toughest part, having him *watch* me make a mistake.

I remember running a heat race at Thompson. My car was good, but not great, so when we had a caution flag, I pitted. Well, after that the

It's 1973, and Eddie Jr. is trying his father's ride, the Judkins #2X, on for size. *(Mike Adaskaveg photo)*

car went worse. When the heat race ended, he came over and said, "What the hell happened?" I told him the truth, which was that on my car—a coil-spring car I had just built—the adjustments you made to the front end were exactly the opposite of the torsion-bar cars we'd been running; in other words, you actually had to turn the bolts in the opposite direction. I said, "Dad, we messed up. We went the wrong way." He looked straight at me and said, "Put this car on the truck. You don't deserve to race today." And he meant it.

Another time, at Thompson again, I had finally gotten a good motor. He came over before practice and said, "Let's go out together. I want you to follow me. I'm going to run a few laps at a speed where I think you'll be comfortable, and then I'm going to wave. When I wave, that means I'm going to go off and do my own thing. You just keep running whatever pace you can handle." So, off we go. We run a few laps, and he waves, but I'm still staying right with him. He waves again. But I'm really going good; in fact, at one point I was able to push him down the straightaway. Now he waves again, points to his head, and motions for me to slow down. But, no, I'm going to stay right with him. Well, the next lap, coming out of turn two, I lost it, spun into the infield, backed into a light pole and knocked myself out. As I came to, he was slapping me, trying to get me to wake up. The track crew guys thought he was mad, but he wasn't, at least not right away; then, as soon as he was sure I wasn't hurt, he showed me how mad he really was. He said, "The next *effin'* time I tell you to slow down, you damn well better *slow down!*"

I've heard people say he was tougher on me than he was on other guys, and I think that's true. As the years went along, I watched him spend so much time with Tony Siscone, and he helped Wally Dallenbach Jr. a lot when Wally drove a modified we'd built. And I remember Mike McLaughlin telling me about being at New Smyrna when he first started racing asphalt, and having this guy come over and offer him some suggestions. Mike had come from dirt racing, so he didn't recognize my father, but they talked a while. After my father left, Mike asked somebody who that guy was, and they said, "Oh, that was Eddie Flemke."

Always the mentor, Flemke counsels Wally Dallenbach Jr. as they observe a Stafford warm-up session in 1981. Dallenbach, known today for his TV work, drove a Race Works modified for a short time. *(Howie Hodge photo)*

We'd be at Stafford or someplace, and some nights there would be a line of people asking my father's opinions. He'd say, "Well, I would try *this*," or maybe, "You might want to check *that*." He would walk 'em through things. Then I'd get my chance to ask him something, after waiting my turn—I got no special privileges as his son—and he'd just pat me on the shoulder and say, "Figure it out, kid."

Sure, that made me mad. I mean, he helped everybody else, and the way I saw it, he wasn't helping me. But, looking back, maybe he *had* to be tougher with me than he was with other people. You know, he did yell at me a few times, but that's probably because whatever he was telling me was something he had told me before. My father didn't mind if someone just learned at a slow pace, but he hated it when somebody wouldn't pay attention. The worst thing in the world for him was to have to say something over and over, and I'm sure I made him do that all the time. It was probably more frustrating for him than it was for me.

Like I said: He sure taught me the hard way. But I thank him for that. Today, I'm smart enough to know *how* he was helping me, even if I couldn't see it back then.

Now, when it came to building cars, the fabricating end of things, he was more hands-on with me. That was the one area where he never left me struggling for answers. He would sit me down and really *show* me things. Sometimes he would even have someone else teach me, if he thought that was a better idea. For example, my father could weld okay, but he knew Bobby Judkins was a *great* welder, so he'd send me to Bobby if I had a question about which welding rod to use or something like that.

The first time my dad and I really worked together a lot, day in and day out, was when he drove the Manchester Sand & Gravel cars for Bill Thornton. In a lot of ways, those were our best times, especially at the start. I mean, I was actually working on race cars for a living—something that was not new to him, but completely new to me—and I was spending time with my father. We put in a lot of hours, but it was a schedule I liked: I'm not an early riser, but I don't mind working late at night, and my father was the same way. Sometimes we'd even ride to the garage together, so there was time for lots of conversation.

And it was fun, because he never stopped thinking, never lost his passion, never lost his drive to try to build something better. He ate, drank, slept, and breathed race cars, and it was neat to see that fire.

He had so much common sense, but he also had a *feel* for things. At some point early in 1977, we were building two new cars, one for me and one for him. They were pretty radical cars for that period. Anyway, we were having this little competition to see whose car would end up lighter. We were actually building them together, but each of us had a few little tricks for our own car. His philosophy was, "Figure out the absolute bare minimum you can get away with for any given part of the

Flemke never lost his zest for pushing the envelope. Here he checks out a new Race Works chassis in the late '70s. *(Mike Adaskaveg photo)*

car, and then cut that in half." And that's how he operated; I'd build a trick, light bracket for the clutch pedal on my car, and the next day he'd have a bracket that looked just like mine, but with holes drilled in it. Well, those cars had leaf-spring rear suspensions, and he made his shackles out of very light steel. That convinced me I should make mine out of aluminum. They came out really nice, and I showed 'em to my father. He said, "Those will never hold up." But I left 'em on the car and, sure enough, those things bent terribly the first night out. Oh, I heard about that later on!

People have asked me, "How would you compare yourself to your father, as a driver?" And my answer is, "I don't. But I can't compare anybody else to him, either."

In my opinion, I never became a race car driver until 1985, because that's when I started running well. I've had people suggest that maybe this was because my father was gone and now I had a lot less pressure on me, pressure from trying to please him. But it wasn't that. I always worried about making him proud, sure, but not to the degree where it messed up my driving. No, it was just a situation where by 1985 I reached a point where I wasn't scared to death of getting hurt in a race car. I was running an SK Modified for Dean Palmer, the engine builder. He used the car to R&D his motors, and I used it to R&D the chassis stuff. We went to Dick Barney and bought back a car my dad and I had built for Dick and Tony Siscone—it was actually the car Tony got burned in at Martinsville in 1982—and we went racing. Well, I knew Tony had been hurt really bad in that crash because of the fire, but I also knew that this car, *my* car, had saved his life. So I felt safer, and as I felt safer,

I went faster. I could feel my whole career change right there. We started winning some SK races, and then later I stepped up to the Tour and won races there, too.

Obviously, I wish my father were there to see that. But I choose to believe that, somewhere, he's watching. And it has helped me tremendously that other people—Pete Hamilton, Ronnie Bouchard, guys who really *knew* my father—have told me over the years, "Geez, your dad would have been proud of you."

There was a lot of pressure having the same name as my father. Well, not *exactly* the same, because we have different middle names; but I've always been a "junior" and I never wanted to dishonor his name. When I was just getting started at Riverside Park on Saturday nights, I remember being at the Spring Sizzler on Sunday and sitting right behind this guy who was laughing and saying to his friends, "Oh, you should have seen Eddie Flemke Jr. last night. He was in all kinds of trouble!" And right around that same time, some reporter wrote that he had learned two things: One, that a Ford could actually be a good racing engine, because John Rosati was winning in NASCAR North with a Ford; Two, he said he'd learned from watching me that "a name a race car driver does not make." Oh, that killed me. *Killed* me. I even talked to my dad about it, and naturally he said just the right thing: "Look, don't worry about it. You're going to be fine, and someday you'll still be racing and nobody's even going to know who that guy was." And, you know, I guess he was right, because I honestly can't remember who wrote that.

But my name, *his* name, means so much to me. There was a Spring Sizzler a few years back when I got into Mike Stefanik on a restart and he lost a few spots, but he came back, passed me for the lead and won the race. And in the victory lane interview he just tore me up, which was fine, but then he had to add something about how my father would have been ashamed. To me, that crossed the line. Say whatever you want about me, but leave my father out of it.

I look at it like, if anyone says I'm not the driver my father was, they're right. He was a million times better than I am. But guess what? He was much, much better than they are, too.

It would be easy for me to quit driving. It wouldn't be easy to walk away from the sport that has given me everything I have, but I could quit the driving part. Don't get me wrong, I want to run well, and I want people to be proud of me; I'm just not *competitive* about my driving, the way I am about the car-building. But one of the reasons I continue driving is to keep that Flemke name out there, because it *should* be out there. On the other hand, if I get to the point where I'm just a field-filler, I'll walk away, because I don't want to tarnish the name. When that day comes I'll just be a car-builder, and I'll be happy with that, because I defy anybody to say I'm not one of the best at what we do at Race Works. Not *the* best, but *one* of the best. I won't compare myself to the

Eddie Jr. has done plenty of winning on his own. He's shown after a 2004 victory at Waterford, a track with lots of Flemke history. *(Howie Hodge photo)*

great drivers, but I will put myself in the Bob Judkins category as a builder, and I think a *lot* of Bobby. And even though I never, ever heard my father compliment me, when it came to the car-building stuff I *saw* his pride, and I *felt* it. I know he approved of the work I did. And, you know, my father is still right there with me in all that. It's not that I walk around thinking what my dad would do in every situation, but I realize that when I see a problem, I sort of look at it through his eyes.

Maybe I just *missed* the mentoring part of our relationship, I don't know. Maybe I blocked it out. See, most of the time when we were kids, my father was joking around. He liked to keep things light, and had such a wonderful laugh; it's like he laughed from his soul. If he *did* try to be serious with me back then, it was usually because he was mad about something, and he might sit me down and talk for an hour. When that happened, I would listen, but I wasn't really *hearing* things. So maybe later on, when his serious talks involved life or racing, my mind just automatically shut off, like a subconscious reaction from childhood: "Uh-oh, he's yelling at me." I mean, he did spend a lot of time with me, but I just never looked at it like he was helping me the way he'd helped all these other guys.

But I do know this: The way I watched him help so many people, that definitely shaped me. Today, I love helping a driver or a car owner who really *wants* to learn, *wants* to improve. The way I look at it, if someone thinks enough of me to ask me a question, that's an honor, and I'm obligated to answer it. That gives me a great satisfaction, and I've always assumed that it did the same thing for my father. And I would be doing his memory a tremendous disservice if I didn't reach out and help these people in any way I could. He would be very disappointed in that.

"Pops was still better than 90 percent of the guys"

Remembering Steady Eddie's amazing autumn of '77

by CLYDE McLEOD

Clyde McLeod was the crew chief of Bill Thornton's Manchester Sand & Gravel #10, the car Ed Flemke drove to the two 1977 victories which, in retrospect, were the grand exclamation points near the end of his brilliant career: the 200 at Stafford on Labor Day, and the Thompson 300 two weekends later. McLeod was also a frequent volunteer crewman on the John Stygar #7 Pinto steered by Flemke to mid-'70s open-competition glory at tracks like Seekonk Speedway, the Waterford Speedbowl, and Plainville Stadium. A Connecticut native, McLeod did multiple stints with Billy Corazzo's Sherri-Cup modified team, working with drivers like Denis Giroux, Brett Bodine, and Mike McLaughlin. Having relocated to North Carolina more than a decade ago, Clyde served as a winning NASCAR Busch Series crew chief for McLaughlin, Todd Bodine, and others. Today, he helps direct the Busch Series program at Dale Earnhardt Inc.

Clyde McLeod

IN THE MIDDLE '70s, there were people who talked and wrote about how Eddie was in the middle of a slump. Well, if it was a slump, it was only by his own previous standards. I mean, go back over the record. In 1976, Eddie won twice at Stafford, won three Plainville opens, and won two Thompson features in a row, including the Icebreaker, where he beat Geoff Bodine. In the summer of '77 he had won a regular Sunday-night show at Thompson, and that's when you had Bugsy Stevens, Ronnie Bouchard, and Geoff Bodine there every week. So that's eight wins in a year and a half, which ain't bad. Like I said, that might have been a quiet period by his standards. But tell me this: Don't you think most modified drivers would have *loved* to be in that kind of a slump?

Steady Eddie tracks down Geoff Bodine in the 1976 Thompson Icebreaker, which Flemke won. *(Mike Adaskaveg photo)*

Clyde McLeod takes a look at the engine, while Pops keeps a watchful eye on things. *(Mike Adaskaveg photo)*

I definitely don't think Pops—and to me, Eddie will always be "Pops"—thought of it as a slump. Sure, we had some mechanical problems, and we had some stupid things happen at times that caused us to not run like we'd wanted to. But in his mind, Pops knew there were reasons he hadn't been winning like he once had, and those reasons were correctable. Some people probably figured it was *him*, but he knew he wasn't done yet. And after the fall of '77, *everybody* knew that, because he won the Stafford 200 on Labor Day weekend and then won the Thompson 300 just a couple weeks later.

To this day, that 300 is a race everybody talks about, because it ended under weird circumstances. The thing people point out is how lucky Eddie was that day, since the race was stopped short because of rain and we happened to be out front. Bugsy Stevens was leading it, and he pitted under a yellow. It was sprinkling at the time, and obviously

Bugsy didn't think it was going to keep raining, but it started *pouring* and that was that. Eddie was now the leader, so he was declared the winner. But, you know, luck is something that has been a part of racing forever; it's a variable that has always been there. I mean, a lot of races have been won by the guy who was running third when the two leaders crashed out, and a lot of races have been won because the heavens opened up at the right time. I'm sure Eddie Flemke lost a bunch of races over the years when his luck had gone the other way, you know?

Besides, the thing a lot of people don't remember is that for most of that day, we'd had *bad* luck. Early on, the car was running fast, and Pops was just pacing himself. It was classic Flemke, running along and happy with his car but not wanting to wear his shit out. Then we had two unscheduled pit stops—one for a power steering pump that was leaking and got us black-flagged, and the other one for a flat tire—and we had to play catch-up. And that was a *tough* thing. One time the race restarted with Eddie up front, but we were actually running at the tail end of the lead lap; Ronnie Bouchard was leading, and he restarted right behind us. Ronnie had won the pole, so he was obviously fast, and we were really concerned about that because we didn't want to lose that lap. But Eddie drove away from him. Now, Ronnie and Eddie obviously had a personal connection, because Ronnie was dating Eddie's daughter, Paula. But Ronnie wasn't about to do him any favors by *letting* him stay on the lead lap; I mean, Ronnie had raced with Pops enough to know that you didn't want to give that guy a second chance. So Ronnie definitely went after him, but at that stage Eddie was just faster.

So, you know, people can talk about the good luck we had at the end, because it was like we came out of nowhere, but it was only bad luck that put us back there in the first place. We definitely had a car that could have run with those guys all day if we hadn't had all that trouble.

In the 1977 Thompson 300, Flemke pitted with power steering woes and again with a flat tire, but came back to win the rain-shortened race. After a wet Victory Lane moment with owner Bill Thornton, the team headed off to celebrate. *(Mike Adaskaveg photos)*

Now, in the 200 at Stafford, we didn't *need* any luck. We had the best car there, and we definitely had the right driver. Eddie was good anywhere he went, but he really liked Stafford. That place was always considered a real driver's track because it was a little bit challenging, and I think that's why he enjoyed it so much. I watched him do some funny things to a lot of really good drivers there; it's like he wasn't just driving his own car, he was driving *their* cars, too. He just felt totally comfortable at Stafford, and it showed.

The other thing we had going for us that day was that, for some reason, Pops *really* wanted to win that race. Back then, everybody ran a zillion races, because the modifieds were basically the weekly division everywhere. That Labor Day weekend, we ran a regular weekly show at Stafford on Friday night, and we finished third behind Ronnie and Geoff. On Saturday, we went up to Oswego and ran sixth in the Bud 200. On Sunday, there was a regular show at Thompson and I figured we'd go there, but Eddie said no. He wanted to stay in the shop in Manchester and work all day to get that car *perfect* for the Stafford race on Monday. I'll bet we worked until one or two o'clock in the morning, and he actually had me go through the valves on the engine *four times*. Every time I'd do it, he'd be quizzing me: "Was that a *tight* 18/1000ths or a *loose* 18/1000ths?" He wanted that gauge to have just the right tug.

Flemke passes Geoff Bodine for the lead in the 200 at Stafford on Labor Day, 1977. He never did give it back. *(Mike Adaskaveg photo)*

And, geez, he was fast that day. We passed Richie Evans to get second, and Geoff Bodine to get the lead. Today, when you think back to modified racing in the late '70s, the first two guys who come to mind are probably Richie and Geoff, because they were winning everything. Wherever you went, any track you could name, they'd be up front. Well, in that 200 at Stafford, Eddie went by *both* of 'em.

It's funny, but once he got by those guys he pulled away a little bit, but not much. I asked him about that later, and he said, "Aw, I was just riding. I had some more left if they wanted to make a run at me." That was his style, of course: Don't show 'em everything you've got.

I remember a lot of things about that September. Most of all, I remember how happy Eddie was. At Thompson, he was not only thrilled by the win, but he just seemed to be in one of his really good moods, a *light* mood. He was certainly not a partying guy, but he even went up to the Clubhouse, which he almost never did. I'll bet Don Hoenig and the staff probably passed out when Eddie walked in! But Bill Thornton wanted to celebrate with a dinner and a drink, and Eddie went along with that. He just *enjoyed* himself.

I think he really felt that with those two wins, he had accomplished something special. He was used to winning races, because he'd done that forever, but very few people gave him much of a chance to win those two big events at that stage in his career. Don't forget, there were a lot of really good drivers at the top of their games then—Richie, Ronnie, Bodine—and most of them were a lot younger than Pops, who was, what, 47 years old? At the same time, so many of the guys who were his own age group had been struggling: Leo Cleary, Freddy Schulz, Fats Caruso. Even Bugsy, who was really fast in '77, had been through a couple of tough years. So you'd hear things, and read things in the racing papers, about these guys being over the hill, Eddie included. I know Eddie heard and read that stuff, and I think it only made him more determined. He really wanted to show that he could run with that hot group, that he could still get the job done.

When he won those races, I think he took some real satisfaction from proving the critics wrong. I mean, even if you wanted to say he got lucky at Thompson, you couldn't deny that he earned the win at Stafford. He was better than the best. Yes, we had a really good car, but he also out-drove everybody there. And, you know, not only was he able to shut the critics up, he was also sending a message to those younger

Steady Eddie roars toward the Stafford checkers, waving to the crowd, as a beaten Bodine follows. *(Mike Adaskaveg photo)*

After his big Stafford score in '77, Flemke was mobbed by well-wishers. Visible are car owner Bill Thornton and son Eddie Jr. *(Mike Adaskaveg photo)*

drivers: "Guys, you're *lucky* I'm 47! If I was your age, I'd be kicking your asses for a long time yet."

I'm sure that in his later years, yeah, maybe Eddie had slowed down a little bit, because every driver does. But he also had a few things happen that maybe made it *look* like he had slowed down.

Don't forget, this was a guy who was basically playing hurt. Eddie always had kind of a bad back, but then he had those two big wrecks in 1974 and '75. His Stafford wreck with the Mystic Missile was a really serious deal. I mean, that's the kind of injury that can really *scare* you. He'd been hurt before—broken bones and stuff like that—but I think this was the first time he'd had an injury that could have ended his career. And the wreck at Star was another bad one. He was driving John Stygar's car, and John and I ran over to where they were getting him out of the car. I remember saying, "Eddie, are you all right?" He said, "I don't think so." They put him in the ambulance and took him to the hospital, and of course he had hurt his back again.

Now, when hurt your back that badly, twice, in that short a time, that's a tough deal. From that point on, you could see that it really bothered him just to get in and out of the car, and I remember him walking around kinda stiff after the races. Like I said, he was playing hurt, and when you get up into your 40s, playing hurt ain't so easy. So that definitely didn't work in his favor.

Flemke and McLeod in conference, 1977. *(Mike Adaskaveg photo)*

On top of that, Pops was stubborn about so many things. I mean, once he made up his mind about something, he could be the most stubborn sonofabitch on two feet. That was the German in him, I'm sure. When he was driving for Bill Thornton, he could have gone out and bought a car, or bought a couple of cars, just picked whatever was the hottest chassis at the time. We had run a Chassis Dynamics car in 1976 and done pretty well, and at the time guys like Rollie Lindblad and Richie Evans and Maynard Troyer were starting to build cars, so there were plenty to choose from. But Pops didn't want to do that; he wanted to build his own car. I'm sure that was his way of saying, "Hey, I outsmarted 'em back then, and I can outsmart 'em today."

He and Little Eddie had the car drawn out. The chassis rails were made out of 2.5 inch square tubing, instead of 2x3 or 2x4, like everybody else was using. And they wanted to have the rails bent, instead of cut and welded in sections like everybody else did. Eddie had learned about a chassis company in Chicago, Boyce Trackburner, that built late model cars and could bend tubing that way. I remember him and Kenny

Bouchard—not the driver, but "Southington Kenny," who worked with Pops and Little Eddie for years—borrowing my pickup truck and driving all the way out to Chicago to get the frame rails bent. It was a really neat design, with everything small and very low, because Eddie, with a lot of input from Pete Hamilton, had really gotten into the idea of keeping the center of mass down low.

Well, right away NASCAR jacked around with him. They didn't like the frame, even though it was legal according to the rulebook. He had to fight with those guys for a long time just to be able to run the thing, so early that season he was racing the old Chassis Dynamics car and fighting with NASCAR on the phone all week. That was definitely a distraction. As I remember, we didn't start running the new car until late spring. At that point, we had a new car that was *completely* different from what everybody else was running, and Eddie was trying to develop it and race it at the same time, which can be kind of a hit-or-miss thing. The car ended up being really good—we won a race at Thompson that summer, and then of course we won those two big races that fall—but first Pops and Eddie Jr. had to get it figured out. So, yeah, that probably cost him a few wins.

And the other thing that went against Eddie was the fact that he was old-fashioned about spending money. He was the kind of person who really looked after the car owner's money, and he did everything he could to keep the cost down for Bill Thornton. That was a nice thing to do, but it hurt us in terms of performance because, in that period, things were changing. The big bucks were really starting to come into modified racing. You had Geoff Bodine driving for Dick Armstrong; you had Ronnie Bouchard in Marvin Rifchin's car; and you had Richie Evans sponsored by Gene DeWitt. Those guys had great motors and great *spare* motors, and they didn't think twice about putting on new tires. If they could go a half a tenth quicker, they'd put on new rubber, no questions asked. All they thought about was winning that race. Eddie, on the other hand, would look at the purse and decide it wasn't worth it to put on two or three new tires just to try to win a regular weekly show. Naturally, Geoff and Ronnie and Richie would finish up front, and maybe Pops would be third or fourth. He would take a lot of pride in the fact that he had saved some money and still finished good, but when you look at it, maybe some of those thirds and fourths could have been wins with a couple new tires on the car. So in trying so hard to watch out for Bill's pocketbook, he gave up a lot.

It was worse, of course, after Thornton got out of racing, and Pops and Eddie Jr. ran their own stuff for a couple years. I wasn't working with him by then, but we were still friends and I paid close attention to what those guys did. If you look at what they had to work with versus what Richie and Ronnie had, they ran good, but now we were in an era when you couldn't win too much without the big money. It always

Flemke chases Stan Greger in a 100-lap open-competition show at Plainville Stadium. Yes, Flemke won. *(Mike Adaskaveg photo)*

bothered me to think that the fans who were just coming into the sport at that time never got to see what Eddie Flemke could do. If you saw that man in his prime, it was sad to see him not winning anymore. I always felt bad about that.

But you know what? I honestly believed he was still better than 90 percent of the drivers he raced with, and just as good as the rest. If he was working with stuff that was even close to what the next guy had, Eddie was going to be tough. When he was *on*, he was *on*, whether he was 25 or 35 or 45 years old.

I can remember him driving one-handed at Plainville Stadium, and winning that way more than once. I'm talking about those 100-lap open-comp shows Plainville used to run, so Pops was doing this against all the Plainville regulars—Dave Alkas, Reggie Ruggiero, Stan Greger, Ronnie Rocco—plus a lot of the top guys from Riverside Park and Waterford. Now, Plainville was a tough track, a flat little bullring where passing was really hard. You couldn't be off your game and win there, and Eddie made it look easy, lapping cars and waving to the crowd at the same time.

Hell, I remember being at Martinsville with Thornton's car when they actually chewed Eddie out for driving one-handed in practice. The NASCAR official came over to me and said, "You tell your driver to keep both hands on the wheel." I could not believe it. I mean, here's a guy who has won hundreds of races, and you want me to tell him what to do out there? But the official said, "*Both hands.*" Well, that was all Eddie needed to hear. He went down the front straightaway a couple laps later, knowing they were watching him, with *no* hands on the wheel, lighting a cigarette. He held the steering wheel with his knee, and had a cigarette in one hand and a lighter in the other. That was his way of saying, "How 'bout this, boys?" Of course, they went nuts and black-flagged him. I'll never forget that.

Eddie was just *so* into racing, always thinking, always one step ahead. I remember him coming out of the pit gate at Plainville before a big open show, and doing 360s—a couple of donuts—as everybody was getting lined up. The crowd went crazy, because he was the big local hero and they thought he was hot-dogging it, but what he was doing was warming up those rear tires. Smart move. He won the feature.

Pops could make a race car do things you didn't believe it could do. He'd figure out a way to make it work, no matter what. You know, when you watch the Cup races today on TV, you hear all this talk about how the best guys are smart enough to search out a line where their cars will work. Well, that was Eddie, even 30 years ago. He was smart enough to say, "Well, I can't pit to adjust this thing, because the race is too short. Maybe if I just move up a little, it'll handle better." He was *deadly* at that.

I loved working with him. He'd be hard on us, yeah. I mean, he was on my ass a *lot*, pushing me. But when the job got done, he was also very good about remembering to pat you on the back. There were times when maybe we'd crashed or blown a motor, and we really had to thrash to get to the next race. But once that race ended and we had done well, he'd smile and say, "How about that? We really pulled off some shit today, didn't we?" He was proud of the times we could all see that our hard work had paid off.

And he was the kind of guy who would watch over the flock, so to speak. He didn't want his guys to stray too far off track, so he'd really look after us. Say we were at Martinsville, and he heard we were out partying; he'd say, "Hey, that's not why we're down here." The next night, he'd come up with something for us to work on back at the motel because he didn't want us going out and getting in trouble. That was pretty sharp of him, because there were a few times when we'd wander over to the Dutch Inn and get hooked up with Richie Evans or Charlie Jarzombek, and then we usually *did* get in trouble. So Eddie kind of kept us all on good behavior. You also ended up learning a lot of family values from him, because there always someone with him—Carolyn, or Paula, or Little Eddie, or Laurie—and you saw the way he looked after them. And, really, if you worked with Pops, he treated *you* like family, too. That might be something good, like buying your dinner just like he'd buy dinner for his kids, or it might be bad, like reprimanding you the same way he'd reprimand his own son or daughter.

You know, I think about that man all the time. I have a little key chain with Eddie's name on it—it was given out as a memorial after he died—and I keep it in a drawer at home, a drawer I have to go into every day. I'll see that key chain, and I'll smile and think about all those good times.

I miss him, boy. He was The Master.

"Geez, it was a great relationship"

An old friend helps launch a new business

by DICK BARNEY

Dick Barney has seen it all in asphalt modified racing, having been around for—actually, having helped pioneer—the evolution of those cars from jalopies to the sleek machines seen today. Barney's ride, whether carrying his famous #14 or the more recent #41, has always been a hot seat. In the coupe days, it attracted stars like Wally Dallenbach, Richie Massing, and Bob Rossell; in the Pinto/Cavalier era, Barney has employed Reggie Ruggiero, Ken Wooley, and most notably Tony Siscone, who drove the Barney car to victory at Martinsville in 1984 and the Flemington Race of Champions ten years later. Ironically, some of Barney's best days came with a driver you may have never heard of. That's because the mega-talented David Haupt usually raced under the nom de guerre of Joe Kelly, who hustled the Barney coupes to key scores at places like Old Bridge and Thompson.

Dick Barney

I'M NOT SURE if we were the very first customers Eddie and Eddie Jr. had at Race Works, but we were definitely *one* of the first. What happened was, Eddie had come to race in the Turkey Derby at Wall Stadium at the end of 1978. It was very cold that weekend, so he asked if he could keep his car at my shop overnight. I was happy to do that for him, and we were close by anyway, so it really worked out. Well, while the car was sitting here, I looked it over closely—which was fine with him—and I really liked it. I was very impressed.

That winter, I happened to call Eddie because I was looking for a new modified, or actually a used one. I had been running a Pinto I'd bought from Richie Evans in 1976, and Richie had raced it for a while

himself before that, so I figured it was time for a replacement. Anyway, I called Eddie, and I said, "Hey, if you hear of a good, solid, used modified up your way, please let me know." He said he'd do that, and that was basically the whole conversation. A week later, Eddie called back and said, "You know, we can build you a car." I told him I wasn't in the market for a new car, and I didn't want to spend too much, and Eddie said, "Dick, I haven't even told you how much we'd charge you!" He went on to tell me how he and Junior were planning on getting into the car-building business, and how we could work something out.

Well, it worked out, all right. We won lots of races together.

Of course, by then I had known Eddie for years. The first time I remember us ever talking was at Thompson Speedway, back in 1965. They used to run these special programs that were a big deal, twin 50-lap features for modifieds. They paid, as I recall, $500 to win each. That was good money in those days, but the best part was that they offered a $500 bonus for winning both races. We went up there with Joe Kelly driving, and we just killed 'em. Joe won the first feature by a mile, and he beat 'em even worse in the second race. Naturally, some of the other teams made a lot of noise about that. They weren't happy, that's for sure.

Kelly soars around Thompson in 1965, winning twin 50-lap features in the Barney #14 and riling up many of the locals. *(Howie Hodge photo)*

Well, we went to get paid, and they only handed me $1,000. I questioned that, and they gave me some kind of bull that we weren't eligible for the $500 bonus because I wasn't one of the regulars, or something crazy like that. I argued, but it didn't do me any good. So I said, "Well, what about tow money? We came a long way!" They handed me 50 cents—that's right, *50 cents*—and said, "That should get you out of the state." I could see I was getting nowhere with these guys, so I took my 50 cents and my thousand bucks and I got ready to leave.

Right about then, Eddie Flemke walked up. He said, "I want to tell you two things. First, I'm not with those guys. What they're doing to you is wrong. Second, you just showed us all we've got a lot of work to do."

That was the start of our relationship, and we became good friends after that. He ran his circuit and we ran ours, but we'd see each other at places like Martinsville, or maybe a special show at a track like Beltsville, Maryland. Of course, I had known Eddie's name for years, and I had raced with him many times. He used to come down to Old Bridge a lot, and I remember racing against him once at Vineland, too.

I'll tell you what I recall about Eddie in those Old Bridge days: I was ahead of the local New Jersey guys, in terms of equipment—I had torsion-bar suspension and disc brakes, all the latest stuff—but one day Eddie showed up with this little blue coupe with a gold "dollar-sign" on the door, and I knew right away it was the lightest race car I had ever seen. I mean, it hardly had any hubs or rotors, and there was nothing on that car that wasn't necessary. I was pretty obsessed with keeping the weight down myself, but you could see that this coupe of Eddie's was as light as a feather. We had some good races together in that period, and later on. He was always a guy to contend with, I'll tell you that. If you beat Eddie Flemke, you knew you'd done your homework.

You know, I always had good drivers. In the days we're talking about, I had Kelly, I had Wally Dallenbach, I had Kelly again, I had Bob Rossell, and I had Richie Massing. Good drivers, all of them.

People ask me all the time how many races my cars have won, but I really have no idea. To be honest, that stuff doesn't interest me. I'm more interested in the next race—you know, what springs I'm going to run, stuff like that—than I am in thinking about the old days. I get these guys who want to talk about the coupes and the fuel injectors, and I tell 'em, "Man, that was yesterday."

Now, talking about a guy like Eddie, that's different. That's stuff you *want* to remember.

What made Eddie such a good driver was that he was very smart about looking at the whole situation. He knew everything there was to know about his car, about the race track, about the other drivers, about *everything*. He was very calculating, and he had everything figured out. He was very talented, yes, but he was also thinking all the time. He wasn't out there just sliding around.

Toward the end of the 1960s and into the '70s, we went through a period when we didn't see each other as much. That lasted maybe 10 years. What happened was, he was sticking closer to home because the New England scene was picking up, and we were doing our own thing here in New Jersey. But, you know, the friendship was still there.

Part of that, I think, was because we had similar interests. I think Eddie and I both liked to quietly do our own thing; we weren't there for the glory, just to win races if we could. We were both really into the *cars*, and trying to make them go fast. I built my own cars and he built his own cars, and I think each of us had his own ideas. We both had cars that were different from everybody else's, if you know what I mean.

Now, when I say I built my own cars, I mean the *whole* car, engines and everything. Unfortunately, the rules in modified racing got to the point where you could use less and less of your own ideas. Today, they've *really* got us confined, but even in the '70s we were starting to see that. I eventually decided that if all you could build in terms of the chassis was something similar to what the next guy had, it was easier to just go out and buy a car. So in 1976, I bought that Pinto from Evans. I had gotten pretty friendly with Richie; I'd known him since the first

Tony Siscone describes the handling of the Barney modified at Thompson, as Flemke and fellow Race Works driver Ray McTeague listen in. That's Robert Barney at the far right. *(Pete Lawlor photo)*

time he ran Martinsville, because I remember loaning him parts there. Bob Rossell drove that Pinto for us, but one week at New Egypt I remember Richie's own car broke, so he ended up driving ours. In fact, he was leading the feature when the thing overheated.

It was after Rossell that we put Tony Siscone in the car. What happened was, I wanted to run both New Egypt and Wall Stadium, and Rossell only wanted to run Wall Stadium. This was in 1978. Well, at the time my partner in the team was Hoyt Morrison, and he called Tony Siscone. I didn't even *know* Tony, so Hoyt and my son Robert called him right from my office. Tony was interested, so we ended up having him in the car at New Egypt, and Rossell in the car at Wall. In '79, Tony ended up driving for us everywhere, and that was our first year with that original Flemke car. The following year they built us another car—they had already come up with some new ideas based on what we'd all learned in '79—and that second car was *really* good. That thing won its first three races, right out of the box.

We had a really good combination going. You had Eddie's brains and Junior's capability as a fabricator; I mean, that kid has always been a very, very talented fabricator. His workmanship is unbelievable. On top of that, we had some input of our own, and, of course, Tony did a great job driving.

You know, Tony and Eddie clicked in a special way. Tony really looked up to that man. Eddie was always so willing to help, as everybody knows, and with Tony he had a guy who was still young and eager to learn, so it was a perfect match.

I've got one funny memory about that: Very early on in our relationship with Siscone, we were at New Egypt, and Eddie came down to help us. It may have been the first time he really had a chance to watch Tony drive. Well, Tony had to go to the tail end of the pack for some reason, and in coming back to the front he got a little over-aggressive. I mean, he hit just about everything on the race track. So at the end of the night, we're standing in the trailer and Eddie says, "You know, the kid is fast and he's good, but he gets into these situations where he tries too hard and ends up running into everybody." Turns out that Tony was standing a little farther back in the trailer, changing clothes, so he heard everything Eddie said. Tony was crushed. *Crushed*. He took it hard. But, you know, I think that probably did him more good than anything, because once he got over hearing it, he *thought* about it. He realized it was fine to be aggressive, but it was not fine to be out of control. So I think that ended up helping him get smoother and better. And, you know, Tony and Eddie got very close; they would always get off to the side and talk.

Back then, Eddie and Junior came to New Jersey a lot, usually with Kenny Bouchard, who worked with them forever. Like I said, we were a very early customer, and we were winning a lot of races, which sold them a few cars. In fact, pretty soon Harry Reed had one of their cars at Wall Stadium, and Tony Ferrante was another early customer, so it was good for Eddie and Junior to be down here. New Jersey was probably *the* hot area for the Race Works cars at that time. And, as far as my own relationship with Eddie, it only got better. Again, we had seen each other a lot in the old days, then not so much for a while, and now it was a regular thing. Plus, I got to know Junior very well, because a lot of the time he was the guy I'd talk to about the cars. I'm joking when I say this, but the only problems we ever had—and they weren't really problems, just discussions—came when we wanted to try something new. A lot of times, Junior and I would agree that we wanted to change something, but Eddie would fight us. Like I said, we each had our own ideas. But, geez, it was a great relationship. They'd come down to the races, and in the off-season I'd go up there to Connecticut and talk with Eddie at the shop.

We were all like family. Eddie and I both had our sons involved, and Tony Siscone was just like family to all of us; he's like a big brother to my son Robert, and like a son to me, and he was also close with Eddie and Junior.

You know, Eddie actually drove for me once. That was in the Thompson 300, in 1981. I wasn't there, so Robert was kind of running

Steady Eddie was a last minute fill-in for Siscone at the 1981 Thompson 300, his one and only drive for old pal Dick Barney. *(Pete Lawlor photo)*

That's Flemke downstairs, with Richie Evans outside in the 300. It was a short day for the Flemke/Barney team, but a day Dick Barney is grateful for. *(Howie Hodge photo, Val LeSieur Collection)*

things. What happened was, Tony had burned his leg in a race at New Egypt, and he had a big blister on it. He was going to try to run Thompson, but it was just too painful. With burns, the next day or two is always tougher than you think it's going to be. Anyway, Eddie was getting toward the end of his career, so he wasn't driving anything that weekend, and they just figured, "Let's put Eddie in there." As it turned out, they didn't end up having a good day, but I like the fact that he did drive one of our cars.

Losing Eddie was tough. *Very* tough. I remember Junior calling me with the news, and I just could not believe it. That's something you don't forget. He was such a good guy, and a good friend. But, you know, I still feel like we're connected, because we've continued to run the Race

Works cars. Junior and I have stayed close—during the week, we always talk—and I really like the way he works. He and his dad were different people, but the one thing in common is that, like his dad, Junior is always *thinking*. He's always mentally building things, engineering things. Those genes were definitely passed along from father to son, very much so. And, of course, Reggie Ruggiero has been Junior's partner at Race Works for a long time, and he came to drive for us in 2004, which has only made the relationship better. I enjoy that. I like maintaining connections that way.

I don't think we'd have accomplished what we have if we hadn't hooked up with Eddie, and then with Junior. And, you know, it was good for them, too. See, it put us ahead of everybody we were running with at Wall and New Egypt, and it definitely helped them get Race Works off the ground.

It's funny to think that maybe none of it would have happened if Eddie hadn't kept his car in my shop for that one Turkey Derby. I'm glad he did.

"I don't think he could have ever walked away from racing"

From grins to grimaces, what was and what might have been

by CAROLYN FLEMKE

Carolyn Flemke, née Goldsnider, was married to Ed Flemke from 1966 until his death in 1984. The years between were among Flemke's most productive, encompassing scores of victories in New York and New England. They were also among his busiest. At the beginning of his second marriage, Flemke was still barn-storming from track to track at an alarming pace, and at its end he was transitioning into another phase of his life, building and selling race cars with his son Eddie Jr. and enjoying a stint as an official at Connecticut's Waterford Speedbowl. While all this was going on, Carolyn was Steady Eddie's steady; she ran the household, shepherded the children—her two, his two, and their daughter Kristy—and, when possible, cheered her husband from the grandstands. These days, Carolyn lives in Bolton, CT, keeping a close and loving eye on her children and grandchildren.

Carolyn Flemke

YOU KNOW, I never once heard Eddie say, "Well, that was my last race." Even when he wasn't driving, and he was busy with other things—building cars, working as an official at Waterford, or whatever—I never heard him say he wasn't climbing into another race car. He always left that door open. If a good ride had come along in that period, I think he'd have done anything to get back in, just to have that one last good effort.

Now, whether he could have stayed with it, I'm not sure. Because, for so many years toward the end of his career, he was in a lot of pain. He had two really bad accidents, one in 1974 at Stafford and one in '75 at Star Speedway, which hurt him worse than most people realized.

Flemke rode out this scary Stafford flip aboard Bob Garbarino's Pinto in 1974. "Some of the guys were white with fear when I got out," he told writer Pete Zanardi. "I just kind of said a silent prayer of thanks." Hours later he was lying in a hospital, with doctors worried about paralysis. *(top, bottom left, Val LeSieur Collection; bottom right, Mike Adaskaveg photo)*

In the Stafford crash, he was driving the Mystic Missile and he flipped very badly. The roof was smashed completely down; in fact, Eddie always said it was a good thing he was so small, because a taller driver would have probably been badly hurt. Naturally, he didn't get treated right away, like he should have. Instead of going to the hospital to get checked out, he just *had* to come home and eat. He'd been very sore at the track, but he insisted that he was fine, so the guys brought him home. He admitted to me that he was in a lot of pain, so I said I'd take him to the emergency room at New Britain General Hospital. He said, "First, can you make me a couple peanut butter and jelly sandwiches?" He knew he might have to stay there at the hospital, and he was worried that he'd missed the evening meal. So he ate two sandwiches and had a cup of coffee, and off to the hospital we went.

I will never forget the look on the orthopedic doctor's face after that Stafford crash. Eddie was lying in the hospital bed with his legs up. The doctor showed up—he'd been off because it was Labor Day weekend, so they had to call him in especially for this—and he stood in the doorway looking very somber. Then he started talking to Eddie, and when Eddie moved his leg a bit, I saw the doctor's jaw drop. He said, "You can move your legs?" Eddie said, "Sure," and he moved them some more. And I could see on the doctor's face that he was stunned.

They took Eddie down the hall for X-rays, and the doctor said, "You don't know how I *dreaded* the ride in for this call. When they told me I was going to see a patient with this specific fractured vertebra, I just knew I'd be telling someone he was paralyzed for life. That's a terrible thing to have to do. When I walked into the room, I was hiding my hands because they were shaking. So when I saw your husband move his leg . . ."

Well, I was so relieved. But then the doctor got very serious and said, "There's no telling how much damage there is. Your husband should have been immobilized immediately. Paralysis could still set in at any time. We'll just have to wait and see. Let's give it three days."

Obviously, there never was any paralysis, but I'm sure there was a lot of damage done. I don't think Eddie ever realized what a lucky man he was, even when I told him what the doctor had said. I mean, they talked about waiting three days, but Eddie was *home* in three days! And, believe it or not, he was back racing in six weeks. The doctor had told him, "You know, I don't recommend that, because you're not fully healed and the slightest hit could badly injure you. And you may not be so lucky next time." But, of course, that didn't stop him.

Then, the next season—actually, it was 11 months later, just under a year—he had the accident at Star. After that crash, Eddie had to wear a back brace. I remember that the first one they gave him was very confining, so he went back to the orthopedic doctor and they came up with a replacement that had more mobility. He wore that brace a great deal, although most people didn't know it. He just didn't let on. If you didn't put your arm around him—or, in my case, if I didn't hug him—it was hard to know it was there. But he got to the point where he was wearing it more and more.

Of course, he did drive for several more years, and he did continue to win races. But he had gotten to the point where it physically hurt him just to climb in and out of the car. You could see the pain in his face, especially after the longer races. And he started going to a chiropractor quite a bit; he didn't like to admit that to very many people, but it was a normal thing for him to do on Mondays. He had a standing appointment there.

My dad, who thought the world of Eddie, would always talk about how it hurt him to mow the grass now that he had gotten old. He'd say, "I used to look forward to doing the lawn, but now I'm tired after an hour." Well, one day Eddie said to me, "I'm starting to understand what your father means. I used to be able to go racing all weekend, and get by with just a nap riding down the road. I can't do that anymore."

I think Eddie accepted the idea that he was at the end of his career,

Oh, my aching back! Steady Eddie grimaces in Victory Lane after the 1977 Stafford 200. Also shown, left to right, are promoter Ed Yerrington, car owner Bill Thornton, and announcer Bill Welch. (Mike Adaskaveg photo)

at least outwardly. He wasn't kicking and screaming about it. But inside, I think it tore him up.

I don't think he could have ever walked completely away from racing. No, not Eddie. He would had been involved in some way.

For example, he really enjoyed the work he did as an official. He had the respect of so many drivers, and I think he appreciated that. He enjoyed the mentoring aspect of it, I know that. And I'm sure he would have been very good in that job, the more he did it.

Even if he wasn't an official, he would certainly have continued to mentor young guys, the same way he mentored Pete Hamilton and Denny Zimmerman and so many others. He enjoyed that sort of thing very much. And it wouldn't have been just drivers; Eddie enjoyed young people in general. I remember the way so many kids—teenagers and guys in their early 20s—would visit with him at the garage, and it was really nice to see that. You know, Eddie was such a humble man. Some people who have that kind of following end up being self-centered, but he never was. He was a regular guy who would never dream of talking down to anyone, and I believe that's why those young people liked spending time with him. I think about that today, and I wish my grandsons were able to enjoy that side of Eddie.

Of course, he would definitely have stayed involved in the car-building business with Junior. He had always enjoyed building cars for himself, so that was just a natural thing to do. Although, you know, I can remember the first time he and Bill Thornton went down to Chassis Dynamics to order a car, which was Bill's idea. Eddie came home and said, "I can't *believe* we're putting that kind of money into a race car. I could build one for Bill instead." I remember him shaking his head. But he understood that things had changed, and that the days of teams building their own cars were gone. So I think he enjoyed the challenge of putting his own ideas into cars, and going into that business with his son.

The one thing I *couldn't* see him doing is just sitting around and relaxing. That just wasn't him. For example, even with all the traveling he did, he *never* wanted to go sightseeing. He used to make fun of the way I liked to stop and do things. Like, when it came time to go to Martinsville, he'd say I should take my daughter Laurie and her girlfriend Penny Kelly, and leave a week early so we could hit all the gift shops and still get there in time for the race. And I remember passing the signs for the Natural Bridge, that tourist attraction in Virginia; I mentioned that just once we ought to stop and see it, and Eddie said, "Let's not rush into this. The thing has been there for hundreds of years, and it'll be there for hundreds more."

No, nothing interested him if there wasn't racing involved. I used to point out how nice it would be to go to Hawaii someday, and he'd say, "But there's no race track there!" Like I said, everything was racing.

He did often talk about one day buying a motorhome and maybe taking it around to the Cup races. Back then, Ronnie Bouchard was still racing, so this would be a good way to keep up with Ronnie and Paula, and of course Eddie knew a lot of the other drivers and mechanics in the Cup series, so he thought that would be fun. He used to say, "As long as we're at the race track by Friday, we can do whatever *you* want to do from Monday through Thursday." Even then, I'm sure all our trips would have consisted of me seeing the sights, and Eddie reading the racing papers in the motorhome. But, you know, that would have been an enjoyable thing for us to do. Eddie thought that would be a wonderful life, just traveling around and going to races.

And, really, why not? His whole *life* had been racing. I understood that from the day we met. In fact, I understood that even before we met.

The story of how we got together is a strange one, because up until we met I *despised* him. See, I had been around racing as a fan for several years. I used to go to Cherry Park with my dad and my brother; in fact, I still remember the frilly dress and patent leather shoes I wore the very first time I went there. Later on, we would go to Riverside Park, where I was a big fan of Buddy Krebs. Buddy drove for Joe Olender, who was my first husband's uncle, and through Joe we got to know Buddy. Well, in those days at Riverside, if Buddy Krebs didn't win, Eddie Flemke did, and sometimes they'd even tangle. So Eddie was not someone I cared for very much. One night, my girlfriend and I actually went out to the parking lot, took out our lipstick, and wrote a lot of not-very-nice things all over the windows of Eddie's street car!

In 1961, I was briefly introduced to him in the infield at Daytona by a friend of mine named Bobby Bennett. Bobby had lived in Manchester, and he was friendly with Don Ponticelli, who owned the "dollar-sign" car. Bobby kept saying, "Carolyn, I really think you should get to know Eddie," and I was constantly telling him, "Look, I'm not interested!" I used to tell Bobby that the only reason he wanted to fix us up was so I could talk Eddie into driving for Donnie. Bobby said, "No, no, I think you'd really like him."

Finally, a bunch of us got together one night, and Bobby brought Eddie along. And you know, once we actually got to know each other, we hit it off right away. This had to be late in 1961. I said to myself, "You know, he's not such a bad guy." We didn't date very much at first, but I would see him at the track, and sometimes he'd say, "Come on, ride to the races with me." Back in the days when Stafford was dirt, he would race there occasionally, and I remember him calling to say, "Hey, I've got a ride this weekend at Stafford. If you want to go, meet me at the rest stop on Interstate 84." I was living with my parents in Bolton at the time, and they thought that was the funniest thing, the two of us meeting at the rest stop. But, see, Eddie didn't know Bolton, and he knew he couldn't find his way to where I lived. So I'd shoot over there, jump in the car with Eddie, and off we'd go.

Stepdaughter Laurie Olender (now Laurie Parsons) was almost always on hand when Pops went to work. Here, it's birthday time! *(Mike Adaskaveg photo)*

He was racing so much in those days that sometimes I wonder how the relationship developed. But we talked a *lot* on the phone, I remember that. And in the off-season, we'd spend a lot of time together with his family and mine. Things went on like that for a long time. I mean, it was five years before we married in 1966.

We both brought children to the marriage. My kids, Laurie and Tim, were born in 1957 and '58, so they were very close in age to Paula and Junior. Kristy, of course, came along later, in 1968. I know that sometimes those kinds of mixed households are difficult, but it wasn't in our case. People have asked me over the years, "How did you make it work?" And the answer is: I don't know, but it *did* work. What made it easier was that the kids just seemed to get along naturally. Eddie and I used to talk about the fact that Laurie and Junior were always together, and so were Paula and Tim. If they played a game, for example, it was Paula and Timmy against Laurie and Junior, so it was my oldest and Eddie's youngest, and then his oldest and my youngest. They stayed close that way for so many years; Laurie went to the races with Junior for a long time, and I remember Paula and Tim once having a whipped cream fight at one of our holiday dinners when they were in their teens. So I would give all the credit for this to the kids, because they *made* it work.

Cake-cutting time at the wedding of Eddie and Carolyn Flemke. Note that Eddie, never one for pomp and ceremony, didn't bother to put down his cigarette! *(Marge Dombrowski Collection)*

For most of our marriage we lived in Southington, first on River Street and later on Loper Street, and those were great days. Eddie and I used to laugh about our "business arrangement." See, I understood, and he *knew* I understood, that racing came first in his life, and it always would. It wasn't that he didn't love me; I *knew* there was love there. But racing had to be first if he was going to be successful. So we had this business arrangement: the garage and the race cars were *his* thing, while the house and the kids were *my* thing. As anyone who knew Eddie will tell you, he was an old-fashioned man. He liked the idea of his wife being at home, looking after the kids and the house, so I was a home-maker.

He was very good at separating the racing side and the home side. Although, there was one race at Thompson when Eddie had a good chance to win and then ran out of gas or something right at the end. I remember telling the kids that they needed to behave on the way home, because their father was going to be in a bad mood. Sure enough, he was very, very quiet, didn't say a word. Then, when we got home, he went outside, fired up the lawn mower and did the whole yard. And I mean the *whole* yard, because when I looked out the window he was taking that mower right through my flower bed! I'm sure he was still thinking about the race, and had no idea what he had just done. And you know something? I didn't say a thing.

But, really, we both respected where the other stood, and we respected the fact that each of us needed to devote our time to different things. I never interfered with his racing, and he never interfered with the way

Baby daughter Kristy put a spring back in Eddie's step. They're pictured together in 1973. *(Mike Adaskaveg photo)*

I ran the house. But he did make one request: After he tripped and fell one night when he got in very late, he said, "The next time you move the furniture around, please call and let me know."

He was still doing a lot of traveling when we were married—just about every weekend, he was racing in New York—but as we got into the '70s most of his racing was closer to home. Instead of going out to, say, Albany-Saratoga and Utica-Rome, it was more like Stafford and Thompson. That was nice.

Now, that didn't mean Eddie was home every night for dinner, or anything like that. He still had things to do to get ready for whatever racing he was doing that weekend. But after Kristy was born, I could see him trying to spend more time at home, to be with her. He knew he had missed out on so much during those "growing up" years with Paula and Junior, so he really enjoyed that time with Kristy. In fact, it got to be pretty difficult, in terms of his timing; I would put Kristy to bed, and he'd come in not long after that. And it's so funny, but she could hear that car pull into the yard, and by the time he was in the door she'd be standing up in the crib, crying, "Dada!" He'd get her up, and the two of them would sit and watch TV together. I can still picture him in that recliner, happy, with little Kristy sitting right next to him. And sometimes they'd even fall asleep together there.

But even though he was home more, and even though he was racing less, his focus hadn't changed. And it never did. Racing was always so important to him. For example, when he was driving for Bill Thornton and Manchester Sand & Gravel, we moved to Manchester; that must have been in 1978. I think he just got tired of getting home so late, because after working until midnight or later at the garage, he had a pretty good drive back to Southington. Then, by the time he was up in the morning, Kristy had already gone to school, so he wasn't seeing her as much as he wanted. Anyway, in that period we discussed what he might do if and when Bill decided to get out of racing; I'm pretty sure Eddie knew it was coming to an end, even before it did. But when we sold our house in Southington, we decided that we weren't going to buy another home. Instead, we'd set aside that money so it would be there if he wanted to run his own car. I'm not sure *why* he wanted to do that at that point in his career, but he did, and I went along with it. We rented a house—it belonged to my brother, who had gotten married and moved—and he and Junior went racing together. That's what made Eddie happy, so that's what we did.

You know, Eddie would have turned 76 years old this past summer, and on his birthday Kristy said it was hard for her to imagine her father at that age. I'm sure that's true for her, because she was still so young,

Another birthday, this time celebrated by a small handful of the early-'80s regulars at the Flemke shop in East Hartford, CT. Watching Eddie slice the cake are, left to right, Kevin Hodge, a barely visible Ray McTeague, Eddie Jr., Davey Orcutt, Jeff Zarrella, Wally Dallenbach Jr., Don McClure, and Eddie Stepensky. *(Pete Lawlor photo)*

Carolyn Flemke and daughter Kristy Boland look over some of the family's scrapbooks in early 2007. *(Mike Adaskaveg photo)*

just a teenager, when he passed away. But I can see it very well. For one thing, I remember his father, Jake, and to me Eddie was very much like his dad; they were both so good at telling stories. And, you know, his father had also led an adventurous life—he'd raced motorcycles, and ridden a motorcycle across country—so they had that in common. I remember, from my earliest days with Eddie, the way the guys would sit around his dad's garage and listen to Jake tell stories. So when I think of Eddie being that age, that's the picture I have: He's at the garage, just like always, and he's telling stories, just like always, only now he's an older version of the same man.

You know, Eddie was a private man, but at the same time he was an open book. He was exactly what he seemed to be. I'm not sure there's anything I know about him that his friends didn't know, too. He was simply a real *person*. No pretense, nothing phony. You don't find enough people like that.

PART FIVE

Legacy

Carolyn Flemke says, "Let me tell you what has stayed with me. We were talking one day about what we might do in our later years, and Eddie said, 'You know, I don't think I'll have to deal with that.' I asked him what he meant, and he said, very seriously, 'I don't think I'm going to be around for all that getting-old stuff.'"

Sadly, Ed Flemke, who had built his career and his reputation on his ability to look down the road, was right one last time.

The year 1984 opened as it always had for Steady Eddie. He had traveled south for Speedweeks, visiting his sister Betty and her husband Van, and of course he had renewed acquaintances at both Daytona and New Smyrna. When he returned home to Connecticut in late February, racing in New England was still a month away: Thompson's Icebreaker and the weekly opener at Riverside Park were both set for the weekend of March 31-April 1.

But it was hardly a static time for Flemke. There were cars to finish up at Race Works, there were always folks stopping by to chat, there were officiating jobs—maybe at the Speedbowl, maybe elsewhere—to consider.

Who knew that there would also be snow to plow? And who knew that this would mean anything?

A rare spring snowstorm blew across the Northeast in the final week of March. For the promoters at Thompson and Riverside, this was a logistical headache; the Icebreaker was postponed, but the Saturday-night show at the Park was still a go. And Flemke? Well, he probably saw the snow as something of a bonus. Eddie Jr. had things handled at the chassis shop, and so this weird weather provided Pops with an opportunity to pick up a little extra cash doing some plowing. To Flemke, who always looked at every angle, this unexpected storm was no different than, say, a Wednesday-night open show at Plainville in the 1970s: just a quick way to pocket some side money.

So he climbed into a friend's truck on Thursday, March 29th, and a long day plowing became a long night plowing. Somewhere around midnight, he stopped home for a coffee, and Fate caught him there.

In the happy times: Papa Ed and little Kristy, 1972. *(Mike Adaskaveg photo)*

Ed Flemke had crawled out of wrecked cars and burning cars. He had flipped over the fence at Southside, gotten thumped around in the biggest Daytona crash ever, and pounded walls at a dozen tracks. He had broken legs at Candlelight Stadium and Albany-Saratoga, and fractured vertebrae at Stafford and Star. Nothing ever hurt him *too* badly. He had traveled thousands of miles in the course of winning hundreds of races. Nothing ever wore him down *too* far. But in the earliest minutes of Friday morning, March 30th, a massive heart attack took him in, of all places, his very own driveway. A newspaper account said he was "found slumped inside the cab of a truck about 12:15 A.M." It was Carolyn Flemke who discovered her stricken husband.

Steady Eddie Flemke was dead at 53.

"He was the baby of our family," says sister Betty Vanesse, "yet he was the first to go."

It goes without saying that the news devastated those closest to Flemke. It also hit like a thud in his favorite sport. Phone calls ricocheted from homes to garages to track offices. Reporters gently pressed Eddie's peers for their thoughts. Leo Cleary, who went back 25 years with Flemke, told writer Matt Buckler, "He won more races on less money than anyone ever has. He was a sly fox, the slyest fox I ever saw."

Less than 48 hours after Flemke's passing, the Riverside season opened as planned. All night long, the pit area was a chilly outdoor version of an

Seymour the Stafford Clown listens in to Flemke and Leo Cleary, who remembered Steady Eddie as "the slyest fox I ever knew." *(Mike Adaskaveg photo)*

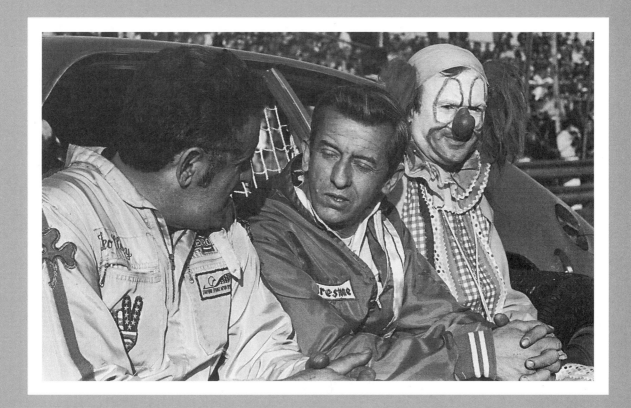

Irish wake, with one Flemke story leading into another. One great line came from Danny Bennett, manning the tire truck for Hoosier distributor Bobby Summers; Bennett said, "Eddie wasn't 53 years old, he was 106. Eddie got 120 seconds out of every minute."

When the public address system called for a moment of silence, the Riverside Park Speedway—a place which gave Flemke some of his first great victories, and in the end gave him his last—fell completely, respectfully quiet. Then the opening modified feature of the New England season was won by Richie Evans, who solemnly dedicated the victory to his old comrade.

The memorial service brought hundreds of mourners to Manchester. "I couldn't believe all the flowers," sister Marge Dombrowski recalls. "They came from everywhere." A touching eulogy was read by Ben Dodge Jr., then one of New England racing's rising promotional minds and a young man whose enthusiasm Flemke admired.

In the days and weeks to come, more tributes followed. *Speedway Scene*, still in its glory days as the tabloid bible of racing in the Northeast, printed a four-page photo spread devoted to Flemke, and columnists in several trade papers reminisced about The Boss. At Stafford, the Spring Sizzler—a race forever connected with Flemke because of his performances in its first two editions—was run in his memory, with Eddie's widow and children presenting the winner's trophy. And as temperatures rose and other tracks opened across the Northeast, racers and fans tipped their hats in various ways.

Then everyone sort of did what Eddie would have wanted them to do. They got on with things. Happily, while they've been getting on with things in the 20-odd years since, those who appreciated the man have not let him slip too far from view.

Flemke is enshrined in the National Auto Racing Hall of Fame; the New York State Stock Car Association Hall of Fame; the New England Auto Racers Hall of Fame; and the New Britain Sports Hall of Fame. And should you ever want to hear a round of Flemke tales, it's easy to get one started. Just sidle up to Bob Judkins, George Lombardo, Junie Donlavey, or anyone who shared a pit area with the guy.

You might be caught off guard by the humility of Bugsy Stevens, who declares, "People talk about the way Eddie helped guys like Pete Hamilton and Denny Zimmerman, but he was one of *my* professors, too. Many times, Eddie took me aside and talked to me, and not just in my early days. That went on right up into the '80s."

You might be touched by the sincerity of his hometown pal Bobby Story, who, despite having run a successful business for decades, says, "I'm 65 years old, but I still think of the time I spent with Eddie as the best days of my life."

Or you might be floored by the emotion of award-winning sportswriter and ex-Star Speedway promoter Russ Conway. In the aftermath of

the 1978 head injury that ended the career of the great Massachusetts racer Ollie Silva, Conway took it upon himself to become Silva's *de facto* caretaker. It was in that capacity that Conway sat beside his friend in the bleacher seats at Daytona the following February. To term it a bleak period in Ollie Silva's life would not be overstating things. "Well, along comes Eddie Flemke, and he spots Ollie," says Russ. "He comes right up and sits down. Pretty soon they're telling stories about all these different races, and Eddie's talking about the time Ollie lapped the field twice in a 100-lapper at Waterford. Oh, man, Ollie lit right up. It was a beautiful day, and I remember Eddie saying, 'Ollie, how lucky can we be? We're down here in the sun, and back home they're freezing their butts off.' I'm not sure how long Eddie sat there; it was probably damn close to an hour. Now, Eddie didn't have to do that, but I think he knew how important it was to Ollie. And I never, ever will forget what he did that afternoon."

Even those who knew Flemke only from a distance seem ever eager to talk about him. In the late 1980s, a short-term stint in IMSA sports car racing brought his son to a street circuit in Miami. "Before the race, this husband and wife came up to me," Eddie Jr. says. "They asked if I was the son of this man Ed Flemke, a guy they had watched years earlier, going back to the '50s. I said, 'Absolutely.' I guess they lived in the Miami area, but they were originally from New England. They had looked at the roster and saw two words—'Flemke' and 'Connecticut'—so they bought pad-

Eddie races alongside Richie Evans, who said upon Flemke's death, "There will never be another one like him." *(Mike Adaskaveg photo)*

To Steady Eddie this was life: a full grandstand, an open seat, and a modified race about to start. *(Mike Adaskaveg photo)*

dock passes and sought me out, just to tell me how much they enjoyed watching my father race."

It is no small trick to have that kind of a lasting impact on people, but Flemke managed it. Richie Evans said, "There will never be another one like him." True enough.

No, he didn't stick around for all that getting-old stuff. But in a life spent around race cars, race tracks, and race drivers, Steady Eddie left plenty of fingerprints behind.

"His sphere of influence was gigantic"

Measuring a great racer, without counting checkered flags

by BRUCE COHEN

Bruce Cohen has done a little bit of everything in racing. In the beginning, he was such a rabid fan that he once led a charging brigade over the fence at Norwood, trying to reach the hated Bill Slater (who later became his close friend). He then worked as a crewman for several drivers, particularly his pal Don MacTavish. In 1972, Cohen joined Dick Berggren and Lew Boyd in noting that most of modified racing's major events were run in the autumn, leaving the springtime wide open; the trio rented the Stafford Motor Speedway from a skeptical Jack Arute, and staged the very first Spring Sizzler. Cohen has also been a car owner, a writer, an announcer, a radio show host and a silent sponsor. These days, he plays an active role with the New England Auto Racing Hall of Fame. Bruce and his very patient wife Linda live in Somerville, MA.

Bruce Cohen

THE LEGACY OF EDDIE FLEMKE, in my opinion, is not the races he won, or the track championships he had. It's not the trophies he left behind. It's the impact he had on people, the sheer influence of the man. He continues to have a very big, very important presence. It's uncanny. I mean, people *still* look up to Ed Flemke. I remember walking through the pits at Thompson Speedway a few years ago, and there was this young kid who had a picture of Eddie on the dashboard of his car. Now, think about that; this was, what, 20 years after the man had passed away?

The strange thing is, it's not as if Eddie was a commanding sort of figure. Physically, he was a short, slight guy, with pretty much the perfect build for a jockey. And, unless he knew you, he was very reserved; he kept to himself. But he was very intelligent, with such a great sense of integrity and such a great sense of right and wrong—"This is the thing *I* should do, this is the thing *we* should do"—that people just came to respect him, whether they were racers, fans or media. Over time, that respect only grew, and his influence just mushroomed.

Look at the way people would seek Eddie's opinions. I'm talking about drivers, mechanics, promoters, you name it. The drivers understood the ability he had to figure out tracks and situations. The mechanics appreciated the way he would freely pass on information. Don't forget, in those days you didn't just buy a car from a builder and call them when you had a question, so good information was hard to come by, especially for younger competitors. But those guys knew that Eddie Flemke would give them the real skinny, the straight scoop on what he thought they should do. And the promoters realized that he looked at the big picture, and that he always had the best interest of the sport in mind.

Over the years, I saw some very capable people seek Eddie out to discuss things with him. Car owners like Bob Garbarino, Art Barry, and Bob Oliver; drivers like Leo Cleary, Ernie Gahan, Richie Evans, and Peter Hamilton; great mechanics like Lenny Boehler and Ray Stonkus; and promoters like Jack Arute. They'd pull him aside and say, "Eddie, what do you think about this?" Now, each of those people was very successful in his own right, and they all had very strong personalities, and yet in so many cases they would defer to Eddie. To me, that's because they simply appreciated how intense and honest he was.

Some of the people he influenced were racers he worked with directly: Hamilton and Denny Zimmerman, and, later on, Evans and Elton Hill, Don Moon and others. Everybody's got a story about the way he helped those guys. I remember the night in 1965 when Thompson finished the season with twin 50-lap features. Hamilton was, without question, Eddie's number one protégé in that period. Pete won the first feature, then started scratch and passed Bill Slater with just a few laps to go to win the second one. Well, Eddie had dropped out of that second feature, and as he watched Pete come from the rear he walked out toward the edge of the track, so Hamilton could see him, and tapped his head as if to say, "Think, Peter, think!"

Now, that's pretty direct. But there are so many more guys he influenced *indirectly*, just because they looked up to him and followed his example. So much of that was because of Eddie's personality. I was always amazed at the way he could talk to the newest go-fer on a pit crew one minute, and the most seasoned big-dollar car owner the next minute, and each time he'd be right on their level immediately. He got along with everybody, other than a certain few racing officials whose names aren't even worth mentioning.

Summit meeting: Bruce Cohen and Ed Flemke flank Bob Garbarino to discuss the modified issues of the day back in the mid-'70s. *(Val LeSieur photo)*

It's been, gosh, more than 40 years since I first got to know Eddie. I started going to Norwood Arena in 1960—the same year NASCAR came in—and he was there with the "dollar-sign" car, John Stygar's coupe. What a car! Blue paint, yellow lettering on the side, triple carburetors. Anyway, I just studied him for a while, and I found myself saying, "Wow, this guy is *seriously* good."

Then he went off to do his Eastern Bandits thing, and whenever he snuck back to Norwood in that period the track announcer, the late Joe Ross, would say over the P.A. system, "And here's Eddie Flemke, who just last night won the feature at Southside Speedway in Richmond!" I thought that was *so* cool, that this guy had been down in Virginia the previous night, and he had obviously driven up the highway all day, and now I was watching him race in Massachusetts. *Wow*.

By 1963 I had started hanging around in the pits—me, a fat little Jewish kid from Brookline—and I would always stand there checking out Eddie and his car. He must have noticed that, because one night he just walked up and said, "Hi, how are you? I'm Ed Flemke." From then on, I'd see him here and there, and I don't think there was ever a night when we were at the same track without the two of us talking.

You know, this is getting off the subject a little bit, but my parents had never liked racing, and could not understood my attraction to it. So one night in 1963, they said, "We're going to come to Norwood this

Norwood nostalgia. From left to right in the foreground are co-owner Greg Mills, Eddie Flemke, track official Angie Nardone, Bobby Humphrey and Jackie Kelly; partially hidden behind Kelly is Henry Wheeler. That's Bruce Cohen leaning on the car, and co-owner Dave Welch standing. *(Bruce Cohen Collection)*

Saturday night, and check this out for ourselves." Well, Eddie happened to be there with his Gray Ghost coupe. He started about 16th, and he won the feature, picking his way through the traffic like he always did. My parents were so mesmerized that they became Norwood regulars, and my mother, who was especially amazed, said, "That guy drives like a boll weevil, the way he just weaves in and out." I don't think I've ever heard Eddie's driving described better; he was just so smooth. Guys like Gene Bergin or Bugsy Stevens or Ollie Silva might have had more spectacular styles over the years, but if you watched Eddie you could see how beautifully he drove. He was *methodically* spectacular.

And smart? God, was he smart. There was a period at Norwood—probably in 1964—when Jack Malone was hot in the #79, a great coupe owned by Greg "Baby Huey" Mills and Dave Welch. Now, Jack was a very good driver who was especially tough at Norwood, and he had won two weeks in a row. Well, on the third week, Jack's leading again, with Eddie right on him, and Jack's mirror-driving the heck out of him. Hey, the guy was leading, and he was going for three in a row, so that was cool. Well, coming into the third turn on the last lap, Eddie braced his knee against the steering wheel and slid his hands from left to right across the top of it, as if he was going to swing to the outside. Jack saw that, drifted up to block, and Eddie snuck right underneath him and won the show. Beautiful.

I've got so many good memories. You know, Eddie in the "dollar-sign," Eddie in the #21X coupe, Eddie in the #10 cars toward the end of his career, and especially Eddie in the #2X of Bobby Judkins, just because to me that always represented the perfect combination of a great car and a great driver.

Was he the best ever in the modifieds? Well, that's such a subjective thing. There are people who always point out that Eddie never won at Martinsville or Trenton. But so what? The guy won hundreds of races, and he beat all the other top drivers in their own backyards at one time or another. Some people might vote for Dutch Hoag because he won Langhorne five times, some for Richie Evans because he won all those NASCAR championships, some for Ray Hendrick because he won so many races up and down the East Coast. That's fine; everybody's enti-tled to his opinion. But I'd put Eddie right up there with any of them. He was one of the premier short-track drivers of his era, and any era.

But, let's face it, it's not the racing we think of when Eddie's name comes up. I mean, sure, behind the wheel the guy was an absolute thrill to watch, but it's that off-track influence we'll always remember. There are still a lot of people around—in the pits and in the grandstands—who

Never one to pass up a chat with Flemke, Bruce Cohen kneels for a pre-race word in 1972. *(Mike Adaskaveg photo)*

In Bruce Cohen's words, Flemke's stint with Bobby Judkins and the #2X "represented the perfect combination of a great car and a great driver." *(Mike Adaskaveg photo)*

were personally touched by that man, and to them it's like he never left, because they continue to follow his examples.

I honestly can't think of another individual who influenced so many people across such a long time span. I mean, this is a guy who had an impact on racing people from the '40s right up until he died in 1984, and he's *still* having an impact today. Forgive me for sounding overly philosophical about this, but there's something mystical about him that's hard to explain.

I will never forget the day I heard Eddie had died. I was at work, and my phone rang at about six o'clock in the morning. It was Bones

Bourcier, and he said, "Eddie Flemke passed away last night." Now, this was right at the end of March, and I cursed him out, saying, "Bonesie, if this is some kind of an April Fool's joke . . ." Of course, I knew right away that he wasn't kidding. And, I'll tell you, losing Eddie really shook me up. It shook up a lot of people.

But I really don't think it was the whole "dying early" thing that made his legacy so strong. I mean, it was incredibly sad that his family lost him at such a young age, and that *we* lost him, because I think he still had so much to contribute to racing. But I think that guy was just *destined* to leave his mark. And today, his is one of the most unusual, and yet most terrific, legacies that we have in racing.

You know, I don't think that man ever truly realized the influence he had on people. I've talked to Little Eddie and Paula about this. I don't believe Eddie ever saw himself as a *leader*, or anything like that. He was a very humble guy. I never thought Eddie had a big ego. Oh, he had a lot of pride—pride in his accomplishments, well-deserved pride in his family, pride in the cars he built and the innovations he came up with —but not a big ego. And he was never *preachy*. Yes, if he was asked, or if he felt like it was necessary, he'd climb up on a soapbox once in a while. But for the most part he would just quietly state his opinion, and that was that.

I just can't say enough about the guy. Once we both got to the point where we weren't bumping into each other every weekend—he wasn't driving as much, and I wasn't going to as many races as I once did—I still made an effort to see him whenever possible. If I had a business trip that took me to Connecticut, I always tried to get the business part over quickly so I could stop in and see Eddie. I just enjoyed sitting there and bullshitting with him. He never talked down to you, never was condescending, and he was always full of good information and good ideas. And yet, you always left scratching your head just a little bit; he always made you think. He *loved* that.

What I mean is, even though we all remember the way he helped his competitors, I always believed he gave them just enough to straighten them out, enough to get them 95 percent of the way there, but then left the last five percent up to them. Not so he could keep his edge over them—because Eddie didn't need much of an edge—but because he just enjoyed getting those people to think on their own. And he was the same way when he was talking about non-racing situations.

I think the last sentence of every Eddie Flemke conversation consisted of the other person saying to himself, "I wonder exactly what Eddie meant by that . . ."

I've often wondered what the guy could have done had he not been a race driver. Sometimes I think he could have been a great surgeon, because he was both so calm and so intelligent. But mostly I think he would have been a fabulous college professor, because a good professor will get his students 95 percent of the way home and challenge them to figure out the last five percent. There's a wonderful 25-cent word I love, "didactic," which basically means someone born to teach or instruct. That's what Eddie was: the ultimate didactic racer.

And yet, you know, Eddie had a fun-loving side, too. Back in the Norwood Arena days, once everyone loaded up after the races, a group of us would race over to the local pancake house. It'd be Pete Hamilton and his gang, Jack Malone and his gang, just a whole bunch of us. Well, one night we all swung onto Route 128—which had just been repaved, so the asphalt was nice and slippery—and Eddie got behind Jack and spun him out. I mean, Eddie rapped him and rapped him until he turned that car right around on the highway. God, we all laughed, including Jack. It was just terrific.

I came to see Ed Flemke as a very dear friend. If you had any kind of a problem on your mind—whether it was business, a social thing, a racing thing—you could never go wrong by either calling him or going down to his shop to visit him. His advice was always sound. There were actually a few times when I *didn't* listen to what he'd said and things went wrong, and later on Eddie said, basically, "I told you so." But he didn't do that in a ball-busting way, never. He was just telling me that I should have thought things through a little better.

I've got a story about him that's kind of funny and kind of touching. There was a period in the early 1970s when I was partying a lot—I mean, an *awful* lot—and Eddie knew about that. He wasn't around to see it firsthand, because, of course, Eddie wasn't a partier himself, but he had heard about this through the grapevine. Well, he pulled me aside at Thompson, and he really ripped me from head to toe: "Bruce, what are you doing? You're acting like a complete jerk. This isn't you." I mean, Eddie wasn't the kind of guy who raised his voice very much, but he got right in my face and he was really animated. It was a very pointed, very one-sided discussion.

I stood right there and listened to him, and by the time he walked away I'd decided he was right. I straightened up my act quite a bit. Oh, I still had a good time, as anyone who knows me will tell you. But I got away from that atmosphere of partying day and night and acting like the ultimate crazy person.

That's how Eddie was. If he cared about you and he saw you were going down the wrong path, he'd let you know that, and he wouldn't pull any punches. But it didn't mean he stopped caring about you. In fact, it was just the opposite; he was only trying to look out for you.

Today, I have a lot of photos of Eddie hanging in my house, right there with Don MacTavish, Gene Bergin, Bill Slater, and all the other heroes. But there's this one particular picture I keep on my desk which shows Eddie in the cockpit of the Judkins #2X coupe, looking so calm and collected. I took that picture at Martinsville in the autumn of 1968.

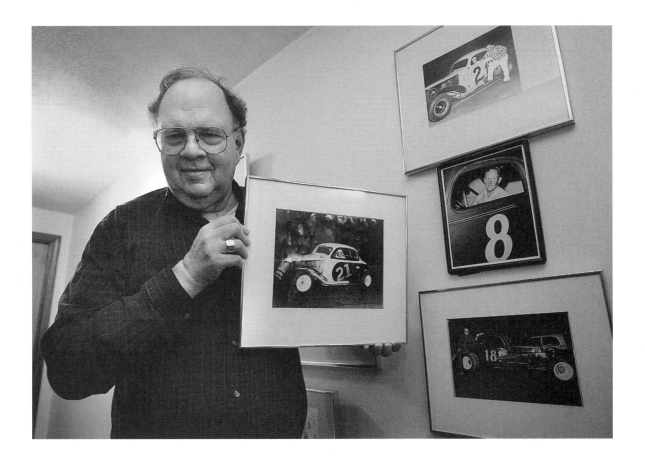

He's waiting to go out and qualify, Mr. Cool, sitting there smoking a cigarette, with his left hand just dangling out the window. It's typical Eddie, looking like it would be impossible to rattle him. Well, that photo has come in so handy. See, I have a volatile temper that I have a hard time controlling in certain situations, and in the last few years I had some business dealings that *really* strained it. And every time I'd get totally aggravated, just ready to explode, I'd look at that picture of Eddie. It's like he was talking to me: "Okay, slow down, think this thing out. Don't go off half-cocked. Use your head."

Just the memory of Eddie has a very calming effect on me.

To me, he transcends his sport, in the same way that when you think about Michael Jordan you don't think only about basketball, and when you think about Tiger Woods you don't think only about golf. They are *inspirational* figures, and Eddie was certainly one of those. I mean, if you were to try to explain him to a stranger, they might think, "Okay, he was a really good short-track driver. Big deal." But to anyone who knew him, or anyone who was influenced by him, he was so much more than that. Like I said, he transcended his sport and the arena in which he competed.

The halls of Cohen's home are lined with shots of his modified heroes. Naturally, Eddie Flemke's image pops up everywhere. *(Mike Adaskaveg photo)*

Outside of my father, I think Eddie was the second most important male figure in my life. What better compliment could you give some-one?

Eddie Flemke might have been small in stature, but his sphere of influence was gigantic. Today, even after all these years, there are guys in the South and guys in New Jersey and guys in garages all over the Northeast who look up to the example he set.

There's a quote from the Talmud, a collection of religious writings that goes back centuries, that says, "There are stars whose light only reaches the earth long after they have fallen apart. There are people whose remembrance gives light in this world long after they have passed away." Now, those lines are maybe a thousand years old, but, really, couldn't those same words have been written about Ed Flemke?

We still think about him. We still talk about him. We still smile about him. And, to me, that's much more important than the fact that he won the Spring Sizzler or the Utica-Rome 400 or a bunch of races here or there.

Lots of guys win races, but there was only one Eddie Flemke.

Afterword by Bones Bourcier

"We tip our hats today to a fellow named Ed Flemke"

(When Ed Flemke joined the New England Auto Racing Hall of Fame as part of the inaugural class in 1998, writer Bones Bourcier gave the induction speech. Struck by the way the lives of all that year's inductees had intersected with Flemke's, Bourcier made these connections the central theme of his speech, which is reproduced here.)

BECAUSE INDUCTION into any Hall of Fame is largely the result of what an athlete has done on his or her field of play, we tip our hats today to the racing career of a fellow called Ed Flemke. We tip our hats to a man whose winning spanned from the late 1940s to the late 1970s. We tip our hats to one of the original Eastern Bandits, to a hero who drove and built some of stock car racing's most innovative machines, to a legend whose smiling eyes lit up victory lanes at more race tracks than most of us will ever even visit.

Estimates at Ed Flemke's career victory total range anywhere from 400 to 600, but no one will ever know for sure. Eddie's most productive days came before tracks kept accurate records, before weekly newspapers allowed fans to follow the careers of their favorite drivers, and certainly before every driver had a publicist or a PR guy to brag about what he had done.

Yet the fact that no definitive records exist to document Flemke's entire career is perfect. Because to define this man's racing life through facts and numbers alone would only serve to shortchange him.

Eddie Flemke was a great driver, certainly. But he was, above all else, a leader, a teacher, a mentor. He brought out the very best in people. If you need examples of that, just glance at the list of names who join him today in being inducted into this wonderful Hall of Fame.

I believe that his peers—heroic drivers like Rene Charland, Bugs Stevens, Bill Slater, Gene Bergin and Ernie Gahan—would tell you that they knew they had to be at their very best if they were going to run with Eddie Flemke. I believe that the great Ollie Silva, who raced with Eddie only occasionally, knew that he had to be at his best when he invaded Flemke's turf, or when Flemke invaded his. I believe that if they were able to join us here today, Bill Welch would say that Flemke made him a better announcer, and Harvey Tattersall would say that in some way, Flemke made him a better promoter.

Eddie simply had a way of making *everybody* better. And he was so good at it that some of the people he made better went on to enjoy a fame even greater than his own.

Ron Bouchard became a household racing name with his upset win at Talladega, but long before he ever went to Alabama he had to battle with Eddie Flemke at Seekonk, Stafford, and Waterford. Richie Evans drove to nine NASCAR modified championships, but first he had to follow Eddie Flemke around Lancaster, Fulton, and Utica-Rome. Pete Hamilton won the biggest stock car race in the world, the Daytona 500, but not until he had learned some valuable lessons from Ed Flemke at Thompson, Norwood, and Albany-Saratoga.

Their own natural abilities allowed Ronnie and Richie and Pete to do what they did. But all three have admitted freely that Eddie Flemke showed them shortcuts on their journeys to greatness. I think Eddie was more proud of that then he ever let on.

He brought out the best in every driver he faced, every mechanic he worked with, every car owner for whom he drove. He brought out the best in a lot of us, simply by setting standards for things like hard work, honesty and integrity.

Not a single day goes by that I don't think of Eddie Flemke, and not a single day goes by without his extraordinary legacy continuing to impact auto racing across New England, and across this nation.

And so we tip our hats today to a man we knew as Steady Eddie, as the Boss, and as just plain Pops. The luckiest among us knew him as a friend. It is a high honor and a personal privilege for me to induct into the New England Auto Racing Hall of Fame the great Ed Flemke.

BONES BOURCIER, February 1998

Ed Flemke Jr. and Paula Bouchard accept the plaque marking their father's induction into the New England Auto Racing Hall of Fame's inaugural class of 1998. *(Howie Hodge photo)*

Index

(Mike Adaskaveg photo)